REBELS AGAINST
ROME

ALSO BY STEPHEN DANDO-COLLINS

*Constantine at the Bridge: How the Battle of the Milvian Bridge
    Created Christian Rome*

*Conquering Jerusalem: The AD 66–73 Roman Campaign to Crush the
    Jewish Revolt*

Cyrus the Great: Conqueror, Liberator, Anointed One

Caligula: The Mad Emperor of Rome

*Rise of an Empire: How One Man United Greece to Defeat Xerxes's
    Persians*

The Ides: Caesar's Murder and the War for Rome

*Blood of the Caesars: How the Murder of Germanicus Led to the Fall
    of Rome*

*Mark Antony's Heroes: How the Third Gallica Legion Saved an
    Apostle and Created an Emperor*

*Cleopatra's Kidnappers: How Caesar's Sixth Legion Gave Egypt to
    Rome and Rome to Caesar*

*Nero's Killing Machine: The True Story of Rome's Remarkable
    Fourteenth Legion*

*Caesar's Legion: The Epic Saga of Julius Caesar's Elite Tenth Legion
    and the Armies of Rome*

REBELS AGAINST
ROME

400 YEARS OF REBELLIONS AGAINST
THE RULE OF ROME

STEPHEN DANDO-COLLINS

TURNER
PUBLISHING COMPANY

Turner Publishing Company
Nashville, Tennessee
www.turnerpublishing.com

Rebels Against Rome: 400 Years of Rebellions Against the Rule of Rome
Copyright © 2023 by Stephen Dando-Collins. All rights reserved.

Cover and book design by William Ruoto
Cover image © Look and Learn / Bridgeman Images

Paperback 9781684427857
Hardcover 9781684427864
Ebook 9781684427871

Library of Congress Cataloging-in-Publication Data

Names: Dando-Collins, Stephen, author.
Title: Rebels against Rome : 400 years of rebellion against the rule of
    Rome / Stephen Dando-Collins.
Description: Nashville, Tennessee : Turner Publishing Company, [2023] |
    Includes bibliographical references and index.
Identifiers: LCCN 2021061674 (print) | LCCN 2021061675 (ebook) | ISBN
    9781684427857 (paperback) | ISBN 9781684427857 (hardcover) | ISBN
    9781684427871 (epub)
Subjects: LCSH: Rome--History--Republic, 265-30 B.C. |
    Rome--History--Empire, 30 B.C.-476 A.D | Civil war--Rome--History |
    Revolutions--Rome--History
Classification: LCC DG254.2 .D36 2023 (print) | LCC DG254.2 (ebook) | DDC
    937/.06--dc23/eng/20220928
LC record available at https://lccn.loc.gov/2021061674
LC ebook record available at https://lccn.loc.gov/2021061675

Printed in the United States of America

For my dearest wife, Louise,
and my longtime New York literary agent, Richard Curtis,
who both know a rebel when they see one.

CONTENTS

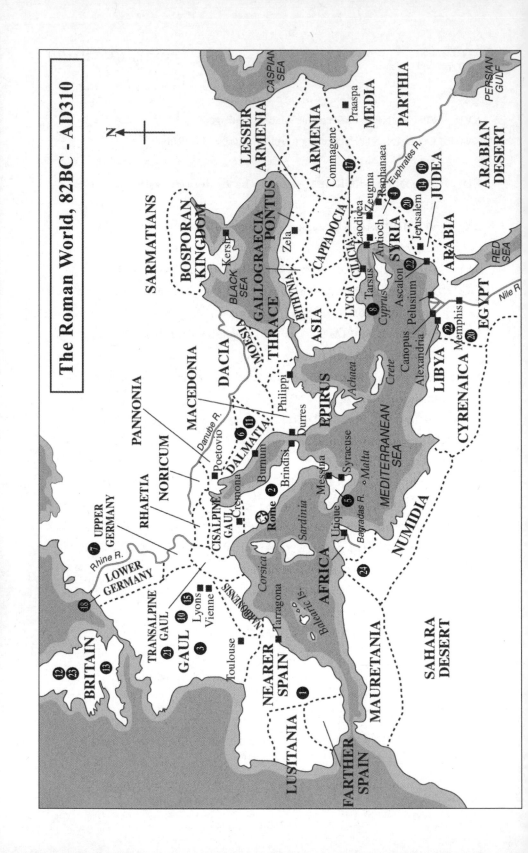

The Roman World, 82BC - AD310

KEY TO MAP

1. Sertorius Revolt, Spain
2. Spartacus Revolt, Italy
3. Vercingetorix's Gallic Revolt
4. Labienus Revolt, Syria and Asia Minor
5. Sextus Pompey Revolt, Sicily
6. The Batos's Pannonian and Dalmatian Revolts
7. Arminius Revolt, Germany east of the Rhine
8. Tacfarinas Revolt, Africa
9. Piso Revolt, Cilicia
10. Sacrovir Revolt, Gaul
11. Scribonianus Revolt, Dalmatia
12. Venutius Revolts, Northern Britain
13. Boudicca Revolt, Southern Britain
14. First Jewish Revolt, Judea
15. Vindex Revolt, Gaul
16. Civilis Revolt, Lower and Upper Germany and Northern Gaul
17. Epiphanes Revolt, Commagene
18. Saturninus Revolt, Lower Germany
19. Simon Bar-Kokhba's Second Jewish Revolt, Judea
20. Avidius Cassius Revolt, Syria and Egypt
21. Gallic Empire Revolt, Gaul
22. Queen Zenobia Revolt, Syria, Asia Minor, and Egypt
23. Carausius and Allectus's British Revolt, Britain and Western Gaul
24. Domitius Alexander Revolt, North Africa

FOREWORD

by Dr. Terry. J. Hannan

*R*ebels Against Rome presents selected but significant events within the Roman empire from 82BC to AD310, a period of over 390 years in human history. This era is significant in the history of human evolution. Italy was not yet a united nation yet the influences of Rome from within the boot of Italy to much of the known world were profound.

The administrators of Rome had extended their domination and cultural influences from Rome, to the Atlantic Ocean, to Britain and north Africa. To the north and west of Rome it dominated the communities in Europe and extended to regions like Bosnia-Herzegovina and Croatia. Further influential extensions were to the Middle East which had become the centres of Judaism and Christianity. This dominant empire needed strong, powerful and intelligent people to manage, control and expand its dominions.

Dando-Collins takes the reader on a sequential journey through the immediate pre-Christian era into the third century AD by creating unique character stories of individuals and closely related social groups, who were able to create this world domination. The decisions and actions of these individuals, both men and women, resulted in long lasting social influences that still affect, into the twenty-first century, the history of many cultures.

Most of their influences required physical and social rebellious activities against those in power in Rome. The motives for rebellion were varied: power seeking, revenge, jealousy, reactions to Roman domination and self-seeking glory.

Many of these rebellious decision makers were visionary. Their outstanding intelligence combined with their ability to make decisions with authority and clarity of thought, allowed Rome to remain dominant in the immediate pre and post Christian eras.

These rebels also had their imperfections and failings. Many of their rebellious decisions were associated with brutal outcomes. Not only to those who were external rebels, but also rebellious individuals within the inner circles of power in Rome. Many of these rebels lost their lives fighting in the rebellions or through self-sacrifice using suicide to escape capture and torture, or the acceptance of failure.

Dando-Collins' stories of these rebels reveals the complexities involved in the management of the extensively distributed empire governed by Rome. These complexities meant that the empire's functioning was inherently fragile because of the individuals involved, such as power seekers within the Roman governing hierarchy and those who were oppressed by Rome's legions. Despite these episodes of rebellion, the power of Rome allowed the empire to survive and expand for centuries.

The ongoing fragility of the empire was facilitated by the presence of strong, intimate familial relationships, sometimes incestuous, as well as jealousy and resentment. Dando-Collins also reveals other sources of rebellious intent. It came from those oppressed by the legions of Rome. The rebelliousness amongst the oppressed was at times facilitated by Rome's affirmations of individuals within these groups. In recognising their talents and intellect, Rome's authorities often appointed them to positions of leadership and made them official members of the Roman society. They could be Gauls, Germans, Jewish, or British. Not all were males.

Dando-Collins documents the emergence of female rebel leaders who were equal to the males in intelligence, strong will and the ability to rule with brutal force. These women, such as Cartimandua and Boudicca, were able to lead rebellions and challenge, and at times, defeat the domination of Roman influence within their societies.

This book is an enthralling read! In his selection of two dozen extensively researched case studies of prominent individuals, Dando-Collins dissects rebellions that regularly changed the course of Roman history. In his writings he reveals the symptoms of revolution, charting the fates of charismatic freedom fighters, power hungry bureaucrats and brilliant generals. He also reveals the brutality used to maintain this power. His words make these individuals real to the reader, beyond simple historical facts. In doing so, Dando-Collins provides a brilliant insight into the way the Roman Empire dealt with the cancer of internal revolt.

INTRODUCTION

What constitutes a rebel against Rome? The rebels on these pages had one thing in common: all were Romans, or one-time Roman allies, who attempted to overthrow Roman rule within the bounds of the Roman Empire. This is in contrast to foreigners who invaded Roman territory or opposed Roman expansion into their countries, men such as Carthaginian general Hannibal, King Decebalus of Dacia, and British king Caratacus.

To claim a chapter here, historical figures had to be genuine rebels, not just a pirate or a bandit with less than noble motives. One supposed rebel not included is Corrocotta, the Jackal, a Spaniard romanticized as a rebel guerrilla fighter by some modern authors. Cassius Dio, the only Roman source on Corrocotta, tells us explicitly that the man was a bandit, not a freedom fighter, during the Cantabrian War of 25–23 BC. Rome's first emperor, Augustus, was so annoyed by Corrocotta's banditry he offered a reward of one million sesterces for his capture. Lo and behold, Corrocotta walked into Octavian's camp and claimed the reward for himself. Octavian was so impressed, he gave the man the money, and let him go. Corrocotta never troubled Rome again.

Not every rebellion is documented well enough to be included. For example, an uprising in Egypt over the winter of 30–29 BC was put down by the Roman prefect of Egypt in just fifteen days. We know nothing about the rebel leaders involved then, or in the AD 293 Egyptian rebellion put down after many months by the emperor Diocletian's deputy Galerius with the help of the future emperor Constantine. So, only those rebels we know about inhabit these pages.

Many of those rebels succeeded, for a time, in humbling Rome. In the end, sometimes after years, other times after only weeks, Rome always prevailed, occasionally through the ineptitude of the rebels, but more often through the skills of Roman generals who rose to the occasion after others had failed.

Some of these rebels were royalty, one a slave. Some were foreigners who served in the Roman army; others were over-ambitious Roman governors. Some were genuine freedom fighters. All had the courage and audacity to oppose the greatest empire the world had known to that time. These are their stories.

REBELS AGAINST
ROME

Portrait of Quintus Sertorius and his "sacred" fawn, by Jose Coroleu, 1881.
© *Look and Learn/Bridgeman Images.*

I. SERTORIUS

REBEL ROMAN GOVERNOR AND GUERRILLA FIGHTER. SPAIN, 82–73 BC

In the spring of 82 BC, a small Roman army reached the foot of the Pyrenees Mountains in today's southwestern France, on the march from Gaul to Spain. Blocking the army's path, a wild Pyrenees tribe demanded that, to pass, the general in command pay a massive toll in gold.

That Roman general was forty-six-year-old Quintus Sertorius, a fine-looking man apart from the fact that he'd lost an eye in battle— just like Hannibal, famed Carthaginian commander of the past. In guile, daring, and self-confidence, few generals throughout history would exceed Sertorius. He was born in Umbria, central Italy, in the territory of the Sabines, who, although they possessed Roman citizenship by this time, were considered by native Romans to be their inferiors. When Sertorius was a teenager, as his father was dying, his mother, Rhea, sent him to Rome to study law and public speaking. His contemporary Marcus Cicero, one of Rome's most noted orators, remarked that Sertorius was a rough and rustic public speaker who lacked polish. But Sertorius's frankness and lack of rhetorical flourish would make him a convincing speaker once he took up military service and discovered a talent for soldiering.

In Gaul, serving as a junior officer in a Roman army locked in battle with invading German tribes, young Sertorius was wounded several times. In one skirmish, he lost his horse. Still wearing his armor, and using his wooden shield as a flotation device, he crossed the Rhone River to escape.

Once he rejoined Roman forces and recovered, he went to his army's commander, consul Gaius Marius, and offered to go in disguise to the enemy camp to learn their plans. Marius allowed him to go to the sprawling German camp dressed in clothes taken from German prisoners and carrying German weapons. With a fine ear for foreign languages, Sertorius had picked up enough German to converse with their ordinary soldiers, and he did so while using his eyes and ears to deduce their numbers and intentions. He returned to his general with the intelligence, which helped the Romans throw the Germans out of Gaul.

Marius rewarded Sertorius with promotion to increasingly important roles. Before long, the young man had command of a thousand troops in Spain, where he again impressed by outwitting and annihilating a local tribe in central Spain after it had initially taken the Romans by surprise. When Rome became wracked in civil war between the faction led by Marius and that led by Lucius Cornelius Sulla, Sertorius found himself on Marius's side, now as a general marching with Lucius Cornelius Cinna in Italy, even though he didn't approve of some of Marius's actions—he approved of Sulla's actions even less. Following the deaths of both Marius and Cinna, with others carrying on the Marian cause, Sertorius was assigned the task of seizing the two Roman provinces in Spain for the Marians. And that was how he had come to the Pyrenees with an army of nine thousand men, to be met with the rude demand for a payment of gold.

Sertorius's subordinates were aghast at this demand from the barbarians, and even more so when Sertorius paid what the locals asked. But Sertorius was both wise and in a hurry. He wanted to enter the Roman province of Nearer Spain before the pro-Sulla governor Flaccus knew that he was coming. A fight with the locals would delay him, and would also ensure that word of his presence in the Pyrenees would probably reach the Roman governor in the capital of Nearer Spain, Tarraco, today's Tarragona, not far along the coast.

"I must buy time, the most precious of all things to those who embark upon great enterprises," Sertorius told his colleagues.[1]

By paying the outrageous toll, Sertorius was able to cross the mountains quickly and reach Tarragona unannounced, forcing Flaccus to flee. Expecting Sulla to dispatch a force from Italy to oppose him, Sertorius sent his deputy Julius Salinator with six thousand men to fortify and guard the Pyrenees passes, while he himself set about winning the support of local leaders, building warships, and arming local recruits. When his troops went into camp that winter, he set up his own tent outside the walls of Tarragona to show that he neither feared the locals nor was to be feared by them.

In 81 BC, a year after Sulla took control of Rome and declared himself dictator with unlimited powers, he decreed that Sertorius and all Roman officers serving with him were traitors and rebels against Rome, subject to a sentence of death, and dispatched several legions under Gaius Annius Luscus to take back Spain. When Annius's army reached the Pyrenees, Sertorius's deputy Salinator was treacherously murdered by a deputy, who then defected to the Sullans. This sent panic through the ranks of Sertorius's troops, and as they deserted their posts, Annius advanced over the mountains. Sweeping all opposition before him, he bore down on Tarragona.

Sertorius, seriously outnumbered, and finding locals deserting him for fear of Sulla's retribution, withdrew from Tarragona and retreated in good order down the Spanish coast with his remaining three thousand men until he reached the port of Carthago Nova, or New Carthage, today's city of Cartagena. There, he and his men boarded the warships he'd built the previous summer and sailed across the Mediterranean to the kingdom of Mauretania, which included much of today's Algeria and northern Morocco. After a number of his men were massacred by locals while foraging for food and water, Sertorius sailed with his survivors back to Spain, only for his ships to be driven away by a Sullan fleet.

So, Sertorius joined with a squadron of pirates from Cilicia, and together they took one of the Balearic Isles from its Sullan garrison. After Annius arrived with a fleet, Sertorius lost most of his ships in a storm as he strove to escape. Yet, despite setback after setback, Sertorius wouldn't give up, even when his pirate allies deserted him and sailed to Mauretania to help Ascalis, a local prince, regain his throne.

In response, Sertorius threw in his lot with the Moorish opponents of Ascalis, and helped them defeat Ascalis and the pirates. When a Sullan force landed to oppose him, Sertorius killed their commander and convinced the Sullan troops to come over to his side. With his enlarged force, he stormed Tingis, today's Tangiers, and took control of Mauretania.

As word of his success spread, chiefs of the tribes of Lusitania, which encompassed much of today's Portugal, sent ambassadors to offer him generalship of their forces in their resistance to the Sullan troops advancing into Lusitania. Sertorius gladly accepted, and in 80 BC he sailed to the Iberian Peninsula with his Roman troops and Moorish volunteers and took charge of the Lusitanian war effort. Soon after landing, he went into battle, routing a force led by the local Roman administrator at the Baetis River, today's Guadalquivir, which runs through Cordoba and Seville to enter the Atlantic Ocean a little to the north of Cadiz.

Marching into eastern Spain unopposed, gathering Lusitanian and Spanish volunteers as he went, Sertorius established his headquarters at an inland mountain town in northeastern Spain called Osca, today's Huesca, occupying a hill on a plateau 1,600 feet above sea level. To reach Huesca, Sertorius's enemies would have to go through narrow mountain passes where they could be easily ambushed. Throughout the Sertorian War, as the Romans came to call Sertorius's reign in Spain, Huesca would never fall to Roman attack.

At Huesca, Sertorius established a senate of three hundred, comprised of Roman senators who fled to join him, Roman settlers, and local nobility. Here, he set up a school at his own expense where sons of Spanish nobility were taught in Greek and Roman fashion. He even created purple-bordered school uniforms for his students—the identifying color of the senatorial class in Rome. Sertorius further enhanced his growing fame after a chieftain gifted him a rare albino baby deer, cleverly playing on the superstitions of locals by declaring that the white fawn was a messenger from the gods. When couriers brought him news, Sertorius hid them away and announced that it was his sacred deer that had imparted the news to him. And when he marched to war, the white fawn accompanied him as his good luck charm.

Making his best remaining Roman troops his personal bodyguard, Sertorius created an army composed of Romans, mounted North African mercenaries, and local Spanish warriors, in Roman-style cohorts. Traditionally, the Spanish fought without helmets or shields, with just leather vests for protection, dashing in to unleash spears before drawing swords for close combat. With this army, and supported by leading native chieftains, Sertorius made Spain his private fiefdom.

The following year, 79 BC, the dictator Sulla took the unprecedented step of retiring, apparently aware of a serious health issue that would claim his life just a year later. He left Rome in the charge of a Senate purged of Marian sympathizers, and, to overthrow Sertorius and reclaim Spain, the Senate appointed Quintus Caecillius Metellus Pius, current *pontifex maximus*, or high priest of Rome, giving him an army for the task. Metellus, as he was known, one of the two consuls elected for 80 BC, was a fifty-year-old, highly experienced general.

On arriving in Nearer Spain, Metellus set up bases at three Spanish cities and embarked on a military campaign against Sertorius. Commanding experienced troops against Sertorius's coalition, Metellus was confident of defeating the rebel, calling him "Sulla's runaway slave." But Metellus would soon discover that his opponent had a few tricks up his sleeve.[2]

Sertorius found the exuberant young men of his Spanish light infantry cohorts eager for battle as soon as the enemy marched up and formed battle lines outside their fortified camp. Addressing the Spaniards, he tried to restrain them using reason, declaring he would only attack when the time and place were right. But he was unable to hold the impatient Spaniards back, and he finally let them go on the attack. While he and his other troops watched from the camp walls,

Spaniards flooded out the camp gate and attacked the Roman troops, who, ironically, had benefited from training and tactics introduced into the Roman army by Marius. Their shield line held firm against every wild Spanish assault.

Sertorius now emerged with his remaining troops, who, keeping strict formation, covered the withdrawal of the exhausted, bloodied Spaniards as they left many of their comrades dead on the field. Once the Spanish youths were all safely back in his camp, Sertorius called another mass assembly. When his soldiers answered the trumpet call, they found their general waiting on his tribunal, the earthen speaker's platform at the camp's center.

With his troops formed up in ranks and files before him, Sertorius had two horses brought onto the parade ground. One horse was an old, lean animal, the other a strong young stallion with a remarkably long, thick tail. Next, he called forward two men from the ranks, one tall and well-built, the other a weedy runt. Giving a signal to the pair, he stepped down to watch the fun. For, Sertorius was about to demonstrate to his followers what would become his most famous lesson, in strategy and in life.

The big man grabbed the tail of the old horse with both hands and began to tug at it with all his might, apparently trying to pull it out. Of course, the horse objected to this and resisted by kicking out at the soldier with its back legs, bringing hoots of laughter from the watching soldiery as the man frantically kept up his efforts. Meanwhile, the smaller soldier had begun to pluck out the hairs of the tail of the young horse, one by one. In time, the tail of the stronger horse was plucked right out, while the tail of the weaker horse remained intact.

"You see, fellow soldiers," said Sertorius, stepping back up onto the tribunal, "perseverance is more prevailing than violence, and many things which cannot be overcome when they are together yield themselves up when taken little by little. Assiduity and persistence are irresistible and in time overthrow the greatest powers—time being the favorable friend and assistant of those who use their judgment to await his opportunity."[3]

From that day on, Sertorius's troops never doubted his judgment or resisted his orders, and the story of Sertorius's horses would enter Roman folklore and be quoted time and again as an example of the rewards of patience and persistence. Sertorius now went on to play a cat and mouse game with Metellus, moving across central Spain as he withdrew west and refused to give battle. By the time Sertorius had crossed the Tagus River, which today forms part of the border between Spain and Portugal, he had left the pursuing army well behind. Metellus, feeling much more comfortable near the coast, which provided supply by sea, had diverted south to add the province of Farther Spain to his control, giving him a solid hold on the Iberian Peninsula's eastern and southern coasts.

Inland, Sertorius camped near a hill where a local marauding tribe, the Characitanians, lived in caves. When the tribesmen chided him for running from the Romans like a defeated man, he rode around their hill announcing that he would show them who was a defeated man. As he and his escort rode, he saw that light dust lying predominantly on the southern slopes of the barren hill rose up in a choking cloud from beneath their horses' hooves. Locals told him that the caves of the Characitanians faced north, and that the north wind brought them cooling relief in summer. Armed with this information, Sertorius now had his infantry dig piles of dust. Filling sacks with the stuff, the troops carried it to the northern side of the hill, creating a huge, dusty mound. Seeing this, the tribesmen roared with laughter, declaring it the most useless siege mound they had ever seen.

But then the wind blew strongly from the north, picking up dust from the mound and blowing it into the caves, and into the mouths, eyes, and ears of the tribesmen, coating their food and turning their water to mud. The following day, as the wind continued to blow, Sertorius had his cavalrymen ride back and forth, stirring up the remaining dust, as his infantry brought fresh sacks around the hill to dump at the horses' feet. On the third day, with the wind still driving dust into their caves, the choking Characitanians came out and surrendered to

Sertorius. In this way, writes his biographer Plutarch, Sertorius proved to his men that "he was able to conquer places by artifice which were impregnable by the force of arms."[4]

With his growing renown, Sertorius was able to gather more Spanish volunteers to his cause. With his enlarged force, he began to progressively stalk Metellus and his army and drive them from Farther Spain. Metellus was slow to make decisions, and largely relied on his heavy infantry, which fought in solid, slow-moving phalanxes, while Sertorius's troops were mostly lightly armed and much more agile. With his rear and his supply lines being constantly harassed by Sertorius's fast-moving fighters, Metellus was outclassed and always at a disadvantage. By 77 BC, Metellus had been driven back, with his army bottled up on Spain's east coast and fearful of emerging from behind city walls, leaving Sertorius in control of Lusitania and most of Farther Spain and Nearer Spain. Just a few coastal cities retained their loyalty to Rome, closing their gates to Sertorius and accepting Roman garrisons.

Meanwhile, in Rome, Marcus Lepidus, one of the two consuls elected for the year 78 BC, had attempted to reverse the reforms of Sulla. Opposed by his fellow consul Quintus Catulus, by 77 BC Lepidus had left the capital and put together an army made up of former supporters of Marius and disaffected country people whose land had been confiscated by Sulla for distribution to his retiring legion veterans. As Lepidus marched on Rome, his colleague Marcus Junius Brutus occupied the city of Mutina, today's Modena, in northern Italy. The Senate appointed Catulus to lead its troops against Lepidus in the defense of Rome and appointed another commander to deal with Brutus—the famous Gnaeus Pompeius, known as Pompey the Great to English-speaking writers and historians.

Just twenty-seven years old, Pompey had married Sulla's stepdaughter—one of the rewards for his sweeping victories as Sulla's youngest and most successful general in the war against Marius. Pompey had also been given the title Magnus, or the Great, by Sulla, for his successes against Marian forces in Italy, Sicily, and North Africa. The son of Strabo, a Sullan general killed by a lightning strike, Pompey had marched for Sulla since the age of sixteen. At the age of just twenty-three he had personally raised three legions in eastern Italy to fight Sulla's opponents. Since then, Pompey had not been defeated. According to first-century Roman soldier Velleius Paterculus, "From the day on which he had assumed the toga [at sixteen] he had been trained to military service on the staff of that sagacious general, his father." Pompey, writes Velleius, possessed "a singular insight into military tactics," and "developed his excellent native talent."[5]

Pompey quickly recalled his recently retired legionaries from their farms and towns and marched on Modena. Marcus Brutus's troops, lacking confidence in Brutus, changed sides and gave him up to Pompey, who sent him into rural banishment after he swore to stay out of politics. When Brutus immediately began to stir up public support for Lepidus, Pompey sent an officer to execute him. His army reinforced with Brutus's men, Pompey then marched toward Rome to support Catulus by cutting off the rear of Lepidus's army.

Catulus, meanwhile, had repulsed Lepidus in a battle at the Milvian Bridge just several miles north of Rome. This had forced Lepidus to retreat up the east coast, only to bump into Pompey coming the other way. At Cosa, eighty miles north of Rome, Lepidus escaped by loading troops onto ships and sailing to Sardinia, where he would die of natural causes. Some of Lepidus's troops and senior officers, including the son of Cinna, succeeded in fleeing to Gaul, led by his deputy Marcus Perpenna Vento, known as Perpenna. There, gathering more troops around him, and fearing that Pompey might come after them, Perpenna marched the troops toward the Pyrenees, intent on entering Spain, where, he knew, the Senate's remaining forces under Metellus were bottled up by Sertorius.

Perpenna had previously governed Sicily for the Marians, and had given it up to Pompey without a fight. He was, according to Velleius, "a man more distinguished for his [noble] birth than for his character."[6]

After Perpenna and his thirty thousand men entered Spain, word reached them that the Senate had sought a commander to lead an army to Spain to restore it to Senate control. Such was Sertorius's daunting reputation, however, that no one had volunteered for the job. So, Pompey had been approached, and was given the same rank and powers that former consul Metellus still held as proconsul, despite being fifteen years too young to be appointed a consul.

When Perpenna ordered his troops to prepare to defend the Pyrenees passes against the approaching Pompey, fear of the young general caused them to rebel. They demanded that Perpenna lead them to join Sertorius, insisting that they would go without him otherwise. Perpenna gave in, leading his troops inland to Huesca, where Sertorius welcomed them, appointing Perpenna one of his deputies. With the addition of Perpenna's legionaries, Sertorius's army now numbered sixty thousand men, with half being legionary heavy infantry with shields, helmets, and armored vests, and the remainder Spanish light infantry.

To aid Pompey's campaign, the Senate decreed pardons for senior Marians who had fled to Sertorius, promising to return the property that had been taken from them when Sulla proscribed them as enemies of the state—if they swore to return to Rome and stay out of politics. Among those who accepted this pardon and left Sertorius to return to Rome was the son of Cinna. As Perpenna and several other senators remained with Sertorius, it's likely they weren't included in the Senate's pardon offer.

In the summer of 76 BC, Pompey arrived in eastern Spain with thirty thousand experienced legionaries, and Sertorius moved to strike a blow before Pompey could link up with his older compatriot Metellus. "While Sertorius bestowed the greater praise upon Metellus, it was Pompey he feared more strongly," writes Velleius.[7]

To drive a wedge between his Roman opponents, Sertorius took part of his army and laid siege to the east coast town of Lauron, which had remained loyal to Rome and was situated between Pompey and Metellus. Pompey marched to the city's aid, and camping close by

Sertorius's camp, hoped to draw him into battle, at the same time sending for Metellus to reinforce him.

Sertorius didn't accept the bait. Instead, he devised a crafty stratagem. There were two places where Pompey's troops could forage for water, firewood, crops, and fodder for their horses and cattle. Sertorius had his light infantry harass every attempt by Pompey's men to use the nearby foraging place, but allowed the Pompeians to forage farther afield unmolested. Then, at night, he secreted 1,200 infantry and 2,000 cavalry in a forest beside the distant foraging place.

At dawn the following day, four to five thousand Pompeian troops marched to the foraging area with a convoy of carts. Around 9:00 a.m., as men began making their way back to camp with loaded carts, those on sentry duty let down their guard and themselves went foraging. Now, Sertorius's troops rose from their hiding places.

As surprised Pompeian troops streamed back along the road, heading for camp, they were ridden down by 1,750 Sertorian cavalry from one direction, their path to camp blocked by the other 250. Pompey, seeing his troops being cut down like chaff before the scythe, sent out an entire legion of six thousand men to rescue the foragers, only for Sertorius to send cavalry circling around behind the legion, cutting it off. The legion, and its commander, met the same fate as the foragers. Pompey lost ten thousand men and his wheeled transport that day, while Sertorius lost barely a man.

"Thus," writes first-century general Sextus Julius Frontinus, "in addition to inflicting a twofold disaster, as a result of the same strategy Sertorius forced Pompey to be the helpless witness to the destruction of his own troops."[8]

Pompey, knowing that Metellus was force-marching his legions to join him, led his remaining troops out to battle Sertorius, who recalled his attackers and formed up his infantry on a hill while leaving his cavalry ranging the flatlands. Perceiving the danger of attacking the hill with Sertorius's cavalry behind him, Pompey held his position.

The news reached Sertorius that Metellus was approaching. Sertorius, determined not to be caught between two forces, withdrew back into the mountains, allowing Pompey to link up with Metellus. Just as Sertorius repeatedly taught his own troops lessons, his punishing example had taught young Pompey the lesson of ambuscade, and here in Spain and in his later career Pompey would himself subsequently ambush opponents with devastating effect.

Sertorius's forces were now divided among several deputies, including Perpenna, and he remained at Huesca while sending them to harass the Romans. His adversaries liaised closely with each other but operated independently, with Pompey covering eastern Spain and Metellus focusing on reclaiming the west.

In the spring of 75 BC, Pompey came to grips with Sertorius's deputies Perpenna and Herrenius outside coastal Valentia, today's Valencia, in southeastern Spain. Perpenna's troops, overconfident after the mauling their side had previously given Pompey's ambushed army, chased withdrawing Pompeian troops and walked straight into an ambush set by Pompey. Perpenna himself escaped back to Sertorius, but his army was savaged.

This same year, Metellus defeated another of Sertorius's deputies, Hirtuleius, at Italica, north of today's Seville. This fired Sertorius to personally lead an army down to Sucro, on the east coast, to face Pompey. A set battle followed, in which Sertorius's left wing was broken and Pompey's troops surged into his camp, as Sertorius led a charge that broke through Pompey's right wing. Pompey himself only escaped after abandoning his horse to the North African cavalrymen who cut him off, slipping away on foot while the Africans argued over the valuable horse and its even more valuable golden decorations.

Then, as Pompey was regrouping his forces, Sertorius fell on the Pompeians looting his camp. But word arrived that Metellus was approaching. "If this old woman [Metellus] had not come up," Sertorius subsequently complained to his subordinates, "I would have whipped that boy [Pompey] soundly, and sent him to Rome."[9]

Sertorius again retreated to the mountains. Metellus was so pleased with this result that he had his troops acclaim him *imperator*, as if he'd won an overwhelming victory. This ancient title, literally meaning "commander," was given to victorious Roman generals on the acclamation of his troops after a great victory. Several years earlier, Pompey had been hailed imperator in North Africa following a resounding victory over Marian forces, and Metellus was apparently jealous of his young fellow general. Accepting congratulations from leaders of every Spanish city he entered, Metellus held lavish victory banquets. But Pompey wasn't celebrating. He knew that Sertorius was far from vanquished.

In the mountains, Sertorius's lucky white fawn had disappeared. When the fawn was found wandering in the night, Sertorius kept its recovery a secret. The next morning he called a meeting of his loyal chieftains and senior Roman officers, and cheerily proclaimed that in a dream the previous night the gods had promised him good fortune. The fawn was then released, and it ran to him, as if sent by the gods. It was great theater, and a morale booster for Sertorius's followers.

Sertorius learned that the armies of Pompey and Metellus were in one body and foraging on the plain below the east coast hill town of Saguntum, today's Sagunto. A century and a half earlier, the Second Punic War had begun there at Saguntum, in 218 BC, and led to the Carthaginian general Hannibal crossing the Alps and arriving outside the gates of Rome. Perhaps inspired by that Roman defeat, Sertorius went on the offensive, bent on preventing his opponents from resupplying. In a fierce struggle on the Saguntum plain, Pompey's best deputy, Memmius, was killed, and Metellus was wounded by a lance. But Metellus's men formed around him and launched a counterattack. This forced Sertorius again to retreat, this time to a city in the mountains, possibly his home base of Huesca. When the opposing troops pursued him, and, camping outside, prepared to besiege him, Sertorius sent to the tribes of Spain seeking additional manpower. As soon as he learned it was approaching, he burst from the city, fought his way through encircling troops, and linked up with his reinforcements.

Sertorius then commenced a roving guerrilla campaign, harassing supply lines, which forced the Roman armies from the mountains. To feed his troops, Pompey went west to set up winter camp in the territory of the Vaccaei in northwest Spain. Metellus went east and crossed the Pyrenees, wintering in southwest Gaul, where food was abundant. From western Spain, Pompey wrote to the Senate seeking aid. He didn't ask for more troops; he asked for money to feed the men he already had, telling the Senate—truthfully—that he had previously expended his personal fortune equipping and provisioning his troops to fight for Sulla. His request was met.

The following spring, the armies of Pompey and Metellus, resupplied and refreshed, resumed the campaign. But Sertorius had come to realize that even if he won set battles, there would always be another Roman army, another Roman general, to contend with. Rome had almost infinite resources, while he did not. Besides, he had become focused on Rome, and on returning to Italy and taking control there. "He was a sincere lover of his country," says Plutarch, "and he had a great desire to return home." The recent death of his mother back in Italy had made Sertorius all the more homesick.[10]

Opponents of Pompey at Rome who were aware of Sertorius's broader ambitions began to express doubts about the vaunted young general's ability to defeat the rebel, predicting it was more likely they would see Sertorius back in Rome than Pompey. Now Sertorius implemented a new strategy. While his troops continued guerrilla war against Pompey and Metellus in Spain, keeping them tied down, he would preserve his military strength for his broader goal of reaching Rome.

But to get to Rome he needed allies. And he seemed to have them. From Rome came letters from ex-consuls, declaring there were great numbers of men at Rome who longed for a change of government. And from the East came envoys of King Mithradates the Great of Pontus, seeking an alliance. Mithradates offered Sertorius a battle fleet if he agreed to return all the Eastern territories that Sulla had taken from him, including the Roman province of Asia, once Sertorius ruled at Rome.

Calling together his Spanish senate, Sertorius asked their opinion of Mithradates's offer. His advisers all eagerly urged him to accept. But while Sertorius was prepared to give Bithynia and Cappadocia to the Pontic king, as, up to this point, they had always been ruled by kings, he couldn't bring himself to give away a Roman province. On the contrary, he wanted to expand Rome's possessions. So, Sertorius proposed that, in return for three thousand golden talents and forty warships, he would send a company of troops and one of his generals, Marcus Marius, a former praetor, to aid Mithradates. Mithradates agreed.

Marius, who, like Sertorius, lost an eye in battle, sailed with his men from Spain across the Mediterranean to the Roman province of Asia, which Marius took control of in Sertorius's name. Serving as one of Mithradates's generals, Marius would defeat a Roman army in Bithynia. Subsequently, in joint command of Mithradates's fleet, Marius would suffer a crushing defeat near the Aegean island of Lemnos, at the hands of Lucius Licinius Lucullus, the famed Roman general sent by the Senate to deal with Mithradates. Marius would swim ashore from his sinking flagship. Captured hiding in a cave, he would be executed by Lucullus.

In Spain, Sertorius's opponent Metellus announced he would give one hundred talents and 100,000 acres of land to the Roman who delivered Sertorius's head. All the while, bands of Sertorius's troops raided Roman communications and supply in Spain before skulking back into the mountains. As Metellus remained idle, seemingly content to see whether his reward offer would pay dividends, Pompey continued to be active, grinding down Sertorius's outstations while avoiding the mountains. In the meantime, many of Sertorius's Roman officers came to despise the life of hit-and-run, seeing themselves as nothing but bandits and fugitives.

When word of Metellus's reward reached the ears of Sertorius himself at Huesca, he suddenly became paranoid. Dismissing his Roman bodyguards, he replaced them with Spaniards. He even became suspicious of his senior Roman officers. As it turned out, he was right to be suspicious. Behind his back, his chief deputy Marcus Perpenna increasingly saw himself as a much more entitled ruler of Spain. As Plutarch remarks in his biography of Sertorius, "There was no man less easy to deal with, or less to be trusted in, than a partner in power."[11]

Eventually, Perpenna talked a number of Sertorius's disgruntled Roman officers into joining him in a conspiracy to remove their leader. In the summer or autumn of 73 BC, Sertorius hosted a dinner at Huesca attended by his senior officers. Midway through the dinner, several guests broke into what appeared to be a drunken brawl, which distracted Sertorius as he lay on the central dining couch. At that point, Perpenna dropped his silver drinking cup. The clatter of the cup on the stone floor signaled several of Sertorius's officers to rise up, producing hidden daggers. While Antonius, the officer beside him, grabbed and secured Sertorius's arms, the others stabbed their commander to death.

Perpenna was now the rebel leader. But he was no Sertorius, and in that murderous instant at Osca the fire of rebellion was doused by Perpenna's vanity. "By this wicked deed he ensured success to the Romans and destruction of his own faction, and for himself a death of extreme dishonor," Velleius observes.[12]

Tribal leaders throughout Spain and Lusitania previously loyal to Sertorius had no confidence in Perpenna, and they sent envoys to Pompey seeking peace. Spanish, Lusitanian, and African elements of Sertorius's army melted away and went home, leaving Perpenna with just Sertorius's Roman units. When the following spring arrived, so, too, did Pompey and his army.

The battle that followed was brief and one-sided. Pompey's troops routed Perpenna's demoralized men. Hoping to save himself, Perpenna surrendered to Pompey. He also handed over the letters the senators at Rome had written to Sertorius urging him to make a bid for power there. Taking the letters, Pompey burned them in front of Perpenna without even reading them, an act for which he would be highly praised in Rome. With his troops clamoring for Perpenna's death, and himself disgusted by Perpenna's dishonorable betrayal and murder of a man he'd personally respected and considered honorable, Pompey ordered the sniveling Perpenna's immediate execution, and the man's head was cleaved from his shoulders.

Most of the surviving Romans who participated in the assassination of Sertorius fled to North Africa, where they were progressively killed by locals. Just a single assassin remained in Spain, in hiding. Years later, he would die, alone, despised and penniless, in a cave.

With Sertorius gone, Pompey set about restoring the provinces of Nearer Spain and Farther Spain to Roman rule. Wild Lusitania would remain outside the Roman orbit for decades to come, but Roman governors would rule again from Tarraco and Cordoba. Years later, one of the governors of Farther Spain would be Julius Caesar, embarking on his first provincial command at the age of thirty-nine. For now, Pompey and Metellus remained in Spain.

Once back in Rome, until his death in 63 BC, the jealous Metellus joined those in the Senate who were opposed to Pompey. But Pompey's conquests, like his fame and power, would only grow. It would be Pompey, for example, who, replacing a floundering Lucullus, would orchestrate Mithradates the Great's final military defeat in the East, after which Mithradates would commit suicide.

As for Sertorius, he would be remembered as a clever but ultimately doomed rebel, a man fated to be opposed by one of Rome's greatest generals.

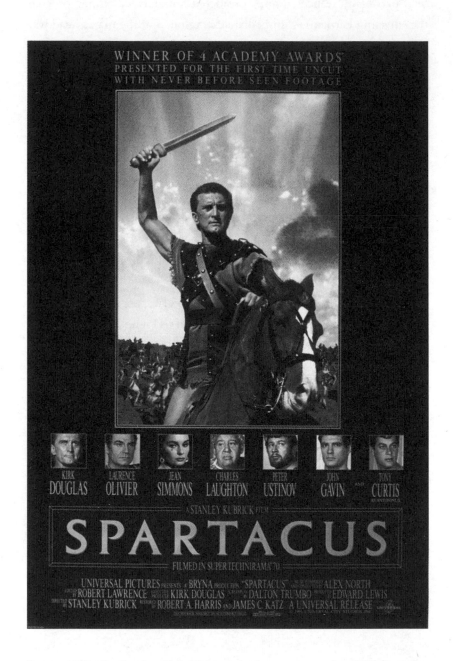

Poster, 1960, for Stanley Kubrick's movie *Spartacus*, starring Kirk Douglas.
Bridgeman Images.

II. SPARTACUS

GLADIATOR, SLAVE REVOLT LEADER.
ITALY, 73–71 BC

In the spring of 73 BC, when Sertorius was still alive and causing Rome headaches in Spain, two hundred gladiators at a slave barracks in Capua, 130 miles south of Rome, rose in revolt against their guards. Armed with knives and skewers from the barracks kitchen, seventy-four gladiators and at least one female slave succeeded in fighting their way out and escaping into the countryside. Their leader was Spartacus. It was a name that would become, and remain, famous.

Around thirty years old at the time of the Capua breakout, Spartacus had been born in Thrace, a kingdom encompassing parts of today's Greece, Bulgaria, and Turkey. As a young man, he served in the Roman army for several years, in one of the scores of auxiliary units that made up half the strength of the Roman military. Until the emperor Claudius made Thrace a Roman province in AD 46, it was ruled by client kings loyal to Rome, who supplied auxiliary units for service with the Roman army, made up of Thracians like Spartacus, men without Roman citizenship.

In Spartacus's case, he almost certainly served in a cavalry wing. Thracians were noted horsemen, and by the first century, Thracian cavalry wings were the most numerous of all the mounted units in Rome's armies, although once Thrace became a province, Thracian units increasingly included a variety of nationalities apart from Thracian natives. Commanders of auxiliary units were frequently members of tribal nobility, and some historians suspect that Spartacus was a well-educated member of the Thracian aristocracy—Spartacus being a recorded Thracian royal family name. In which case, this Spartacus, the escaped gladiator, would probably have commanded a cavalry wing of five hundred horsemen in his army days. This would explain Spartacus's later aura of authority, his skilled horsemanship, and his solid grip on Roman military strategy and tactics.

Modern historians suggest that Spartacus was among the Thracian and Macedonian auxiliaries known to have been brought to Italy in 83 BC by Sulla to support his legions in his civil war against Marius. At some point during Spartacus's military service, perhaps only a year or two prior to the Capua breakout, he was accused of a crime, which caused him to desert the Roman army. He became a roving bandit. Exactly where is not recorded, but the fact that he ended up in a slave market in Rome suggests it was in Italy. After he was captured, apparently reasonably soon after his desertion, he was sentenced to enslavement and put up for sale.

It was Spartacus's fate to be spotted at a Rome slave market by Gnaeus Cornelius Lentulus Vatia, whose business interests included his own gladiatorial "school," or company. Spartacus's physique made him an ideal candidate for Vatia's school in Capua, from where he would be hired out to fight in the arenas of Italy. He was trained as a *murmillo*, a class of gladiator who fought naked to the waist and barefoot, but which was the most heavily equipped of the gladiators. He went into the arena with a helmet and arm and shin guards, and the same heavy shield and short sword used by legionaries on the battlefield. Ancient Roman graffiti found in Italy indicates that Spartacus may have occasionally also fought mounted, in spectacles in which cavalry was pitted against infantry. His background as a cavalryman would certainly have equipped him for that.

The 1960 Hollywood movie *Spartacus* cast Peter Ustinov as Vatia (called Batiatus in the movie), the *lanista*, or owner, of Spartacus's gladiatorial school, and depicted him in frequent contact with his gladiators. In reality, many Roman senators and members of the Equestrian

Order invested in gladiators as just one of their business interests, and had little to do with the men who fought and died for them, leaving that to their gladiatorial managers. Julius Caesar had his own gladiatorial school, and despite the millions of words written about him there is no account that shows him taking more than a cursory interest in his gladiators.

An unnamed Thracian woman cohabiting with Spartacus at the gladiator barracks, probably a slave, escaped with him. Once the runaways left Capua, they headed south toward Neapolis, today's Naples, on the Bay of Naples. The wild slopes of volcanic Mount Vesuvius, six miles east of Naples, had long been home to bandits, and Spartacus and his companions climbed the single road that wound up the mountainside and made camp on the summit, 3,700 feet above sea level, looking out over the towns on the Bay of Naples. From there, they could see the approach of any army sent to recapture them.

After being recaptured, runaway slaves were often returned to their masters. Some were sentenced to death in the arena—usually the older, less useful ones, who were sent unarmed in bunches against wild beasts in amphitheaters to entertain the masses. More than a century after Spartacus, the emperor Caligula was driving his chariot south of Rome heading for Pozzuoli to make a state visit to Sicily, when he passed a contingent of chained prisoners, apparently recaptured slaves, being herded along the highway toward Rome and death in the arena.

When one elderly prisoner called out to Caligula asking him to give him a quick death then and there on the end of a sword, Caligula cynically called back, "So, you consider yourself alive in your present state?"[13]

An escaped slave who turned to armed rebellion against Rome could expect no mercy if captured. Spartacus and his followers had no illusions about what would happen to them if they were to be retaken. Their only hope was in fighting to stay free until they could somehow leave Italy and return to their homelands.

From Vesuvius, they raided estates throughout central Italy, freeing other slaves and building and arming a force numbering in the thousands. Appointing two deputy commanders, Crixus and Oenomaus, Spartacus organized and trained his recruits in military fashion. He divided his men into companies, appointing company commanders, creating standards, and choosing trumpeters who would signal movements on the battlefield and sound the change of watches in the camp at night. Female and child slaves would have been among those freed, and these became the companions of the outlaws, their cheerleaders in victory and their solace in adversity.

In the autumn of 73 BC, the Senate sent a force of three thousand infantrymen to deal with Spartacus and his troublesome slave rabble. This was led by Gaius Claudius Glaber, one of the eight praetors elected that year in Rome. Praetors were Rome's highest-ranking judges, sitting in judgment in the courts. Only the two elected consuls were more senior than the praetors at that time.

Some authors, when pondering why a praetor and not a consul would be sent with troops to counter the slave revolt, have assumed that Glaber's men were little more than hastily assembled militiamen, forgetting, or not knowing about, the existence of the Praetorian Guard. In this era, Rome's legions were levied from citizens as needed, both at Rome and throughout the Roman world. At this moment, Rome's legions were engaged in the war against Sertorius in Spain and against Mithradates in the East. The only standing military force in Rome at this time was the Praetorian Guard, so called because it answered to, and was commanded by, the praetors.

Considered an elite force, the Praetorian Guard would fall into abeyance during the later civil war between Caesar and Pompey, only to be revived by Mark Antony following Caesar's death. The three thousand troops led south from Rome by praetor Glaber were without doubt men of the Praetorian Guard. Imagine the shock in Rome, then, when it was learned that after Glaber and his Praetorian Guard cohorts had camped within sight of Mount Vesuvius, placing guards on the single road to Spartacus's summit camp, they were routed.

Spartacus's followers had woven rope ladders from the shoots of willow trees commonly used in basket making, and Spartacus and his best men had used them to climb down steep cliffs, assuredly at night. Then, with the Roman sentries looking toward the mountain, the gladiators had launched a surprise attack on Glaber's camp from the plain. Several cohorts gave way to an attacking force of less than one hundred men. Those Praetorians not butchered in the camp beat an inglorious retreat, fleeing north as Spartacus and his men captured and looted the Roman camp. Of the Roman commander we hear nothing more, and it is likely Glaber was killed in his *praetorium*, his headquarters tent.[14]

The Senate quickly appointed another praetor, Publius Varinius, to command a new campaign to deal with the Spartacans, and gave yet another praetor, Lucius Cossinius, the job of raising levies in support of Varinius. As Varinius slowly marched south, adding new recruits as he went, he sent his deputy, the senator Lucius Furius, on ahead with a two-thousand-man advance guard, again almost certainly from the Praetorian Guard. Several decades later, when Octavian and Mark Antony were allies, the Praetorian Guard would number eight cohorts, each of one thousand men. If this was also the size of the Guard in 73 BC, it means that just three thousand men remained behind at Rome to guard the Senate and its senators.

Heading for Mount Vesuvius, an unwary Furius marched into a rebel ambush, apparently in Campania. Furius seems to have perished as his men fled. At the same time, Spartacus had kept the praetor Cossinius under surveillance. Cossinius, who was supposed to be levying troops, was unaware that Spartacan spies were among the slaves around him, and had taken time off to relax in the bath of a villa outside Pompeii on the Bay of Naples, within sight of Vesuvius. There, Spartacus found him and killed him.

As for Varinius, he was still moving slowly south with two forces made up of raw recruits. One he led; the other was commanded by his *quaestor*, or adjutant, Gaius Torianus. Out of the blue, Torianus's camp was raided by Spartacus's men, and then Varinius's own camp was hit.

Stunned by the defeats and losses, and by the way the rebels seemingly came and went at will—often in the night—Varinius dispatched Torianus back to Rome to report to the Senate. Meanwhile, Varinius himself pulled together four thousand surviving Praetorians and raw recruits from all the bloodied forces that had been sent against Spartacus, and built a fortified camp near the rebels.

Spartacus and some ten thousand followers slipped away from their camp in the night, leaving campfires blazing, corpses tied to stakes "standing guard," and a single trumpeter sounding the changing of the watches through the night. Once Varinius realized he'd been fooled, he withdrew to await reinforcements, but goaded by his troops, who were anxious for revenge, he soon set off after the rebels. The best they could do was trail in the wake of Spartacus's marauding army, which sacked town after town and freed more slaves, adding them to their ranks.

But Spartacus's increased numbers brought division in his ranks. His deputy Oenomaus had been killed. Now Spartacus's surviving lieutenant, Crixus, a Celt, sided with a faction of troops who wanted to go up against Varinius and take the slave revolt to all of Italy, for blood and for booty. Spartacus, however, argued for avoiding battle and heading north to the Alps, from where they could all go home. Staying and fighting Rome, with all its resources, he said, could only end badly for the rebels.

A vote was called for. When it was taken, few stood with Spartacus. The vast majority, especially the latest recruits, lusted for the lives and wealth of their former masters. Besides, many of these men were the sons of slaves and had been born in Italy. Unlike Spartacus, they had no homeland to return to. Accepting the results of the democratic vote, Spartacus agreed to lead his men against Varinius—but he would do it in his own time. He instructed his followers to make careful preparations to ensure victory, and to increase their numbers by recruiting shepherds. The rebel army turned south and marched to the southern region of Lucania, recruiting and looting as it went.

Varinius followed with his four thousand Roman troops, only to walk into an ambush. Varinius's personal attendants, his six Praetorian lictors—a role often held by retired centurions—were captured along with Varinius's symbols of office, his *fasces*, which Spartacus would adopt as his own symbols of power. Even Varinius's horse was captured, although he himself escaped. His routed force fared no better, with a number of military standards among the trophies secured by the rebels that day.

Back in Rome, in late 73 BC, the alarmed Senate met and issued orders for the recruitment, equipping, and training of four new legions, totaling 24,000 men, to combat Spartacus, whose name was now a household word in Italy, spoken in fear and dread by everyone but the slaves. Already, 150,000 citizens were marching in Rome's legions in Spain and the East. The *conquisitores*—literally, "searchers"—Rome's recruiting officers, who ranged throughout northern and central Italy looking for citizen recruits between the ages of seventeen and forty-six, were not as particular as they might have been in less threatening times. Some of the men they rounded up were volunteers, but many were forced recruits, or "levies"—which is the origin of the word *legio*, or legion. Every town was required to keep up-to-date lists of citizens of legion age. If a man could march and carry a sword and shield, he was selected.

The new legions were to be ready by late March the following year, traditionally the time of commencement of spring military campaigns. This gave the new legions' centurions three months to batter discipline into their new legionaries—to train them in the use of their weapons, the trumpet calls that dictated legion movements, and the battlefield formations designed to bring them victory.

Those three months over the winter of 73–72 BC also gave Spartacus time to prepare. New recruits flooded to him from the lower classes, and by the spring of 72 BC his rebel force numbered at least forty thousand. Some accounts put his followers at as many as 120,000 by the following autumn, a large proportion of them noncombatants.

In the spring, this rebel mass moved into the Bruttium region in south-west Italy. But Spartacus and Crixus were again at loggerheads. Spartacus wanted to push up the mountainous spine of Italy to achieve his longtime goal, escape from Italy via the Alps. Crixus wanted to remain in southern Italy raiding and pillaging.

Agreeing to disagree, they created two forces, with every rebel free to choose which leader he followed. Spartacus had the reputation and charisma of an unbeatable general, so it is no surprise that three-quarters of the rebels chose to march north with him that spring. The remaining twenty-five percent, eager for spoils, remained with Crixus in the south as he moved his raids into today's Puglia region.

When intelligence of this split reached Rome, the Senate agreed that the two consuls for that year would each lead an army of four new legions against the rebels. Gnaeus Cornelius Lentulus Clodianus, known as Lentulus, would shadow Spartacus's force, while the older consul, Lucius Gellius, a man in his sixties, would quickly march south to seek out and destroy Crixus's force, then wheel north to reinforce Lentulus for a strike against Spartacus.

Gellius, taking two legions, quickly achieved the first part of his brief. Surprising Crixus's smaller force near Mount Garganus in Apulia, Gellius's raw legionaries overwhelmed the overconfident rebels. Although they reportedly fought extremely tenaciously, Crixus and two-thirds of his men were killed in the battle. News of the victory electrified Rome—at last, the tide was turning against Spartacus. Or so it seemed. But Spartacus was no Crixus, and would prove harder to defeat.

While Gellius was achieving his success in the south, his fellow consul Lentulus had located Spartacus's larger force in the Apennine Mountains northeast of Rome. As the victorious Gellius marched north to cut off a Spartacan retreat, Lentulus placed his legions in Spartacus's path, blocking the way north, and began to push south through the Apennines. In theory, Spartacus was now trapped between the two senatorial armies. But his army of at least thirty thousand men—including a cavalry element, which the Romans did not possess—was more than a match for Lentulus's force. Deciding to deal with Lentulus before Gellius arrived, Spartacus prepared an ambush at a site in the hills, which some believe was a little south of what is now Florence.

Surprising Lentulus's unprepared legionaries on the march, Spartacus led his men as they rose up from hiding and charged. The legions, strung out along a mountain road, broke under this charge, with legionaries turning and fleeing into the wilds. Among the many Romans who fell that day were the two senators commanding Lentulus's legions, with the silver eagle standards of their legions falling into rebel hands. With the rebels occupied looting Lentulus's baggage train, Lentulus was able to escape with some of his men.

As soon as Spartacus was able to regroup his booty-laden force, he turned south and ambushed Gellius as he was coming north. Gellius's new legions, full of bravado after the victory over Crixus, were likewise overrun, and Gellius and his surviving troops recoiled in disorder. Three to four hundred captured Roman legionaries were subsequently forced by Spartacus to fight each other to the death in gladiatorial games, staged there in the mountains in honor of his dead comrade Crixus. While gladiatorial games had by this time become a blood sport, originally they were staged as a funeral rite to honor fallen Roman heroes. Spartacus's games were the ultimate insult to the Roman Senate—Roman citizens forced to fight and die for the entertainment of escaped slaves.

Spartacus and his undefeated army now entered the River Po Valley north of Mutina, today's Modena. The Po was the border between Italy and the province of Cisalpine Gaul, today's northern Italy. Here, the rebels were confronted by the Roman governor of Cisalpine Gaul, Gaius Cassius Longinus, and his garrison, which involved at least one legion and perhaps two. The battle is likely to have taken place north of the Po, because by law the governor could not cross into Italy without Senate permission.

Again, the slave army overwhelmed Rome's professional soldiers. As Cassius Longinus and the bloodied remnants of his force reeled back, leaving behind the silver eagle standard of a legion, the path was left open for Spartacus and his men to reach the Alps. From there, Spartacus's men could turn left and head into Gaul, or turn right, and head for the Balkans, Greece, and Spartacus's homeland of Thrace. But then Spartacus did a strange thing. Turning away from the open northern escape route, he marched his army back into Italy. His goal, it would be claimed, was Rome itself. Certainly, the people of Rome believed that he was coming to take their city; panic reigned in the capital.

In the meantime, the consuls Lentulus and Gellius had linked up and reformed their four shattered legions—combined they now had twenty thousand men—when they learned that Spartacus had marched to Italy's east coast and was in the Picenum region, a lush, wealthy farming district.

It is highly likely that Spartacus quite deliberately marched through Picenum, rather than sticking to the mountains. Picenum was the home territory of young Pompey the Great, who was currently off in Spain consolidating Roman rule after the deaths of the rebels Sertorius and his successor Perpenna. In Picenum, a twenty-three-year-old Pompey, still seven years short of Senate entry age, had raised and equipped three legions at his own expense for Sulla. Those three units, known as Pompey's 1st, 2nd, and 3rd Legions, had helped Pompey win the civil war for Sulla and were currently with him in Spain. Perhaps, like the funeral games of Crixus, Spartacus's march through Picenum was a deliberate insult to Rome, a demonstration that he was even greater than the idolized young general the Romans called "Great," who could not even defend his homeland.

In Picenum, Spartacus's larger army engaged in a set-piece battle with the depleted legions of Lentulus and Gellius. This was a surprising departure for Spartacus, who had relied on ambush and surprise so often in the past. But, as the Romans were to find out, Spartacus had a trick up his sleeve. Lentulus, in overall senatorial command because he'd served as a consul earlier than Gellius, who had come to the consulship late in his career, occupied a hillside with a double battle line. In a wild mass, the rebels charged up this hill time and again, without breaking through, although the senatorial forces suffered heavy casualties in holding their ground.

But Spartacus had discreetly divided his force. While one division kept Lentulus busy on the hillside, other rebels succeeded in getting around behind the senatorial troops unseen. They then attacked the consuls' lightly defended marching camp, within view of Lentulus on the hilltop. Fighting their way into the camp, Spartacus's men ransacked it, with some rebels emerging wearing the spare white and scarlet cloaks of Roman tribunes and generals, seized from baggage in the camp.

Now, too, Lentulus saw that, far from being rabble, Spartacus's troops were in disciplined cohorts, handpicked for this operation, and those cohorts were now marching on his position from the devastated camp. To avoid being attacked from front and rear and being surrounded, Lentulus was forced to order a full retreat, and he and his men abandoned the hill and withdrew in a semblance of order.[15]

Now Spartacus again changed his mind. Instead of heading across the Apennines to Rome, as the Senate believed he would, with winter approaching he marched all the way back to southernmost Italy, familiar territory, where some survivors from Crixus's army would have been in hiding. Another Roman army came against Spartacus upon his arrival there, and again the Romans were repulsed. Spartacus ended 72 BC unconquered—but trapped in southern Italy.

With Lentulus and Gellius both having been embarrassed by the rebels, in the autumn of 72 BC the Senate appointed a new commander to lead its forces against Spartacus, the immensely wealthy senator Marcus Licinius Crassus. In his forties now, Crassus had previously supported Marius in the civil war before changing sides to support Sulla. He had proved one of Sulla's most reliable generals, commanding the dictator's right wing in the Battle of the Colline Gate, which had delivered Rome to Sulla a decade before the name Spartacus was spoken in the Senate. Crassus was jealous of the fame and popularity of Sulla's other leading general, Pompey. So, the fact that the humbled sitting consuls Lentulus and Gellius were Pompey's friends and supporters made Crassus's acceptance of Roman military command in Italy all the sweeter when they offered it to him.

Like Pompey in Spain, the Senate gave Crassus *imperium*, the full powers of the Senate, in his area of operations. This meant that he wouldn't have to refer back to the Senate for approval of any of his actions; he was a law unto himself. Over the winter, Crassus recruited in Italy and trained six new legions. By the spring of 71 BC, Crassus and his new army of more than ninety thousand recruits and survivors of the previous year's campaign against Spartacus were on the move, marching south. Simultaneously, Spartacus moved north from Lucania toward them.

In Picentia, which stood between Campania and Lucania, Crassus detached the two surviving legions from the previous year's battles under a senator named Mummius, sending them south to circle around behind Spartacus but not engage him. Mummius, proving too greedy for glory and dismissive of the rebel army's lethal abilities, disobeyed Crassus's orders. As soon as Mummius saw an opportunity for battle, he sent his two legions against the much larger rebel force. Predictably, they were smashed by Spartacus's troops. Many legionaries threw away their weapons and ran, abandoning their eagle standards.

After Mummius and thousands of survivors fled back to Crassus's camp in Picentia, Crassus issued new weapons to the runaways and made them give a solemn promise never to throw them away again. Then his demeanor changed. First, he humiliated Mummius; how, we aren't told. Then he decimated the first five hundred men to arrive back at camp following the disastrous battle, the men who had been the first to flee and desert their comrades. Historically, to decimate meant to reduce by ten percent. Under Roman military law going back to the fifth century BC, all the men under sentence of decimation drew lots. One in ten would randomly draw a short straw, and the remaining ninety percent would be forced to club the unlucky ones to death. Years later, Julius Caesar and Mark Antony would decimate their own mutinous legions. There in Picentia, at a parade before the entire army, four hundred and fifty of Crassus's troops duly executed fifty of their own comrades. The message to Crassus's remaining men was clear.

Crassus now suddenly broke camp and marched south, perhaps at night, and fell on a force of ten thousand rebels that had been left by Spartacus to shadow him. After a fierce battle, during which they stood their ground to the end, only nine hundred rebels survived to become prisoners; 9,100 were killed. Crassus had his first victory against Spartacus, even if Spartacus himself was not present. On hearing of the defeat, Spartacus retreated south with his main force. The rebels kept going until they reached the Tyrrhenian Sea at the port of Regium, today's Reggio, and Crassus and his army warily followed.

As it happened, outside the Sicilian port of Syracuse across the Messina Strait, pirate vessels commanded by a Cilician named Heracleo had defeated a Roman battle fleet. Tens of thousands of Cilician pirates were ranging the Mediterranean, and before long they would control the sea lanes that Rome depended on for supply. Spartacus the rebel reached out to Heracleo the pirate. The pair met and made a deal. In exchange for gold, Heracleo's ships would ferry two thousand of Spartacus's men to Sicily, where Spartacus intended to free more slaves from their Roman masters to increase his numbers. But as soon as Heracleo had his gold he sailed away, without keeping his part of the bargain. Never trust a pirate!

Spartacus then tried to build rafts to ferry men to Sicily, but they proved a failure. The rebels were forced to retreat into the hills and winter there. While they were camped, Crassus caught up to them and bottled up the rebels on a mountainous peninsula, which was just thirty-five miles across where it joined the mainland. The Roman general created a trench line from sea to sea and created a major fortified defensive position on Melia Ridge, fifty-five miles inland from Regium, dominating the coast road below. There, the Romans wintered, and waited.

Early in 71 BC, well before spring, Spartacus launched an all-out attack against the Roman position on Melia Ridge. Crassus was ready, and lured the attackers into a trap amid carefully prepared fortifications. Crassus had received reinforcements of cavalry and, more importantly, archers and slingers. Where these specialist auxiliary troops originated is unknown, but they quite possibly came from Crete, which was renowned for its slingers. In any case, they brought him a stunning victory. Unable to come to grips with the Romans on the walls of Crassus's well-placed fortifications, Spartacus's men were cut down in droves by arrows and other missiles.

By day's end, the rebels had fled, leaving behind twelve thousand dead. Crassus would claim he only suffered three fatalities that day. Smarting from his first defeat, Spartacus set up camp on the coast, still trapped on the peninsula, and a stalemate developed as each side eyed the other. Crassus was in no hurry. He had the rebels where he wanted them.

In Rome, however, the people were becoming impatient. Why were Spartacus and his army still at large? Why wasn't Crassus crushing them? Rome's popular assembly, made up of plebeians, voted to recall Pompey the Great and his legions from Spain to deal with the rebels. The Senate rubber-stamped the popular vote, and a message was sent, calling on Pompey to return with all haste. Crassus later claimed he advised the Senate to recall Pompey, but in truth the last thing he wanted was to share the glory of ending the slave revolt with Pompey, let alone surrender it to him wholesale.

Probably from Roman scouts boasting to rebel outposts that Pompey was coming, Spartacus learned that a formidable Roman general was marching into Italy with his seasoned legions to deal with him. The rebel leader promptly sent a message to Crassus, offering to end hostilities and become Rome's ally. Crassus dismissed the offer out of hand. So in February 71 BC, Spartacus waited for a stormy night, and with some of Crassus's troops absent on winter furlough and Roman sentries keeping their heads down in the storm, he led a breakout from the peninsula.

Using rocks, tree branches, and the bodies of prisoners and cattle, his men filled in part of the entrenchments designed to fence them in, then scurried inland. The breakout was discovered after the men were well advanced, and Crassus fell on the rebel army's rear, causing heavy casualties. But Spartacus and the majority of his men succeeded in escaping in the night.

Intent on heading back north to the Apennines, Spartacus led his men into Lucania. Since basing himself on Mount Vesuvius at the beginning of this war, he'd been more comfortable in the mountains, occupying the high ground. Crassus had likewise achieved victory at Melia Ridge because he'd held the high ground.

But now the rebel leadership experienced another rift. Two of Spartacus's deputies, Castus and Gannicus, led as many as thirty thousand booty-minded Celtic and German rebels in breaking away. They headed off to Calabria, in the "toe" of southwest Italy, taking with them much of the loot captured from the legions they'd defeated over the past two years.

In March, Castus and Gannicus's army was encamped on Mount Camalatrum in Calabria when, in the woods, two women spotted six thousand Roman troops from Crassus's army circling behind the rebels' lakeside camp. Once the women raised the alarm, the rebels turned to face the threat, only to be attacked from another direction by Crassus's main force. Then, from higher ground, the six thousand legionaries attacked. Castus and Gannicus, caught between the two Roman forces, were in dire straits. But then help arrived. Hoping to reunite his forces, Spartacus had tailed the breakaways with his main army, and they now launched into the fray.

Crassus was forced to withdraw, but he followed the rebels as they linked up and marched into Lucania, where their two forces camped separately but near each other. Crassus had finally learned to be as tricky as Spartacus, and near the town of Cantena at the foot of a mountain he sent some cavalry to divert Spartacus's attention. Crassus's remaining cavalry attacked the Celts and Germans, then turned tail and galloped away, apparently in disorder. The men following Castus and Gannicus gleefully gave chase, only to run straight into an infantry ambush. The Celts and Germans stood their ground and fought, but they were surrounded. Castus, Gannicus, and thousands of their men were killed. The destruction of this second rebel force gave Crassus a crushing victory. From the rebel camp, five legionary eagles, twenty-six lesser Roman military standards, and five of the six *fasces* lost by the praetor Varinius were recovered by Crassus's troops.

Spartacus, unable to reach his comrades in time, withdrew his army. It is believed that he marched into Bruttium, seeking the protection of mountain heights. Crassus sent a force of infantry and cavalry to keep on the rebels' tail, but Spartacus could still bite. He suddenly swung on the force on his heels and attacked it, shattering it. One of the two Roman commanders, seriously wounded, had to be carried away by his men.

The rebels then changed direction. Spartacus turned southeast toward Italy's Adriatic coast and marched for Brundisium, today's Brindisi, a port that throughout Roman history served as the departure point for Romans heading to the East. Once again, with the plunderers Castus and Gannicus gone, Spartacus was thinking of escaping Italy. Then news reached him that a Roman army led by Marcus Lucullus, the younger brother of the Roman general Lucius Licinius Lucullus, who was at that time conducting Rome's war against Mithradates the Great in the East, had just landed from a fleet in Brundisium, summoned home by the Senate to help end the Slave War. These troops were coincidentally arriving back from successful operations against the fractious Bessi tribe, in the north of Thrace, Spartacus's homeland.

News of this Roman force's arrival less than two hundred miles to their southeast caused a mutiny in Spartacus's ranks. Hemmed in on three sides, with Crassus behind them, Lucullus in front, and Pompey approaching from the north, the mutineers were spoiling for battle. "Fight or die" was now their motto. Though Spartacus wanted to avoid battle, he gave in to his men yet again. Mounting his horse, and with his cavalry around him, Spartacus led his army toward Crassus's army. With the rebels marched women and children, the camp followers, including Spartacus's own female Thracian partner, and three thousand prisoners, all of them Roman citizens. These were mostly captured soldiers, but probably also some landowners for whom there would have been hopes of negotiating ransoms.

On hearing of Spartacus's turnaround, Crassus increased the pace of his troops, advancing to do battle with the rebels before Pompey or Lucullus arrived on the scene to steal his victory. In the valley of the Upper Silarius River, the two sides sighted each other and made camp. As was then standard practice for a Roman army on the march, Crassus ordered a trench and rampart dug around his camp. Seeing this, some of Spartacus's men spontaneously dashed to the attack. But the digging legionaries didn't flee. Grabbing their weapons, they defended themselves as the camp's guard cohorts rushed to their support. As the rebels withdrew in disorder, Crassus ordered the sounding of the trumpet call "Battle Order."

Hearing the trumpet call, Spartacus likewise ordered his men to prepare for full-scale battle, then sent for his horse.

"If I win today," he declared before his gathered thousands, "I will have many horses, and good ones, from the enemy. If I lose, I will not need any." Drawing his sword, he killed his horse on the spot, making it blatantly clear that he wouldn't be deserting his men by riding away when the fighting became hot.[16]

As both sides formed battle lines across the valley, Spartacus pinpointed Crassus himself—his personal standard held high by his standard-bearer so that every Roman soldier could see where his general was. Crassus also stood out in his scarlet *paludamentum*, the richly embroidered cloak of a Roman army commander. (Three decades later, Julius Caesar would lose his scarlet *paludamentum* in Alexandria Harbor during a desperate battle against the Egyptians.) Almost certainly, Crassus positioned himself on the right wing, the usual place for commanding generals in Roman battle lines, where the best legions were stationed.

Spartacus, with his personal bodyguard, positioned himself on his own left wing, immediately opposite Crassus. Forced by his own men into a set-piece battle, Spartacus had run out of tricks. With both sides equal in number—forty thousand men each—Spartacus decided that his only option for victory was to kill his opposite number, Crassus, which would surely demoralize the Roman rank and file and send them running.

The rebels charged first, sweeping across the valley grass in wild-eyed abandon. With a roar and the clash of shield on shield, the two lines swept together like two converging waves. Spartacus led the men of his wing in hacking a way through the Roman legionaries in his path, only to find a fresh Roman line waiting in closed-up ranks, shields locked together. Spartacus drove on single-mindedly toward Crassus, slaying two centurions who barred his way. But the rest of his army was not making such progress.

All around him, Spartacus's bodyguards fell. Elsewhere, rebel fighters were being driven back. Roman troops surrounded Spartacus. A small javelin pieced him in the thigh. Unable to stand, he dropped to one knee, but keeping up his shield, he continued to swing his sword. Inevitably, the target for scores of javelins and swords, the rebel commander fell. A victorious roar went up from legionaries on Crassus's wing. Spartacus's men knew what this meant. He was dead. The loss of their heroic leader devastated the slave army. Seized by panic, many threw away their shields and ran for the hills.

The day brought an overwhelming victory to Crassus. He lost a thousand men in the battle, but as many as thirty thousand rebels had been killed with their leader on the battlefield, or in the pursuit that followed. Their bodies were left to rot where they fell. Spartacus's

3,000 Roman prisoners were freed, while three groups of slaves totaling 6,000 men were hunted down in the nearby hills and captured. Another 5,000 fled north to Etruria, today's Tuscany. There, within days, they walked into Pompey and his legions, who had marched all the way from Spain. Pompey unleashed his hardened legionaries on them, taking no prisoners. This last remnant of Spartacus's once feared army was swiftly wiped out.

In April, Crassus arrived in Capua, the scene of Spartacus's original breakout, marching his six thousand rebel prisoners with him. He then proceeded to crucify every one, lining the road from Capua to Rome with them, their eventually decomposing corpses signaling to all remaining slaves in Italy that this was the fate of runaways and rebels. The women and children who had followed Spartacus's army would have been returned to slavery.

The victors soon had their rewards. In July, Crassus and Pompey were elected consuls for the following year, 70 BC, effective January 1. In addition, for his success in Spain against the Spanish rebels under Sertorius, Pompey was awarded a Triumph, the glorious parade in a golden chariot through Rome's streets awarded by the Senate to generals who killed at least ten thousand foreign foes in battle. In accepting the award, Pompey made history, not only as the youngest-ever recipient of a Triumph but also as the first member of the Equestrian Order, which ranked below the Senatorial Order, to celebrate a Triumph. His much older colleague in the Spanish war, Quintus Metellus, was also awarded a Triumph, as was Marcus Lucullus for his victory in Thrace. But because Crassus had defeated slaves, he only received an Ovation, a second-class Triumph in which the general rode on horseback in his victory parade.

Before long, at the behest of the Senate, Pompey and his crack legions would sweep the Cilician pirates from the sea, returning the Mediterranean to Roman control. In the East, Pompey would go on to wrap up the war against Mithradates and awe the Parthians, establishing the eastern border of the Roman Empire at the Euphrates River and turning Syria into a Roman province. He would conquer Judea, and set client kings on thrones throughout the East; in Egypt, he enthroned Ptolemy XII, father of Cleopatra, giving him from his legions a Roman bodyguard, which was headed for a time by his eldest son, Gnaeus. Pompey's conquests would also double Rome's annual income via taxes from the East.

As for Crassus, in the coming years he would partner Pompey and Julius Caesar in the so-called First Triumvirate, which effectively ran the Roman Republic. But when he thirsted for glory and led a Roman army into Parthia in 53 BC, he and his son perished at the hands of the Parthians at the Battle of Carrhae, with twenty thousand of their legionaries killed and ten thousand captured. The defeat rocked Rome and obsessed Romans for a generation until those ghosts were set to rest by Tiberius, stepson of the emperor Augustus, who in 20 BC successfully negotiated the return of the sacred Roman standards captured by the Parthians at Carrhae.

No educated Roman ever forgot the names of Pompey or Crassus, one lauded as a great hero, the other, despite his defeat of Spartacus, with a legacy of failure in Parthia. Yet, who today has heard of Pompey, the general and statesman who reclaimed Spain for Rome and pacified and greatly expanded the Roman Empire in the East, or of Crassus, the general responsible for one of the worst Roman defeats in Roman history? Yet, because of a memorable Hollywood movie that was far from historically accurate, the name of Spartacus is still known today.

Colossal 1865 statue representing Vercingetorix, Mount Auxois, France.
Photo © Josse/Bridgeman Images.

III. VERCINGETORIX

GALLIC REVOLT LEADER.
FRANCE, 52 BC

In the summer of 52 BC, two opposing armies climbed onto the Gergovian Plateau, 1,200 feet above sea level and six miles south of the modern-day city of Clermont-Ferrand in central France. One was a legionary army led by Julius Caesar, Roman governor of Cisalpine Gaul, who over the past six years had conquered all of central and northern Gaul, subjecting the long-haired Gallic tribes to Roman rule.

The other army, made up of thousands of Gallic rebels, was led by Vercingetorix—a name meaning "king who was victor in a hundred battles." This title was applied to him by his followers. We don't know his actual name. We do know that at this time he was in his late twenties or early thirties. We also know, from a gold coin he minted the same year, that he was clean-shaven, with curly hair tumbling over his ears, and large eyes. He was the son of the late chief of the Averni tribe, whose capital, Gergovia, lay on the Gergovian Plateau. Vercingetorix's father had attempted to rule over all of Belgic Gaul, only to be put to death by the tribes for his ambition.

For several years, Vercingetorix had been a faithful Roman subject. Caesar had even called him a friend. But in January 52 BC, when Vercingetorix learned that the Carnute tribe of today's Orleans had revolted against the Romans, he had urged his uncle and other Averni leaders to do the same. They had ejected him from Gergovia as a troublemaker, but the young prince had gone around to other tribes, inciting them to rebel. Sure enough, that spring, tribes from Paris to the Bay of Biscay had risen against the Roman occupiers, and Vercingetorix returned to Gergovia as the head of a rebel army, evicting his uncle and taking charge.

This uprising had forced Caesar to hurry back to Gaul from his winter quarters in northern Italy. Marching on Orleans, he besieged the town, rapidly taking and looting it. At a council of war, Vercingetorix and other tribal leaders agreed to make a stand sixty miles southeast of Orleans, at today's Bourges. Sending 10,000 men to support the 40,000 residents of Bourges, Vercingetorix camped a day's march away with his main army, as Caesar besieged the town. One wet night, the legions came over the walls of Bourges. Only eight hundred Gauls survived.

Caesar then divided his army of ten legions, giving half to his deputy Titus Labienus to deal with rebel forces along the Seine River to the northwest. He marched with the remainder to take Vercingetorix's capital, Gergovia. Vercingetorix, realizing the Roman general's intent, also set off for Gergovia. Both armies took five days to reach the plateau, but Vercingetorix arrived first, occupying the town and building several fortified camps. When Caesar learned that ten thousand Aeduan tribesmen were approaching from today's Burgundy to reinforce Vercingetorix, he marched four legions twenty-four miles in a day to intercept them, and convinced them to join his forces.

Back outside Gergovia, Caesar made a cunning feint, sending one legion plus mule drivers on their pack animals imitating cavalry across the skyline. This drew away thousands of rebels, enabling Caesar to attack and overrun three Gallic camps. But when Caesar had "Recall" trumpeted, only one legion obeyed. The others surged to the walls of Gergovia. When the deceived rebels turned back and rushed to fall on these legions' rear, Caesar sent the ten thousand Aeduans to extricate his men. However, the trapped legionaries, thinking the Gauls were rebel reinforcements, panicked and withdrew in disorder, as the rebels gave chase.

Caesar personally led the 10th Legion, a unit raised by him in Spain and considered his best, in making a stand. He repulsed the rebels, but lost seven hundred men of the 8th Legion that day, including forty-six centurions. The Gauls would claim they came close to seizing Caesar himself. A century and a half later, while visiting the Averni, the historian Plutarch would be shown a sword purported to have been dropped by a fleeing Caesar.

Four years after this battle, while fighting the civil war against the Roman Senate, Caesar would remind his 10th Legion of this day, calling on them to find the same valor: "If you do, you will turn our loss to gain, as happened at Gergovia."[17]

While Caesar was forced by Vercingetorix to withdraw from the plateau, his deputy Labienus had won a battle near today's Paris, only to be forced to withdraw under threat of being cut off. The two Roman forces linked up and withdrew south. Vercingetorix sent Gallic cavalry in pursuit, but Caesar's cavalry turned and routed them, capturing several rebel leaders. Stung by this, Vercingetorix marched his army to Alesia, the fortified hilltop town of the Mandubii tribe on the plateau of Mont Auxois, thirty miles northwest of today's Dijon. Inspired by his Gergovia success, young Gauls flocked to join Vercingetorix at Alesia, increasing his army to eighty thousand men.

Caesar never rejected an opportunity when it was offered. Delighted to have the rebels cooped up in one spot, he swung his enlarged army of eighty thousand legionaries, auxiliaries, and cavalry around and marched to Alesia. There, surrounding the rebels, his legions dug a ten-mile, double-sided entrenchment line around Alesia, with twenty-three wooden forts along its length. To meet this challenge, tribes between the Loire and Saone rivers, assembling a massive relief force of 250,000 infantry and 80,000 cavalry to aid Vercingetorix, marched on Alesia.

Roman forces now found themselves trapped in their entrenchments between Vercingetorix on the hill and a counter-encirclement by the hordes of newly arrived rebels below them, but they stubbornly fought off every attack from without. Then, Vercingetorix mounted a desperate attack down the hill with sixty thousand men. This should have broken through Caesar's trench line, but Caesar had cool heads among his deputies. These included Labienus, Marcus Brutus—by some accounts Caesar's illegitimate son, and later one of his lead assassins—and Caesar's newly arrived young adjutant, his quaestor Mark Antony. They led reserves to wherever they were needed, steadying resistance. As the fighting raged, Labienus, spotting a weakness in the rebel lines outside the encirclement, urged Caesar to launch a counterattack at that spot.

Following Labienus's advice, Caesar led a picked force in a sudden attack from his entrenchments, which broke through rebel lines below him. His troops then swung left and right and chewed into the Gallic lines. Gauls outside the Roman lines broke and fled, chased across the plain by the cavalry now released by Caesar. Some Gauls escaped, among them King Commius of the Atrebates in Belgic Gaul, but Caesar would boast that his men captured so many rebels that day he was able to give every one of his 50,000 legionaries a Gallic slave. Another 20,000 Gallic captives would be sent back to their two tribes in return for tribal submission.

Vercingetorix retreated back up to Alesia, but, with the town out of food and water, his remaining men knew their fate was sealed and laid down their arms. The rebel leader came riding out of Alesia alone, in his best armor, and was conducted to Caesar, who, with his legions formed up, sat on a campaign chair to receive him. Dismounting, Vercingetorix removed his sword belt, helmet, and armor, and presented them to Caesar. He then sat at Caesar's feet as his surrendering men tramped down from Alesia and were chained around wrists and neck by waiting Roman troops. Vercingetorix himself was then chained and led away.

Unrest continued into the following year, but without a figurehead like Vercingetorix it was sporadic and uncoordinated. In central Gaul, Caesar ruthlessly dealt with renewed resistance at Orleans and Bourges. In the north, Labienus defeated rebellious Treveri Germans of Belgic Gaul. In the southwest, when the town of Uxellodunum, near today's Vayrac, rebelled, Caesar overran it and cut off the hands of every male captive. By year's end, the revolt was over, and the Gallic tribes resumed paying Roman taxes and giving over their youth to serve as auxiliaries in the Roman army. It has been estimated that a million Gauls died in Caesar's Gallic conquest.

Some rebel leaders were killed, some were pardoned in return for submitting their tribes to Roman rule. King Commius of the Atrebates fled to Britain, where he assumed rule of Belgic Gauls who had settled there earlier, living out his days in Britain. Vercingetorix lived as a Roman prisoner for another six years, until he became the star attraction in the street parade of Caesar's AD 46 Triumph at Rome. Caesar liked to boast of his magnanimity, but he didn't spare Vercingetorix—the rebel was garroted following the parade, as Caesar attended a celebratory banquet.

Caesar's able deputy Labienus would abandon Caesar once his commander crossed the Rubicon in 49 BC to rebel against the Senate of Rome. He took most of Caesar's Gallic cavalry with him to the senatorial side, many of them men who'd fought for Vercingetorix.

But, as you will see, the Gauls were not done with revolt. Several times more in the coming centuries they would rebel against Rome.

Marc Antony.[1]

From a Roman bust of Marcus Antonius (Mark Antony), who commanded efforts to defeat Labienus. © *Look and Learn/Bridgeman Images*.

IV. LABIENUS

ALLYING WITH PARTHIA AGAINST MARK ANTONY. MIDDLE EAST, 42–38 BC

As the Liberators, Caesar's assassins Marcus Brutus and his brother-in-law Gaius Cassius, gathered their forces in Macedonia in the summer of 42 BC to go to war against the Triumvirate—Caesar's successors Octavian Caesar, Mark Antony, and Marcus Lepidus—Brutus simultaneously dispatched a young tribune from his army on a delicate mission to the East.

Quintus Labienus was the son of Titus Labienus, Julius Caesar's able deputy in his conquest of Gaul, who'd defected to the senatorial side once Caesar went to war against the Senate. Now, three years after his father's death in the 45 BC Battle of Munda in Spain against Caesar, young Labienus, despite inheriting his father's features—a long face, a long nose, and furrowed brow—was only in his twenties and inexperienced. But his cavalry specialist father, despite having been on the losing side, was still well regarded by the Parthians, whose army was based around cavalry. This was why Brutus sent Labienus's son East, to try to convince the king of Parthia to support the Liberators against the Triumvirate and supply troops.

Labienus Jr. was politely received by Parthia's King Orodes II, but the king delayed any response to his request for troops as he awaited news of affairs in Macedonia. Once word arrived that the Liberators' army had been defeated by the army of the Triumvirate that September, at Philippi in Macedonia, and that both Cassius and Brutus were dead, Quintus Labienus, now a fugitive, was permitted to remain in Parthia as the king's guest.

Two years later, word reached Labienus that Antony was lounging in Egypt with his lover Cleopatra and neglecting the administration of the Roman East. Labienus was able to convince the Parthian king that most of the Roman troops in the East had previously marched for Cassius and Brutus, and would come over to him if he led a Parthian army into the Roman provinces west of the Euphrates. So, Orodes gave Labienus a sizable force, and appointed his handsome and well-liked son and heir, Pacorus, as co-commander.

Sure enough, once the Parthian army crossed the Euphrates many Roman troops stationed in Syria flocked to Labienus's standard. He took city after city as garrisons came over to him without a fight, as he'd predicted. Only the coastal city of Tyre held out, while Apamea and Antioch both came over to Labienus after some initial resistance. Just one of Antony's officers, Decidius Saxa, offered resistance, but Pacorus's cavalry swept away his troops, and Saxa fled.

As Labienus pursued Saxa north into Cilicia, and with Syria having been rapidly removed from Antony's control, Pacorus and his Parthian troops turned south, occupying Judea and placing a Jewish king of their choosing on the kingdom's throne. Meanwhile, Labienus marched northwest. With a force of mostly local levies, he overtook Saxa, capturing and executing him, then took a number of Cilician cities. To the immediate north, Lucius Munatius Plancus, Antony's governor of Asia, fled to the province's Aegean islands. Emboldened by his successes, the conceited young Labienus now produced coins at the Apamea mint that declared him an *imperator*, an honor bestowed by acclamation on a victorious Roman general by his own troops. Furthermore, he styled himself Parthicus ("victorious in Parthia"), as if he had defeated the Parthians rather than allied with them.

In the spring of 39 BC, Labienus passed triumphantly from Cilicia into the province of Asia. Expecting to bring it under his control with little effort, he marched with a force of primarily raw Cilician draftees. But the young rebel was in for a surprise. Mark Antony hadn't bothered to personally intervene in this crisis. He'd headed for Italy to aid his wife Fulvia and his brother Lucius in their conflict with Octavian. Instead, to deal with Labienus and the Parthians, Antony dispatched Publius Ventidius, an experienced general and protégé of Caesar, with several legions.

Ventidius moved rapidly. Landing in Asia with an advance party of light infantry, he didn't wait for his legions, instead marching south with the men he had—and Labienus barreled straight into him. Unnerved by this sudden appearance of determined opposition, Labienus led his troops in a retreat to the foot of the Taurus Mountains, and Ventidius followed.

Both forces camped close to each other for several days, as Labienus sent for Parthian cavalry, and Ventidius, encamped on a hill, awaited the arrival of his more heavily armed legions. Reinforcements for both sides arrived on the same day, but the Parthian cavalry, scornful of Roman infantry, immediately galloped up the hill and attacked Ventidius's camp without even communicating with Labienus.

Ventidius's legionaries were ready, and in their compact lines they advanced at a steady walk. With shields raised, javelins flying, and swords jabbing, they drove the Parthian riders back down the hill. Many Parthians were knocked from their saddles and trampled by comrades in the chaos that followed. Galloping away, the Parthian survivors deserted their Roman allies.

Labienus formed up his dejected infantry outside his camp, intending to defend it, but by nightfall neither side had gone on the offensive. In the darkness, Labienus and his men attempted to slip away, but Ventidius, having been alerted by a deserter, was waiting for them. He killed some of Labienus's men, and others quickly surrendered. Labienus, dressed as a civilian, succeeded in escaping, and went into hiding in the Cilician wilds.

Sending his cavalry ahead, Ventidius marched south to deal with the main Parthian army. At a mountain pass between Cilicia and Syria known as the Cilician Gates, just twenty miles from the city of Tarsus, Ventidius's cavalry was surrounded by the Parthian garrison. It took

Ventidius arriving with the infantry to defeat the Parthians and kill their commanding general, Phranapates. Ventidius then marched into Syria and Judea, clearing it of Parthian forces, while Prince Pacorus withdrew across the Euphrates.

Meanwhile, a search had been going on for Labienus in Cilicia. It was led by Demetrius, a freedman of Julius Caesar whom Antony had assigned to Cyprus. Demetrius seems to have gone to Cilicia on his own initiative to track down Labienus. After some time, perhaps months or even a year or two, Demetrius located the fugitive and arrested him. Labienus was, we know, executed, although the specifics of time and place haven't survived. He would have been taken by Demetrius to Ventidius or Plancus, who possessed the authority to put him to death.

The following year, 38 BC, Antony's general Ventidius lured Pacorus and a Parthian army back across the Euphrates with a ruse, and in the Cyrrhestica district of Syria between the Euphrates and Orontes rivers, his legions roundly defeated the twenty-thousand-man Parthian force, killing Pacorus. Some historians would claim that Labienus was also killed in this Battle of Cyrrhestica, but Cassius Dio's account of the arrest by Demetrius appears more likely.[18]

For one thing, following the Battle of Cyrrhestica, Ventidius had Pacorus's head paraded around the cities of Syria, Cilicia, and Asia, which had supported Pacorus and Labienus, to demonstrate the foolishness of cooperating with invaders. Had Labienus been killed in this same battle, it is logical that his head would have suffered a similar fate.

We don't know what reward Demetrius received for capturing Labienus the rebel, but the Senate awarded Ventidius a Triumph for defeating Pacorus and his Parthians, a fitting reward for Rome's greatest victory over Parthia since Crassus's legions had been crushed by the Parthian cavalry decades earlier. It was a victory that would convince Mark Antony to personally invade Parthia and Media in 36 BC, with disastrous results for his legions.

Gold aureus coin issued by Sextus Pompey when prefect of the Roman fleet, showing his late father, Pompey the Great (left), and brother Gnaeus Jr. *Photo © Raffaello Benahi/Bridgeman Images.*

V. SEXTUS POMPEY

DEFYING OCTAVIAN AND THE TRIUMVIRATE.
SICILY AND THE EAST, 42–35 BC

O n July 1 of the year 36 BC, the same year that Mark Antony was invading Parthia in the east by land, three Roman fleets set out on the first stage of a massive amphibious invasion of Sicily, a Roman province that for the past six years had been in the hands of a charismatic young man by the name of Sextus Pompeius, or Sextus Pompey, as later historians call him. Now thirty years old, Sextus was the youngest son of Gnaeus Pompeius Magnus, Pompey the Great, one of Rome's greatest generals and politicians, who had been called out of retirement by the Senate in 49 BC to counter the revolt initiated by Julius Caesar.

When his father was defeated by Caesar at the 48 BC Battle of Pharsalus in Greece, seventeen-year-old Sextus was at Myteline, capital of the Greek island of Lesbos, with his stepmother, Cornelia. After Pompey arrived at Lesbos in a humble grain ship after escaping from Greece, Sextus had traveled with his father in a small fleet of warships to Egypt, only to witness his father's brutal assassination by the Egyptians. Sextus had escaped by sea to North Africa, where he joined his father's cavalry commander, Titus Labienus, once Caesar's deputy, and Publius Attius Varus, the Senate's governor of Africa. Caesar had subsequently landed in Africa with his best troops, and in April 46 BC defeated senatorial forces and their North African allies at the Battle of Thapsus. Sextus had escaped with Labienus and Varus to Spain, joining his brother Gnaeus, ten years his senior, who had earlier gone to Spain to coordinate opposition to Caesar there.

While Pompey the Great had been almost universally loved and admired by Romans—even his opponent Caesar had cried on hearing of his assassination—Pompey's eldest son, Gnaeus, was a boastful young man who wasn't taken seriously by many senators. Gnaeus's military experience was negligible—although as a military tribune he had commanded the Roman bodyguard of King Ptolemy XII of Egypt—when he'd apparently had an affair with the king's teenage daughter Cleopatra. As for Sextus, he had been too young for anyone to notice or form an opinion of him before this point. Nonetheless, the luster of their father's name caused much of the population and several of Caesar's legions in Spain to defect to the brothers and the senators who had escaped to Spain, forcing Caesar to hurry to Spain and campaign against them.

At the desperate March 45 BC Battle of Munda in southern Spain, Caesar had defeated the army led by the Pompey brothers in what proved to be the last battle of that civil war. Even though the last senatorial generals, including Labienus and Varus, died at Munda, both Pompey brothers escaped. Gnaeus, wounded, was tracked down and killed in southern Spain that April by Caesarian forces. Sextus, who was separated from his brother following the Munda defeat, survived in Spain for a time by resorting to banditry, then succeeded in escaping by sea to the island of Sicily, where he found many supporters with fond memories of his father.

Just eleven months later, Caesar was dead, assassinated at Rome by sixty senators who styled themselves the Liberators. As Caesar's great-nephew and adopted son, Caesar Octavian, and Caesar's deputy Mark Antony went to war against Liberator leaders Cassius and Brutus, Antony worked out a deal to prevent young Sextus Pompey from throwing his name and support behind the Liberators. Under this deal, the Senate paid Sextus reparations for the properties of his father that had been seized by Caesar—Antony had personally acquired Pompey's city house in the Keels district in Rome—and appointed Sextus to the post of Prefect of the Western Fleet, giving him command of the Roman warships then based in the western Mediterranean at Massilia, today's Marseille in the south of France.

Sextus grabbed this opportunity to win the loyalty of the men of the fleet, seeing this as a power base he could use to his own advantage, while at the same time preserving his own skin. He even made sure that the coins minted at Marseille to pay the marines and seamen displayed his name and head, and sometimes those of his late father and brother. Once Octavian and Mark Antony had defeated Cassius and Brutus at the 42 BC Battle of Philippi, they set about shoring up their control of the Roman Empire, in 41 BC setting up the Board of Three for the Regulation of the State. Consisting of Octavian, Antony, and the *pontifex maximus* Marcus Lepidus, this board, called the Second Triumvirate by later historians, divided the empire among themselves.

Only now did the Board of Three's triumvirs realize that young Sextus Pompey was a thorn in their side with his powerful fleet, so, to keep him onside but deprive him of his fleet they appointed him governor of Sicily. Sextus happily took the post, and was welcomed by the legions stationed in Sicily. He himself welcomed senators who scurried to Sicily to join him, among them his father-in-law, Lucius Scribonius Libo, as well as his own wife, Scribonia, and his widowed sister, Pompeia, and her children; Pompeia's husband, son of the late Sulla the dictator, had been killed by Caesarian forces in Africa.

But instead of relinquishing command of the fleet as the triumvirs had expected, Sextus took the fleet with him to Sicily. Sextus's fleet, writes Velleius, quickly doubled overnight when the fleet that had previously sailed for Cassius the Liberator fled from Greek waters to Sicily to join him. The admiral who initiated this, Statius Murcus, was executed by Sextus when his existing admirals, the freedmen Menodorus and Menecrates, jealously circulated false reports about Murcus's loyalty.

Sextus began building more warships in Sicily, mostly triremes, the tried and tested Greek battle cruisers that carried 170 rowers with three banks of oars, thirty deck crew, and ten to twenty marines. To crew these ships, he welcomed thirty thousand escaped slaves from throughout Sicily and Italy, paying them to sail for him or train as marines. As his captains and admirals, he chose freedmen of his late father who had a talent for warfare at sea.

With his fleet of hundreds of warships, Sextus then annexed Sardinia and blockaded the ports of Italy, starving Rome of grain supplies from Egypt and Africa. At the same time, he landed his troops along the coast of Italy, raiding Italian towns like a pirate, and capturing merchant vessels. All of a sudden, Sextus Pompey, this wily young man in his twenties with charisma and a famous name, was a serious threat to Octavian, Antony, and Lepidus. More than one Roman historian, such as his contemporary Sallust, would suggest that Sextus now had the makings of a genuine rival to the triumvirate, and was a potential sole ruler of Rome.[19]

Sextus's domination of Rome's vital sea lanes drove the triumvirate to the negotiating table in 39 BC. On a promontory at Misenum, a port not far from Rome on the west coast of Italy, with his powerful fleet anchored in the bay and troops of the triumvirs lining the shore, Sextus sealed the Pact of Misenum with Octavian and Antony. In return for ending his blockade of Italian ports, clearing the seas of pirates and paying an agreed amount of annual tax to Rome, Sextus's realm would be enlarged to include Corsica and Achaea in southern Greece. In addition, he required that all senators and equites who had either joined him in Sicily or been sentenced to death by the triumvirate for supporting the Liberators be pardoned, and the tens of thousands of escaped slaves who were serving in his navy be granted Roman citizenship. Plus, he personally would be made an auger at Rome and be appointed consul within the next several years. Satisfied with these concessions, Sextus gave his sacred oath, as did Octavian and Antony, to abide by the agreement.

What's more, to cement a three-way familial alliance between Sextus, Octavian, and Antony, Sextus betrothed his infant daughter Pompeia to three-year-old Marcus Marcellus Caesar, Octavian's nephew and closest male relative—the son of Octavian's sister Octavia, wife of Antony, also making Marcellus Antony's nephew by marriage.

Following their conference, each of the three leaders threw a dinner for the others. Sextus went first, hosting Octavian and Antony aboard his huge flagship, a battleship with six banks of oars. As a smiling Sextus greeted his guests, he said that, today, they were dining on his keels—a play on words based on the fact that Antony now possessed the house of Sextus's father in Rome's Keels district, where Sextus had grown up, while Antony and his dinner guests were now aboard the ships of Sextus's fleet.

As the men were wining and dining convivially, reclining on divans on the ship's deck, one of Sextus's admirals leaned close and whispered in his ear. This middle-aged former slave, identified as Menodorus by Appian, our most detailed source on him, but called Menas by Velleius Paterculus, Plutarch, and Cassius Dio, had once been a freedman of Sextus's father.

"Shall I cut the cables," Menodorus whispered to his commander, "and make you master not only of Sicily but of the whole Roman Empire?" In other words, Sextus could sail away with Octavian and Antony as his prisoners.

Sextus, a handsome young man, as his father had been at his age, with a slight hook to his nose and a stubbly beard, looked at Menodorus for a moment. "This might have been done without telling me," he then replied, also in a low voice. "Now we must rest content. I do not break my word."[20]

Sextus duly returned to Sicily and terminated his naval blockade. He showed no interest in more personal power than had been agreed at Misenum, but Octavian had no intention of giving young Pompey a long-term share of power. In signing the Misenum Pact, Octavian was merely buying time. Immediately, he began a program of warship construction, and in 38 BC conducted secret negotiations with Menodorus, whom Sextus had appointed his governor of Sardinia and Corsica, after the duplicitous and ambitious admiral had sent a message offering to betray Sextus and hand over Sardinia and Corsica to Octavian.

To confirm this step, Octavian summoned his fellow triumvir Antony, who was then in Athens, to a meeting at the port of Brundisium, today's Brindisi, in southeastern Italy. Antony came by sea for the meeting, but Octavian was delayed. Without waiting for Octavian, Antony sailed back to Greece, but he left Octavian a letter urging him to remain faithful to the pact with Sextus. In addition, Antony promised to punish Menodorus if he betrayed his master Sextus. Antony's warmth toward Sextus seems to have stemmed from the fact that Sextus had saved Antony's mother, Julia, from the clutches of Octavian in Italy on one of his earlier raids, and had subsequently sent her safely to Antony at Athens. This appears to have occurred during the 41–40 BC Perusian War in central Italy, when Antony's brother Lucius and his then wife Fulvia had gone to war against Octavian.

Ignoring his brother-in-law's advice, Octavian finalized the treacherous deal with Menodorus in 38 BC, and the admiral duly handed over control of Sardinia and Corsica, bringing a squadron of seven of Sextus's warships with him to Octavian. Menodorus's reward was Roman citizenship, admittance to the Equestrian Order, a golden crown, and employment as one of Octavian's admirals. Both Octavian and Sextus accused each other of breaches of the Misenum Pact, but for the later historian Tacitus, there was no doubt who was at fault: "Octavian cheated Sextus with a spurious pact," he writes.[21]

Octavian's construction of triremes at Ravenna on the northeast coast of Italy and at the port of Rome proceeded apace. He also ordered an army of several legions to march from the Balkans, where they had been stationed since the 42 BC defeat of the Liberators at Philippi, to join him for an amphibious invasion of Sicily in the spring of 37 BC. All his ships and troops were to assemble at the start of the summer at

Rhegium, today's Reggio, a Calabrian port on the Strait of Messina, opposite Sicily.

To command his navy, Octavian appointed two leading senators who'd been firm supporters of the late Julius Caesar. Lucius Cornificius, who was to bring the newly built Ravenna ships to Reggio, had led the 43 BC Senate prosecution in absentia of Caesar's assassins. The new ships built outside Rome were placed in the hands of Gaius Calvisius Sabinus, one of only two senators who had attempted to physically defend Julius Caesar when he was assassinated beneath the statue of Pompey the Great in Rome's Theater of Pompey in 44 BC. The triumvirate had appointed Calvisius a consul in 39 BC, and now he took charge of the new west coast fleet bolstered by the seven ships Sextus's turncoat admiral Menodorus had brought to Octavian. As Cornificius set sail from Ravenna, Calvisius, with Menodorus as his deputy, sailed from the Etruscan coast opposite Corsica, with both fleets aiming for the final assembly point, Reggio.

Cornificius's Ravenna fleet joined Octavian at Tarrantum, today's Taranto on the boot of Italy, and from there Octavian set sail with Cornificius and his fleet for Reggio. In addition, "the infantry was sent on the march to Rhegium," as Appian would write, "and great haste was displayed in all quarters." Once both fleets and numerous legions linked up at Reggio, Octavian planned to embark on his amphibious invasion of Sicily.[22]

Sextus Pompey, meanwhile, only learned that Menodorus had betrayed him once Calvisius's ships were at sea and heading his way. Remaining in the sheltered port of Messana, today's Messina on the northeast coast of Sicily, with just forty warships, Sextus dispatched his freedman admiral Menecrates with the bulk of the fleet to intercept Calvisius and Menodorus off the west coast of Italy.

Several days later, just to the north of the Bay of Naples, as nightfall was approaching, Calvisius spotted the massive fleet of Menecrates farther out to sea, heading north to intercept him. Calvisius quickly put into a bay off the town of Cumae, while Menecrates sailed on and anchored for the night at the island of Ischia, twenty miles north of Neapolis, today's Naples. Calvisius wasn't sure whether Sextus's admiral had spotted his fleet, but next morning, to be on the safe side, he placed his outnumbered ships in a defensive half-moon formation in the bay, wings forward, with Calvisius in command on the right wing and Menodorus commanding the left.

Sure enough, at daybreak, Menecrates came up with his fleet and immediately launched a full-frontal attack. His broad charge drove the ships of Calvisius's half-moon back, forcing the sterns of many onto the rocky shore. Then Menodorus came out with his ship from the left wing to challenge Menecrates, who eagerly accepted the challenge, the two having been great rivals in the service of young Pompey.

With their crews shouting at the top of their voices, the two ships charged each other like knights in a joust. When they violently collided, Menodorus's prow was damaged by the underwater "beak" of his opponent's ship, while the oars along one side of Menecrates's ship were sheared away like broken matchsticks, causing untold injuries to the rowers inside the hull. Grappling hooks quickly bound the two ships together, as missiles were launched from both sides. Menodorus's vessel, being the higher, had the advantage in the engagement. Both commanders were wounded, and as Menecrates's ship was being captured he jumped into the sea with an iron Spanish javelin in his thigh, never to be seen again.

While Calvisius led ships of his right wing in pursuing several of his opponents out to sea, Menecrates's deputy Demochares came in close and set fire to many of Calvisius' ships stranded on the shore. With nightfall, Demochares, grieving the loss of his commander Menecrates, led his fleet back to rejoin Sextus at Messina. Apart from Menecrates and his flagship, Sextus's fleet was without loss, while Calvisius had lost numerous ships. The Battle of Cumae, as it would be called, was a resounding tactical victory for Sextus.

Meanwhile, Octavian was heading through the Strait of Messina on his way from Taranto, with Cornificius's fleet, loaded with troops, when Sextus came out of Messina with his forty ships to challenge him. Despite heavily outnumbering Pompey, and ignoring the advice of Cornificius and other subordinates, Octavian turned his fleet away and sailed into Reggio, saying he wanted his reinforcements of ships and legions to reach him before engaging. Once at Reggio, Octavian learned of the disastrous Battle of Cumae, but the message brought by small, fast boat was that Calvisius was sailing to join him with those of his ships he had managed to save. On learning this, Octavian again put to sea and pushed on, aiming to clear the Strait of Messina and link up with Calvisius off the southwestern coast of Italy.

Sextus spotted Octavian's fleet passing Messina, and by this stage Demochares had rejoined him with the bulk of his ships. So, Sextus, having supplemented his marines with legionaries aboard his vessels, set sail from Messina with his entire fleet. At rapid rowing speed Sextus overtook Octavian's ships from astern, as, hugging the Italian coastline, Octavian approached the promontory of Scyllaeum, which marked the northern exit point of the Messina Strait. Running up beside Octavian's fleet, Sextus attacked opposition ships all along the line and challenged Octavian to turn and fight.

Instead, Octavian ordered his captains not to engage, and led his fleet into one of the two sheltered coves that lay on either side of the massive rock at the end of the Scyllaeum promontory, three and a half miles across the Strait of Messina from Sicily. Here, all Octavian's ships anchored with their prows pointing defensively seaward. Scyllaeum, in today's Calabria, was named for the legendary monster Scylla, part beautiful girl, part sea monster, who wrapped its tentacles around sailors and dragged them down to the depths of the ocean. A ruined fortress on the promontory and the town below it (present day Scilla) reputedly dated to the time of the Trojan War.

Sextus detached his admiral Demochares to attack Octavian with part of his fleet. Demochares sent two ships against every one of Octavian's, throwing Octavian's crews into consternation. Appian writes that, in trying to escape, Octavian's ships "dashed against the rocks and against each other and began to fill with water. And so these ships were lost, like those at Cumae, without striking a blow."[23]

Octavian himself leapt to shore from his flagship after it hit the rocks, and he set about dragging his floundering seamen and soldiers from the water. With as many men as he could gather, he then climbed to the top of the high, rocky promontory of Scyllaeum, which offered protection against infantry attack.

Octavian's deputy Cornificius wasn't prepared to go down without a fight, and without awaiting orders from Octavian he cut his cables and led a squadron that rowed for the open sea to do battle with Sextus's admiral. Cornificius himself made straight for Demochares's flagship, and ramming it, he captured it, while Demochares escaped by jumping onto another of his ships, which had come to his rescue.

At this point, with nightfall approaching, Octavian's admirals Calvisius and Menodorus hove into sight with the ships they had salvaged from the defeat at Cumae. Sextus saw them first, and ordered his fleet to withdraw to Messina for the night. After sunset, Octavian and his men lit fires on shore, which were spotted by the troops of the 13th Legion, marching all the way from Illyricum to Reggio to reinforce Octavian's invasion force. It is highly likely that Octavian was also expecting the 4th Legion from Illyricum, but through a mix-up the marching orders for the 4th had been sent to the 6th Legion in far-off Spain, which would turn up in Italy weeks later. The men of the 13th, learning of the battle off Scyllaeum that day, followed the light of the campfires to join Octavian and provide food and aid to his seafarers, with the legions' centurions creating a makeshift tent for Octavian himself.

This battle in the bay had cost Octavian half the ships of Cornificius's Ravenna fleet, while Sextus had lost just the single vessel of Demochares. It had been an overwhelming second successive victory for Sextus, and back at Messina his Roman-citizen legionary troops hailed him *imperator*, as they had after the victory at Cumae. Years before, Sextus's father, Pompey the Great, had also been hailed imperator by his legions. The word *imperator* literally means "commander," and would eventually morph into the English word "emperor." To be hailed imperator by his troops was the highest honor a Roman general could achieve apart from being awarded a Triumph by the Senate, and Octavian, once he became the emperor Augustus, together with all future emperors, would claim exclusive right to the title.

To celebrate this latest victory over Octavian, Sextus would quickly issue new coins from the Messina mint, on which he would declare himself "Great and Pious Imperator for the Second Time." One side of the coins depicted the *pharos*, or lighthouse, of Messina, which sat on Sicily's Cape Petorus, at the northern entrance to the Strait of Messina. A statue of Neptune, god of the sea, stood atop the lighthouse. The Pompeius family claimed descent from Neptune, and from this point forward Sextus proclaimed himself a descendant of the god and wore a navy blue cloak in celebration of his twin naval victories over Octavian.

Also depicted with the lighthouse and Neptune on Sextus's coins were a war galley, the dolphin standard of his marines, and the eagle standard of a legion. The reverse side of Sextus's coins featured a depiction of Scylla the sea monster with a ship's rudder in her hands, giving Scylla a portion of the credit for Sextus's victory while placing the battle at Scyllaeum. Since the nineteenth century historians have incorrectly labeled this sea battle the Battle of Messina; clearly, it should be known as the Battle of Scyllaeum.

The day after his latest calamitous sea battle, Octavian looked down over the bay from the Scyllaeum promontory to see "some of his ships burned, others partly burned, others still burning, and others broken in pieces, and the sea filled with sails, rudders and tackle. While, of the ships that were saved, the greater part were damaged."[24]

Despite his crushing Scyllaeum loss, Octavian didn't lose heart, ranging Calvisius's newly arrived vessels in front of his own shattered fleet to defend against fresh attack by Sextus, as he himself set about repairing his damaged ships. He guessed—correctly—that, as in the past, Sextus would not return to capitalize on his victory and deal the *coup de grace* to Octavian—a decision for which later Roman historians such as Appian would severely criticize Sextus.

Then, at midday, as Octavian's seamen were working on repairs, a storm blew up from the south. It dashed Octavian's anchored ships against each other and drove many onto the rocky shoreline. To avoid the fate of the others, Menodorus took his squadron of massive flagship and six triremes out to sea. The following day, after riding out the storm, he would sail for Messina with his squadron, to rejoin Sextus—he had been miffed that Octavian had made him subordinate to Calvisius, and planned to change sides yet again in the belief that, with his rival Menecrates dead, Sextus would make him his most senior admiral.

At Scyllaeum, the storm raged on into a black, moonless night, only to abate just before the following dawn. Locals could remember no storm as violent at that time of year. "The greater part of Octavian's ships and men were destroyed by it," Appian writes of the event. After sunrise, Octavian departed the scene of carnage and headed overland for the port of Vibo, farther north, leaving subordinates to repair as many ships as possible and then take them to Puteoli, today's Pozzuoli, near Rome.[25]

Sextus's popularity on Sicily was increased by his twin victories at sea, while doubts were expressed at Rome as to whether Octavian could overcome his audacious rival. Determined to prove his critics wrong, Octavian dismissed Calvisius, blaming him for Menodorus's double defection and making him the scapegoat for the disasters at both Cumae and Scyllaeum. He set about regrouping, planning to relaunch his invasion of Sicily the following year. To achieve this, Octavian stole slaves from friends to crew his repaired ships, and made a deal with Mark Antony to swap twenty thousand of his legionaries then in Italy, including the men of the newly arrived 6th Legion, for 120 of Antony's warships. In addition, Octavian's sister Octavia, who was by then Antony's wife, convinced her husband to give Octavian another ten ships in exchange for one thousand men picked from Octavian's Praetorian Guard cohorts in Rome.

As overall naval commander for his 36 BC Sicilian operation, Octavian appointed his loyal and dependable school friend Marcus

Agrippa, who, like Octavian, was just twenty-seven years of age. In 39 BC, Agrippa had served as a consul at Rome, and the following year had gone to govern Gaul, where he had put down unrest in Aquitania before leading a military expedition across the Rhine into Germany. Agrippa quickly set about a crash program of building especially large new ships and training new crews at Lakes Avernus and Lucrinus, near the Campanian port of Pozzuoli, the arrival point for much of Rome's grain from Egypt and Africa.

During the spring of 36 BC, Sextus, who was expecting Octavian to again attempt to invade Sicily, sent Menodorus on a scouting mission with his seven-ship squadron. Ranging along the west coast of Italy, Menodorus raided Pozzuoli, capturing guard ships at Octavian's shipyards and sinking grain ships anchored in the bay, causing general confusion. But Menodorus was bitter that Sextus had failed to make him his most senior admiral, and had decided to betray him yet again. At a meeting with one of Octavian's officers on an island he arranged the third defection of his squadron.

When Menodorus was presented to Octavian, he begged his forgiveness. Octavian did forgive the man's previous multiple betrayals, and, while dismissing the captains of Menodorus's ships, he took Menodorus himself, his vessels and crews back into his service. Over the winter, Octavian had lost the crews of twenty-three of Antony's ships at Taranto in southern Italy to an epidemic, and was desperate for ships. However, being no fool, Octavian kept Menodorus under close watch from that day forward.

Ships and troops for the new Sicilian invasion were not ready until the summer of 36 BC, but by the time the operation got underway that July, the forces Octavian had pulled together in little more than a year were immense, involving well over a thousand warships and cargo ships and some 150,000 troops—twenty-one legions, 5,000 auxiliary light infantry, and 20,000 cavalry. It was the largest Roman amphibious operation since Sextus's father had put twenty legions aboard warships to defeat the Cilician pirates. Against this force, Sextus was able to field an army of twenty-one legions and several thousand cavalry, while his navy was roughly the same size as that of his opponents.

The bulk of Octavian's force originated in Africa, where the third triumvir Marcus Lepidus assembled sixteen legions—four newly levied in Africa, plus twelve veteran legions that, according to Velleius in his *Compendium*, were down to no more than half strength after years of civil war service. The 14th Legion was in fact fielding just one thousand men; Octavian had recruited up to five thousand new levies for the unit in Cisalpine Gaul, but they were still in Italy. Even though Lepidus possessed one thousand cargo vessels and seventy warships, they were only enough to ferry his dozen veteran legions, five hundred Numidian cavalry and their horses, and a large quantity of war supplies in one hit, so Lepidus ordered his cargo ships to return to Carthage for the remaining four legions after the first twelve units had landed.

Simultaneously, as Lepidus's massive fleet set sail from North Africa on July 1, Octavian sailed from Pozzuoli with another fleet, offering sacrifices and pouring libations into the sea from his flagship to seek the blessing of Neptune, Sextus's family deity. On the same day, 107 of the ships sent by Antony sailed from Taranto under the command of Antony's admiral Titus Statilius Taurus.

Sextus would soon gleefully proclaim that Neptune clearly favored him, for, three days after the three invasion fleets set out, another storm lashed the seas around Sicily, with southerly gale-force winds halting Taurus's fleet and forcing him to turn around and flee back to the shelter of Taranto. Lepidus was just then unloading troops on Sicily's northwest coast, and a number of his cargo vessels were capsized by monstrous seas. Nonetheless, Lepidus got most of his tens of thousands of troops ashore unopposed and commenced operations against the city of Lilybaeum, today's Marsala, on the west coast of Sicily. Marsala held out for Sextus, but Lepidus took several nearby towns.

Octavian's fleet, running down the Italian coast from Pozzuoli to Vibo, where it was to take on board Octavian's legions, was also caught at sea by the storm, and was forced to put into a bay near Veleia, in Campania. The wind then changed and drove many of Octavian's ships onto the shore. Thirty-two of his major warships with up to six banks of oars were sunk or dashed to pieces on the rocks, as were a number of his single-bank Liburnians. The only compensation for Octavian was that the majority of his crewmen were saved.

Octavian set about repairing on the spot those ships that could be salvaged, sending all his spare crewmen to Taranto to man some of the twenty-three ships of Antony's that had lost their crews to disease. He himself hastened to Vibo with his undamaged ships. From there he sent two legions under the command of Marcus Messala Corvinus, a former officer in Antony's service, to land on Sicily's east coast at Taormina, just south of Messina, in support of Lepidus, who intended to advance on Messina from the northwest. Octavian also ordered Taurus to transfer his ships and troops farther along the boot of Italy from Taranto, to be able to cross the Strait of Messina and land at Taormina at short notice, and sent three legions to the strait to await orders.

Octavian himself remained at Vibo, visiting regional towns, recruiting retired veterans, and keeping his legions busy drilling. At the same time, knowing that many ordinary Romans retained considerable sympathy for the Pompey family, he sent a senior officer to Rome to assure everyone there that he had everything under control and the defeat of Sextus was only a matter of time.

Sextus kept the majority of his warships in the safe anchorage of Messina harbor until he knew Octavian's invasion plans, sending small squadrons to patrol the Messina Strait and the Tyrrhenian Sea north of Sicily. Once Lepidus was ashore in Sicily with twelve legions, he sent his fleet on the three-day return voyage to Carthage to collect his four new legions. Having encountered no naval opposition on the first voyage, the sail-powered cargo ships embarked these four legions, then set off without their warship escorts, which dawdled after them. The transports were within sight of Sicily's northern coast when one of Sextus's scouting squadrons came upon them. Without hesitation, the captain in command, Papias, charged toward Lepidus's crowded troopships.

The masters of the troopships assumed the approaching warships belonged to Lepidus and had been sent to guide them to shore, so instead of scattering, they steered straight toward Papias's squadron. The warships swooped on them, ramming and raining burning missiles on one troopship after another. The result was carnage. Later historians wouldn't even glorify the encounter as a battle. It was a massacre, for none of Lepidus's troopships were armed. Some forty of these vessels were sunk, burned, or captured by Papias's squadron. Those of Lepidus's men from the ill-fated ships who swam to shore were killed by Pompeian troops once they reached the beach. The remainder died on their ships or drowned.

It was another major victory for Sextus. Two of Lepidus's new legions occupying the leading troopships were wiped out, with as many as twelve thousand troops and an unknown number of sailors perishing in the sea or on Sicily's shore. As Papias sailed back to Messina with captured cargo ships and tidings of his victory, Lepidus's remaining troopships were fleeing back to Carthage. The two surviving legions subsequently re-embarked and sailed under escort to successfully join Lepidus in Sicily—one almost immediately, the other somewhat later.

It was August by the time Octavian at last sailed from Vibo with his repaired and augmented fleet and a number of embarked legions, with Agrippa as his deputy. After putting into the island of Stromboli off the north coast of Sicily, he learned from scout ships that Sextus had large land forces spread along Sicily's northern coast and a naval squadron under Demochares at Mylae, today's Milazzo, due south of Stromboli and just twenty-seven miles northwest of Messina. Deciding that Sextus must himself be at Milazzo, Octavian sailed back to Vibo, picked up three more legions, then sailed to link up with Taurus at Scyllaeum, planning to combine their forces and cross the strait and land at Taormina, south of Messina, catching Sextus between his land forces and those of Lepidus to the northwest.

Sextus was actually still at Messina, but having learned that Agrippa had moved from Stromboli to occupy the island of Marettimo, just off

Milazzo, he immediately dispatched his freedman Apollophanes from Messina with a readied squadron of forty-five warships to reinforce Demochares at Milazzo, and set sail himself for Milazzo shortly after with another seventy warships.

The next morning, before dawn, Agrippa sailed from Marettimo Island with half his fleet, intent on doing battle with Demochares's forty ships. But when Agrippa arrived off Milazzo later that morning, he found, to his surprise, 155 of Sextus's ships waiting for him, arrayed for battle. In the night, the squadrons of Apollophanes and Sextus had arrived to join Demochares, with Sextus himself landing at Milazzo. Agrippa immediately placed his largest battleships in the center of his line and sent small, fast ships rowing hard to bring the rest of his fleet from Marettimo and alert Octavian that Sextus was at Milazzo with a large part of his navy.

As Sextus climbed a hill behind Milazzo, two fleets of roughly equal size faced off within sight of the town. From his vantage point, Sextus would watch proceedings and send orders to his admirals using signal flags. Both sides had prepared carefully for this year's naval campaign, equipping their warships with wooden towers in bow and stern from which embarked legionaries and marines would fire catapults and launch javelins during close-quarters combat. The ships of both sides looked alike. So that their own ships could recognize each other in the heat of battle, the fighting towers had been painted identifying colors—Sextus's were likely blue, Octavian's, red. Agrippa would have reminded his men that here off Mylae in 260 BC, a Roman fleet had delivered the inaugural defeat to a Carthaginian fleet in the First Punic War. As Sextus and his supporters were also Romans, he probably told his men the very same thing.

Admirals' standards rose in the sterns of flagships, and to a blare of trumpets both sides charged forward. Perspiring rowers bent their backs. Thousands of oars rose and dipped to the battle speed dictated by the rhythm that their timekeepers down below pounded out with mallets on wooden blocks. Agrippa's ships were mostly large craft of up to six banks of oars, which made them heavy and slow, but they were strong and resistant to ramming. Sextus's warships were generally smaller, lighter, faster triremes, and they had the more experienced crews. But while Sextus's ships could nip in and out like greyhounds, Agrippa's ships were solid bulldogs equipped with more firepower, and carried more legionaries and marines for boarding enemy craft.

Some ships made frontal attacks, others rowed in from the flank, and soon the sea was congested with a mass of hundreds of ships, as, here and there, rammed craft from both sides began to take water and founder. After this initial rush, the battle would come down to close-quarters combat, as grappling hooks flew and one vessel was drawn to another. Agrippa's larger ships were soon dominating Sextus's smaller craft, and as boarding parties came flooding down Ravens—boarding planks with spikes on the end that lodged in the decks of opposition ships and held fast—Sextus's outnumbered men were pushed into the sea. There, small rowboats, the tenders of each warship, which had been launched for the purpose, plucked many swimming men from the water.

Agrippa spotted the standard of Sextus's captain Papias, the man who had delivered Lepidus's fleet such a horrific blow, and rowed straight for it, ramming the trireme beneath the bow and shattering the timbers of the hold, below the waterline. As the sea rushed into Papias's ship, the trireme quickly sank, trapping and drowning rowers of the lowest bank of oars. Oarsmen of the upper banks had to smash holes in the deck above them to escape. Papias himself jumped to a ship of his squadron that came alongside to rescue him. He continued the fight from its deck.

On shore, Sextus was alerted that the rest of Agrippa's fleet was en route from Marettimo Island to join the battle, and signaled his fleet to withdraw in good order. His captains did, regrouping to mount a charge, then backing off, then again charging. Gradually, taking one step forward and two steps back, they pulled away from Agrippa's less maneuverable craft and cunningly ran into the shoals where the

Mela River entered the sea. Agrippa's ships, heavier and with a deeper draught, couldn't follow.

Agrippa anchored offshore to blockade Sextus's 125 ships, considering a night attack with the incoming tide—until his officers talked him out of it because his ships would risk running aground and becoming sitting ducks. So, in the evening, Agrippa reluctantly ordered a return to Marettimo, sending a courier ship to Octavian to announce that he had achieved victory over Sextus's fleet.

Agrippa's departure allowed Sextus's ships to put to sea in the darkness and return to Milazzo and Messina. Sextus had lost thirty of his smaller ships in this engagement, which future historians would call the Battle of Mylae, and Agrippa had lost five of his battleships. While the battle had been a tactical victory for Agrippa, neither fleet was incapacitated, and in reality it was little more than a draw. Sextus sent messages to his captains praising their crews for their day's work.

"You fought against walls rather than against ships," Sextus declared, doling out rewards and assuring his crewmen that for their next encounter he would increase the height of his fighting towers to equal those of Octavian's. Plus, the next time they went against Octavian's bulky ships, he said, he would make sure they fought where the waters of the Messina Strait emerged into the Tyrrhenian Sea in a strong current, which the larger ships would find difficult to handle, giving Sextus's more agile ships the advantage. After supper at Milazzo, Sextus sailed back to Messina in the dark.[26]

While the Battle of Mylae was being fought off the Sicilian coast, Octavian had transferred from Scyllaeum to Leucopetra, or White Rock, today's Punta del Pellaro at the extreme southwestern point of the Italian mainland. From there, he was preparing to make a night crossing of the strait to land at Taormina when word arrived from Agrippa telling of his success off Mylae. Assuming from the glowing report that Sextus's fleet had been shattered, Octavian waited until the next day. Accompanied by all the troops his ships could carry, he made a safer daylight crossing, which, he believed, befitted a victor.

Octavian landed where the Alacantra River enters the sea near Taormina with three legions, two thousand retired legionaries from military colonies in southern Italy and five hundred cavalrymen without their horses, intending to send his ships back to Italy to pick up more troops and horses. As he himself was coming ashore, he slipped and fell. Quickly pulling himself to his feet without assistance, he brushed himself down. But, in landing there, he had made an even greater, more injurious slip, for he had sailed into a trap.

In the late afternoon, Octavian's troops had only just commenced making camp when, to their general's astonishment, Sextus arrived with his fleet—the fleet Octavian believed to have been destroyed—and blockaded the bay. At the same time, Sextus's cavalry swept in from one flank and his infantry took up positions on the other. As night fell, Octavian found himself trapped at the landing place.

That night, Octavian, determined to break out, left Cornificius in command of troops onshore and boarded a small, fast ship. Without raising his personal standard, which would have given him away, he set sail accompanied by his warships in an attempt to break through Sextus's blockade. That attempt didn't go well. In a running battle that continued into the daylight of the following day, Sextus's speedier ships ran riot. Some of Octavian's warships were captured and burned; others raised their sails and, with a following wind, fled for Italy, contrary to orders. When Octavian's crews swam to shore from their sinking ships, they were killed or captured by Sextus's cavalry, with Cornificius too afraid of the cavalry to send his infantry to rescue the seamen.

Twice during the sea battle, Sextus's flagship passed close to Octavian's small ship, ignoring it as it went after bigger fish. The fighting only terminated with the onset of the next night. Later historians, particularly those favorable to Octavian, rarely mention this battle—an embarrassing defeat for Octavian personally. They offer no figures for Octavian's losses in ships or men, and none give it a name. Because it was fought off Tauromenium, as Taormina was then known, we might call it the Battle of Taormina. Even Velleius, who was not yet born but would later serve under Octavian, admits that "a serious defeat was received near Tauromenium, beneath the very eyes of Caesar [Octavian]."[27]

Not for the first time in this war against Sextus, "Caesar's own person was endangered," and Octavian had to abandon his own ship. By nightfall, he was in a small rowboat, a tender, his ship apparently having been sunk. Transferring from one small boat to another to avoid being recognized, and accompanied by just his armor bearer, Octavian landed the next day on a remote stretch of coast on the Italian side of the Strait of Messina, "shattered in mind and body," according to Appian in his *Histories*. On reaching Reggio, he pulled himself together and sent a message to Agrippa urging help for Cornificius's trapped army, at the same time ordering the three legions waiting at the strait to cross and reinforce Cornificius at Taormina.

Cornificius, meanwhile, had decided not to risk annihilation by remaining where he was. Setting off overland with his army, heading north to link up with Lepidus's legions, he took a mountainous inland route. After four waterless days of hard marching in stifling midsummer heat, under attack from Sextus's troops all the way, Cornificius's legionaries were on the verge of giving up when they were reached by three legions put ashore by Agrippa on the north coast and sent to rescue them. Agrippa, after giving his crews a few days' rest at Marettimo Island following the Battle of Mylae, had sailed with his entire fleet and landed his troops at Tindari, west of Cape Milazzo, which he swiftly captured from Sextus's garrison.

Within days, Octavian once again crossed the Strait, bringing more legions. Landing near Messina, he linked up with Lepidus. Their combined land forces outnumbered those of Sextus, who was reluctant to commit to a major land battle. With his navy having fought loyally and successfully for him for years, Sextus had more confidence in his fleet than his legions. He boldly sent Octavian a message, challenging him to a sea battle with three hundred ships a side. With a single roll of the dice, it would be winner take all.

As the location for the battle, Sextus nominated the waters off the town of Naulochus, which no longer exists. Located between Milazzo and Cape Pelorus on the northeast tip of Sicily, Naulochus offered a safe harbor and was not far from where the Messina Strait and Tyrrhenian Sea met, which Sextus considered favorable waters for him. Octavian, no sailor himself and despite having lost every single naval encounter against Sextus over the past eighteen months except for the Battle of Mylae, nonetheless "considered it cowardly to refuse," according to Appian in his *Histories*, and he accepted the challenge. The date for the battle was set for September 3, 36 BC, little more than a month since Octavian and Lepidus had launched the invasion of Sicily.

In the days leading up to the battle, both sides worked feverishly to prepare and arm their ships. Sextus would have kept his word to his crews and increased the height of his warships' fighting towers. On Octavian's side, Agrippa had been experimenting with a secret weapon designed to prevent Sextus's faster ships from darting in to launch missile attacks against his packed decks and then pulling away again before Octavian's ships could get close enough to deploy boarding parties.

Called the *harpax*, the "grabber" or "robber," Agrippa's invention was a vast improvement on the standard grappling hook. Fired by catapult, it was a large iron device, not unlike an anchor, that flew across the water and whose end-spikes lodged in the timbers of an enemy ship's stern. A rope extended back to the ship that fired it. This rope was wound around a manually operated winch, and as this was wound in, the enemy ship was hauled closer, for boarding. To prevent the opposition from cutting the winding rope, a long iron shaft extended back from the spikes. Only later would the Romans themselves develop a counter to the harpax—scythes on long poles that could be used to reach out and cut the winding rope. But when Sextus's fleet assembled for what became known as the Battle of Naulochus, Sextus was entirely ignorant of the harpax, and had no counter for it.

On the September day of the battle, with the weather fine and the sea comparatively flat, Sextus, Octavian, and their armies took positions along the shore at Naulochus, the legions lining up to watch the battle like the audience at a sporting contest, with both sides separated by a suitable distance. On the water, Agrippa would be commanding Octavian's fleet, while no single admiral was in overall command of Sextus's fleet.

Sextus's three hundred ships appear to have arrived first, not long after dawn, forming a long, neat line nearest the shore, which would allow Sextus's captains to run for shore to beach their ships if they were holed in battle and taking water. When Agrippa's ships arrived, they faced off opposite their stationary opponents, one-on-one, backing water to keep their positions. In addition to their marines, the ships of both sides had been loaded with legionaries, all keyed up for the contest, as their comrades on land cheered them on. This was like no naval battle before or since.

With a roar from their crews, the six hundred ships of both sides launched forward at the same time. After the losses at Mylae, Sextus had clearly instructed his trireme captains to avoid getting too close to Octavian's ships, for they sped past their immediate opponents spewing burning arrows, then swung about for another, closer run, this time without using fire, which could endanger their own craft in close. Only Sextus's few larger ships attempted to ram their opponents.

Soon, Agrippa's captains were using their secret weapon. Harpaxes flew long distances to harpoon opposition ships in the stern after they passed, then slowly reeled them in. Once they had been caught by a harpax, Sextus's captains ordered their rowers to back water to prevent their ship from being drawn in. In answer, Agrippa's ships also backed water. The larger ships, with more rowers, invariably won this tug-of-war. Before long, more and more of Sextus's crews found themselves alongside larger enemy ships, trying to repel boarding parties. The sea fight developed into a series of desperate struggles on the decks of hundreds of stationary ships, as tenders picked up men floundering in the sea amid debris and corpses.

A new problem emerged. The troops of both sides, all being Roman, were identically clad and armed. To identify friend from foe once they were fighting hand-to-hand with sword and javelin on deck, each side had been issued with a watchword for the day. But once one side heard the other side's watchword, they yelled it too, to fool their opponents and gain the upper hand. Inevitably, it wasn't long before allies were killing each other in error.

The battle was a stubborn and protracted contest along a drawn-out line of warships, and for a long time no one on shore could determine who was winning. As a ship went down here or there, there would be a roar from men on sea and land. But was it a ship of the blue fleet, or of the red fleet? On the water, Agrippa was eventually able to discern that more of Sextus's ships were foundering than his own—in the end, it would prove that twenty-eight Pompeian craft were sunk on that day, to just three of Agrippa's.

This freed up some of Agrippa's ships to gang up on their surviving opponents, and he personally led a charge that sank several triremes and broke the Pompeian line. A number of Sextus's ships now dumped their fighting towers overboard to lighten their load, and ran for the Messina Strait. Agrippa was able to cut off most of these fleeing ships and drive them to the shore. Just seventeen of Sextus's triremes succeeded in escaping, heading at all speed for Messina. A cheer rose up from Octavian's watching legions, and a universal groan from Sextus's troops. Those of Sextus's ships that beached themselves were abandoned by their crews, who fled inland. In their wake, Agrippa's men landed and either stove in or burned most of the enemy ships, towing some undamaged craft off the beach to employ them in Octavian's service.

Sextus had seen enough. Shocked by the comprehensive defeat, which saw 283 of his warships sunk, destroyed, or captured, he removed his armor, blue cloak, and the commander's insignia around his waist, and in civilian clothes, rode away with a cavalry escort, accompanied by his closest associates. With his departure, Sextus's infantry and cavalry at Naulochus surrendered to Octavian under terms that were quickly agreed.

Heading for Messina, Sextus dispatched orders to Plenius, his commander at Marsala on the west coast, to march around the south coast of Sicily with his eight legions and meet him at Messina. Hundreds of merchant vessels lay in the harbor at Messina, many captured by Sextus in his piratical days, others added only recently from Lepidus's devastated troopship fleet; these could carry some fifty thousand men. Sextus's plan was to load these vessels with Plenius's legions and sail for Spain, where, he knew, many Spaniards who venerated his late father would flock to his banner, and he would take Spain the way he had taken Sicily.

Once Sextus reached Messina, he was convinced by associates that his Spanish plan was unworkable. Even if Plenius and his legions could march from Marsala to Messina without being intercepted by the legions of Octavian and Lepidus, the journey would take days, and by that time Agrippa would have arrived off Messina with his victorious fleet and cut off escape by sea.

That night, the seventeen triremes that had escaped from Naulochus to Messina were loaded with Sextus's treasure and valuables, which he'd packed in readiness for a hurried departure. Sextus then sailed out of Messina, taking his wife, daughter, sister, and sister's children with him, along with his father-in-law, Libo, seven other loyal senators, and several thousand troops from the Messina garrison. Instead of heading for Spain, he turned south and sailed for the Greek islands of the Aegean, Mark Antony's territory, hoping to make Antony his ally against Octavian and Lepidus.

As Sextus abandoned Sicily, his general Plenius followed orders and marched to Messina with his legions. There, they took refuge behind the city's substantial fortifications. With Lepidus's troops sealing off escape by land and Agrippa and his fleet blockading the harbor, Plenius commenced surrender negotiations. While Agrippa sent to Octavian for orders, Lepidus quickly accepted Plenius's surrender, joined Plenius's legions with his own, then let the combined army sack pro-Sextus Messina.

Sailing to Lesbos, Sextus took up residence at its capital, Myteline, where he and his stepmother had been left out of harm's way by his father during the war between Caesar and the Senate. Now Sextus was very much in harm's way, and in need of an ally or an escape route. Learning that Antony and his legions had recently been driven out of Media by the Parthians and Medes, and that Antony had retreated with his tail between his legs to Alexandria to be with his lover Queen Cleopatra of Egypt, Sextus dispatched envoys to Antony, seeking to serve as one of his generals against the Parthians. At the same time, hedging his bets, he sent envoys to the king of Parthia, offering to become one of his generals against Antony. As a third option, he sent envoys to the kings of Pontus and Thrace to open up a potential escape route to neutral Armenia.

Unfortunately for Sextus, his envoys to Parthia were captured en route by Antony's troops. When Sextus's envoys in Alexandria arrived to make their case for Antony employing their master—reminding him that Sextus had rescued Antony's mother years before and that Sextus's daughter was betrothed to Antony's nephew —Antony confronted them with the captured envoys to the Parthian king, who revealed details of their duplicitous mission. Without sending a response to Sextus's proposed alliance, Antony delegated Marcus Titius, who knew Sextus well, to deal with him. Should Sextus show no hostile intent, Titius was under orders to treat him honorably, as long as he submitted to Antony. But if Sextus took up arms against Antony, Titius was to wage unrelenting war against him.

Marcus Titius had a complex background. His father, the senator Lucius Titius, had supported the Liberators, and after their defeat in 42 BC he had fled to Sextus in Sicily. But Marcus, a more hot-blooded fellow, had taken up sea piracy in the Western Mediterranean, then the area under Sextus's control as prefect of the fleet. Two years later, Marcus had been captured by Sextus's admiral Menodorus off the coast of southern Gaul. Sextus had usually executed pirates, but because Marcus's father was in Sextus's entourage, Sextus had spared him, and

Marcus had joined Lucius and Sextus in Sicily. Another two years later, Marcus and his father were among those pardoned by the triumvirs as part of Sextus's terms for the Pact of Misenum, and both men had returned to Rome. There, Marcus had become a client of Antony, who subsequently took him along to the East.

By the spring of 35 BC, Sextus, having received no reply from any of his envoys, lost patience and sailed from Lesbos with his entourage. As Lesbos was part of the Roman province of Asia, encompassing much of today's northwestern Turkey, Sextus landed on the coast of mainland Asia and paid his respects to Antony's provincial governor, Gaius Furnius, once a close friend of his father. Furnius received Sextus hospitably but, becoming concerned when Sextus began drilling his troops in public, sent to adjacent provinces for forces of his own. When these troops arrived, Sextus plotted to kidnap their commanding general to use as a bargaining chip, but this plan was leaked to the other side.

Caught out and, according to Appian, inspired by Labienus's recent rebel successes in the region, Sextus decided to go on the offensive. Occupying the city of Lampsacus, near modern Lapseki, south of the Hellespont in Asia, a city populated by Italian legion veterans, he quickly recruited locals to add to his small existing force, creating an army of three legions plus two hundred cavalrymen. He then lay siege to the nearby coastal city of Cyzicus. This jolted Governor Furnius into action. Marching from his capital city of Ephesus, Furnius camped his army close to Sextus's force. Sextus, launching a surprise attack on the front and rear of Furnius's camp, forced Furnius himself to flee. With many of the governor's men volunteering to serve Sextus, the rebel increased his army and marched east to the cities of Nicomedia on the Sea of Marmara and nearby Nicea, taking both without a fight.

Suddenly, Sextus was looking like a real threat to Antony. He even attempted to bribe a unit of Italian cavalry sent to Antony by his wife, Octavia, who remained loyal to him despite his widely known affair with Cleopatra. But the opposition was mounting. First, the gold intended for the cavalry troopers was intercepted. Then, seventy of the warships Antony had loaned Octavian for use against Sextus hurriedly sailed to Asia. At the same time, Titius arrived from Syria with 120 warships loaded with thousands of troops. The entire task force met at Marmara Island in the Sea of Marmara.

Made aware of the size of the forces against him, and without a substantial navy or any cavalry to speak of, Sextus decided to move inland and fight a guerrilla war. After a tearful parting from his wife, little daughter, and his sister and her children, who were to remain behind, apparently at Nicomedia, he burned his seventeen warships, armed their 3,700 seamen and put them in his army, and prepared to march into the province of Bithynia to the northeast. All but one of the senators with him were against this, urging him to surrender to Titius and beg Antony's mercy. When Sextus refused to listen, the senators, including Sextus's father-in-law, Libo, despaired of him and deserted, going to Titius and throwing their allegiance behind Antony.

Undaunted, Sextus marched his little army into Bithynia's interior. On his heels, with Furnius in command, the combined forces of Titius and Furnius followed. One night, after Sextus had slipped his army from its camp, Furnius gave chase, trapping him on a hill. Yet there was still a sting in the scorpion's tail: in the night, Sextus crept down into Furnius's camp with three hundred men and caused mayhem. Again he went on the run, and again his opponents caught up with him and encircled him. Out of supplies, Sextus sought a meeting with Furnius, whom Sextus trusted as a good friend of his father's. The pair met on opposite banks of a small river, their conference taking place over its rushing waters.

When Furnius called on Sextus to beg Antony's mercy, Sextus responded, "I will surrender to you alone, Furnius, asking merely your pledge that you will conduct me to him in safety."

"Surrender yourself to Titius," Furnius replied, "to whom these matters have been entrusted by Antony. The pledge which you ask from me you can ask from him."[28]

Twice in the past, Sextus had saved Titius's life, first after he had been captured by Sextus's admiral Menodorus, second, when Sextus had secured a pardon from the triumvirs for Titius and his father. Despite this, Sextus didn't trust that Titius would preserve his life. So, Sextus offered to surrender to Furnius's deputy, Amyntas, but this offer, too, was rejected—it was Titius, or nothing.

Once again, Sextus made a covert night departure from his camp, leaving campfires burning and trumpeters signaling the watch changes. With his most faithful men, he set off on foot for the coast, intent on burning Titius's fleet. Just a single senator had remained with Sextus—Marcus Aemilius Scaurus, whose mother had once been married to Pompey the Great. But even Scaurus deserted him now, going to the Antonians and telling them which direction Sextus had taken.

In daylight, Furnius's deputy Amyntas overtook Sextus with 1,500 cavalry. Seeing the hopelessness of the situation, most of Sextus's surrounded men surrendered. Now, too, Sextus surrendered to Amyntas, unconditionally. As Sextus was taken to Titius in chains at Miletus on the west coast of Anatolia, all his troops swore loyalty to Antony. And, as Sextus had feared, Titius ordered his execution. Sextus was promptly beheaded there in Miletus.

Some later historians surmise that Antony ordered Sextus's death post-capture, or that his governor of Syria, Lucius Munatius Plancus, ordered it in Antony's name. Appian suggests that Sextus could have been executed by Titius without Antony's knowledge, because Antony's lover Cleopatra was warm to the Pompey family—Pompey the Great had restored her father to the Egyptian throne, and as a teenager she had apparently had an affair with Sextus's elder brother Gnaeus when he commanded Ptolemy XII's Roman bodyguard.[29]

Cassius Dio, two and a half centuries later, wrote a report, unconfirmed by earlier Roman histories, indicating that Titius did ask Antony what to do, and that Antony responded from Egypt that Sextus was to be put to death, only to change his mind and subsequently send a reprieve. Dio says the second courier arrived first, with the reprieve, and when the first courier arrived with the undated execution order, Titius acted on that.[30]

Sextus was right to distrust Titius. Not only did he execute Sextus despite owing him his life, but five years later, on the eve of the 31 BC Battle of Actium, Titius deserted Antony and Cleopatra and participated in their defeat by Octavian. As his reward, Titius was made a consul by Octavian that same year. On his return to Rome, Titius celebrated Octavian's victory with games in the Theater of Pompey, only to be driven from the theater by a riotous crowd angered by his execution of Sextus and his gall in celebrating in the theater built and paid for by Sextus's father.

Menodorus, who had once captured Titius and twice betrayed Sextus, died in Octavian's campaign against Pannonian tribesmen just months after Sextus's execution. In 35 BC, too, another Sextus Pompeius, an otherwise little-known and unremarkable paternal second cousin to Sextus Pompey, was made a consul by Octavian. This was Octavian's little joke—he had promised in the Misenum Pact to make Sextus Pompeius a consul, and he did. Just the same, he ignored the citizenship granted by the same Senate-ratified pact to the thirty thousand former slaves who sailed for Sextus, sending them back to slavery under previous masters or their heirs. Those not claimed were executed. As a permanent reminder of his defeat of Sextus, Octavian placed a golden statue of himself atop a column in Rome's Forum, decorating the column with beaks from Sextus's ships.

Once Sextus fled Sicily, Marcus Lepidus had attempted a coup. "The most fickle of mankind," in the words of Velleius, Lepidus required all forty legions in Sicily to swear loyalty to him exclusively.[31] But Octavian had gone to Lepidus's camp, and moving among the rank and file convinced them to support him instead, with Sextus's former troops leading this swing to Octavian. Lepidus, deserted, was stripped of power by Octavian. Retaining just the title of pontifex maximus, he was exiled to a small town in southern Italy, where he would die. With both Sextus and Lepidus removed, just one man stood in Octavian's path to total power: Mark Antony.

Sextus's wife, daughter, and sister were never heard of again. Antony probably permitted them to live in his realm for the next five years, but Octavian would have had them executed following his defeat of Antony and Cleopatra, to leave no descendant of Pompey the Great to one day challenge him. Certainly, Sextus's daughter never married Octavian's nephew Marcus Marcellus; Octavian later married the boy to his own daughter, Julia. Nonetheless, the Pompey family would be revered by Romans for generations, as beacons of Rome's lost democracy. While some distant Pompey relatives would later achieve high office, none would be as great as Pompey the Great, and none would shake the Roman world the way bright, bold Sextus Pompey did for seven memorable rebellious years.

Had his last sea battle off Sicily ended differently, Sextus may well have defeated Octavian and become sole ruler of Rome, with the Pompey dynasty, not the Caesar dynasty, creating the foundations of imperial Rome.

Roman bust of Tiberius when Roman general leading efforts to defeat the revolts of Bato of Pannonia and Bato of Dalmatia. © *Luisa Ricciarini/Bridgeman Images*.

VI. THE TWO BATOS

FREEDOM FIGHTERS. DALMATIA AND PANNONIA, AD 6–9

In the late winter of AD 5–6, several thousand men of military age from the Daesitiates tribe gathered at a Roman camp in their homeland of Dalmatia. They were answering a summons to be inducted into the Roman army as auxiliary soldiers, with twenty-five years' paid military service to Rome under the emperor Augustus, the former Octavian, lying ahead of them.

The adjacent regions of Dalmatia and Pannonia, later separate Roman provinces, had been incorporated into the single new Roman province of Illyricum in 14 BC by Augustus, after he personally annexed by force an area taking in much of today's Serbia, Croatia, Bosnia, and Slovenia, and parts of Austria and Hungary.

By AD 6, Augustus had been reigning as emperor of Rome for thirty-three years, and his declining health meant he no longer took the field in command of Rome's army. For several years, Augustus's eldest stepson, Drusus Caesar, had led successful campaigns east of the Rhine River against Germanic tribes, but his promising career had been cut short on campaign east of the Rhine when he fell from his horse and broke a leg, and gangrene set in. Following the death of Drusus, his younger brother Tiberius Caesar had led Rome's legions on annual campaigns beyond the Rhine and Danube Rivers, in which they marched as far as the Elbe River, defeating and bringing to terms German tribes in numerous battles.

Over the winter of AD 5–6, Tiberius wintered at Carnuntum on the Danube with elements of five legions. His force included half the cohorts of the 20th Legion—later granted the title Valerius Victrix, making it the 20th Strong and Victorious Legion—which had been taken from their normal station in Pannonia to add to his army. His plan was to launch a two-pronged attack against the Marcomanni tribe, one of the most aggressive of Rome's German foes, in the spring of AD 6. When Tiberius crossed the Danube with his legions, Gaius Sentius Saturninus, governor of Upper Germany, planned to launch a simultaneous attack from Mainz on the Rhine, with both forces linking up in the Bohemian homeland of the Marcomanni in the modern-day Czech Republic, taking the Germans by surprise.

To support this campaign, new auxiliary units were being levied in various parts of the empire, including Dalmatia. Revolt had flickered in Dalmatia and Pannonia over the twenty years that Rome had been overlord of the indigenous tribes, but Roman garrisons had always quickly and brutally snuffed it out. Now, however, as Roman historian Cassius Dio writes, as the Daesitiates gathered to answer the call for recruits they realized how numerous they were and how feeble was the Roman garrison that remained in their territory.[32]

Spontaneously, led by their chieftain Bato, tribesmen turned on the Roman centurions sent to train them, and killed them. The Daesitiates were hardy natives of the mountains of today's central Bosnia and Herzegovina. They spoke their own dialect as well as Latin, and were quite literate. All we know about Bato was that he was a mature man with an adult son. Bato's plan was to drive the Romans from Dalmatia, and, initially, he led raids in his region, robbing Roman citizens, massacring Roman traders, and wiping out a large vexillation of Roman auxiliaries stationed in the area, taking their arms.

Whether it was inspired by the revolt in Dalmatia or it occurred independently, the Breuci tribe, to the northeast, in Pannonia, also decided to rise up against Rome at this time. They elected two nobles as their war leaders. One, coincidentally, was also named Bato; the other was Pinnes. This Bato of the Breuci would emerge as the principal leader of the Pannonian tribes that joined the rebellion. We know nothing about him, neither his age nor his stature. But he appears to have been younger than the Dalmatian Bato, who would have come from his tribal elite; and would have been known for his military skills.

Two Pannonian armies were created, perhaps not from design but from conflicting and divergent objectives. Unlike Bato the Dalmatian, who merely sought to free Dalmatia, Bato's grand plan was to bring together, arm, and train a large force, clear Roman forces from Pannonia, and then march into Italy and attack Rome itself. The objective of his colleague Pinnes was more limited. Pinnes wanted to attack and plunder Roman interests in the neighboring Roman province of Macedonia, which had no garrison. Bato of the Breuci, bringing all the Pannonian tribes into a rebel league, also contacted his Dalmatian namesake, sealing an alliance between the Pannonians and Dalmatians. While the Pannonian rebels would follow their Bato's direction, the Dalmatians under their Bato would operate independently and with their own objectives.

Velleius Paterculus, a Roman officer who fought in this war against the Batos, would remark on how quickly the Pannonian rebels turned intent into action: "It came to pass, by Hercules, that no nation ever displayed such swiftness in following up with war its own plans for war, and in putting its resolve into execution."[33] By the summer of AD 6, with Bato the Breucian recruiting and training tens of thousands of Pannonian tribesmen, Pinnes led his force into Macedonia, raiding and pillaging towns, villages, and farms. Bato, seeking sole command of Pannonian forces, soon rid himself of Pinnes by betraying him to the Romans.

Farther south, once Bato of the Daesitiates garnered victories and arms, his Dalmatian following quickly grew, and by autumn he led an army of twenty thousand Dalmatians to the Adriatic coast to attack Salonae, near today's Split, capital of Rome's province of Illyricum.

Opposing Bato, commanding a force of five thousand men made up of the five remaining cohorts of the 20th Legion and five cohorts of auxiliaries, was the province's governor, Marcus Valerius Messalla Messalinus. According to Dio, writing in the third century, Messalinus went to Germany when half the 20th Legion's cohorts were transferred there to serve in Tiberius's German campaigns in AD 5, but Velleius Paterculus, who took part in the war, makes it clear that the governor had remained at Salonae and led the fight against the Dalmatian rebels.[34]

The Dalmatian Bato received a serious head wound from a sling-stone in this battle, which helps explain the fact that his force, deprived of his leadership, was driven off by the vastly outnumbered Roman defenders. Velleius writes that Messalinus "routed and put to flight more than twenty thousand."[35]

For this victory, Messalinus would be awarded Triumphal Decorations by the emperor. But Bato was not finished. Recovered from his wound, and realizing the futility of taking on the Roman military on its terms, he regrouped his men and dispatched rebel parties that overran and sacked Roman communities all the way down the Adriatic coast to Apollonia in Greece.

Meanwhile, similarly with a force of twenty thousand, Bato the Pannonian besieged Sirmium, modern Sremska Mitrovica. This city, just inside the Pannonian provincial border with Moesia, controlled the Sava Valley as well as the important highway that passed through it to Siscia to the northwest and Italy beyond. Sirmium held out, and on Augustus's orders was relieved by a force led from the Danubian province of Moesia by its governor, Aulus Caecina Severus, known as Caecina. But news that Sarmatian and Dacian tribesmen had flooded across the Danube in his absence and were now raiding throughout Moesia prevented Caecina from capitalizing on his success. Turning about, he hurried with his troops back to his province.

Despite Caecina's success at Sirmium and Messalinus's at Salonae, by the winter of AD 6–7 there was little Roman territory in Pannonia and Dalmatia that hadn't been devastated by fire and sword at the hands of rebels led by the two Batos. Velleius writes that there were 800,000 native peoples in Pannonia and Dalmatia at this time, and of these he estimates that 209,000 had taken up arms against Rome by the time the revolt ended, with 9,000 of them mounted.[36]

With much of the Adriatic coast opposite Italy in rebel hands, there was panic in Rome. Even Augustus, a seasoned military commander, was shaken, telling the Senate, "The enemy might appear in sight of Rome within ten days."[37]

Augustus ordered Tiberius to cancel his planned operations in Germany for AD 7 and urgently march for Pannonia with five legions. He also ordered three legions stationed in Moesia and two from the East to march to Pannonia with supporting auxiliaries and allied cavalry, to link up with Tiberius. In addition, a total of ten thousand retired legionaries living in Italy, who were subject to emergency military service as members of the Evocati reserve, were being recalled to their standards. Also in Italy, thousands of freedmen, former slaves of military age, were commandeered from their male and female owners in proportion to those masters' means, armed, and formed into auxiliary military units.

The deputy commander of this force from Rome was a young man of thirty, the previously mentioned writer Velleius Paterculus. His grandfather had been a close friend of Tiberius's father, Tiberius Claudius Nero, and Velleius's family became clients of Tiberius's father and then of Tiberius himself. Velleius's elder brother Magius Celer Velleianus was already a senator and commanded a legion in Tiberius's army. Velleius himself had recently returned to Rome after a decade's military service, initially as a tribune with a legion in Thrace and Macedonia. Later, still a tribune, he accompanied Augustus's adoptive son Gaius Caesar to the East and met the king of Parthia. Since AD 4, having been promoted to prefect, Velleius had commanded an auxiliary cohort and then a wing of auxiliary cavalry on the Rhine under Tiberius, serving in his German campaigns of AD 4 and 5.

Velleius had returned to Rome hoping for an appointment as a quaestor, the adjutant to a provincial governor. This was the last stepping-stone on the path to membership in the Senate. "I was now, at the end of my service with the cavalry, quaestor designate," he wrote, "though not yet a senator." To his surprise, Augustus put him in command of the freedman cohorts enlisted in the scramble to arms in Rome.[38]

As Velleius's superior, in overall command of the mixed force of freedmen and recalled legion veterans from Italy, Augustus appointed twenty-year-old Germanicus Julius Caesar, nephew and adopted son of Tiberius. Germanicus, grandson of Mark Antony, had married Agrippina the Elder, granddaughter of Augustus himself. This union of the Julian and Claudian families, between grandchildren of the two final opponents in the civil war that had rocked Rome and destroyed the Republic, was a union made in heaven as far as Romans were concerned. Germanicus was athletic, brilliant, handsome, and hugely popular, and word that he was leading the reinforcements being sent to Pannonia from Italy to link up with his uncle and adoptive father, Tiberius, had a calming effect on the populace.

In the spring of AD 7, four Roman armies converged on Pannonia to combat the revolt. From the Rhine, Tiberius arrived in northern Pannonia and set up camp at Siscia, today's Sisak in Croatia. The then existing fortress of Siscia occupied an island at the confluence of three rivers, the Sava, Colapis, and Odra, and Tiberius immediately set about strengthening the position to make it his center of operations. Germanicus, accompanied by Velleius, would join Tiberius there with his force of twenty thousand recalled veterans and new freedmen recruits from Italy.

From Moesia came the governor Caecina, returning with elements of three legions and auxiliary cohorts. From Asia came another commander of consular rank, Silvanus Plautius, bringing two legions—including the 7th, which was then based in Galatia—plus auxiliaries. These two legion forces combined before reaching Pannonia, and their five legions were joined by Roman ally King Rhoemetacles of Thrace, who led a large contingent of Thracian cavalry.

The two Batos, learning of the approaching Roman army from the East, with its forty thousand troops, combined forces and lay in wait at the Volcae Marshes, west of today's Mitrovica in the Sava Valley. Their intent was to prevent the Roman force from linking up with Tiberius. As the army of Caecina and Plautius made camp at the Volcae Marshes, the rebels descended on them en masse. The Roman cavalry, which had the task of defending the legionaries as they dug the ditch and walls around the camp, attempted to intercept the horde of rebels, which seemed to appear from nowhere. When King Rhoemetacles's horsemen stood their ground, however, this cavalry force was overwhelmed, and took heavy casualties. Other auxiliary cavalrymen bolted from the scene, leaving the camp builders unprotected and allowing the rebels to fling themselves onto the unfinished camp.

In this chaos, the Roman generals were unable to exert their command over the separated troops. Legion tribunes and first-rank centurions were cut down as they attempted to defend their bunched legionary eagle standards. A camp prefect in command of one legion vexillation and several prefects of auxiliary units were surrounded and cut off. It fell to the ordinary legionaries to mount a counterattack, often without their standards to rally behind. With the men of one legion yelling encouragement to those of another, the legionaries succeeded in charging and driving the rebels from the camp, saving the day. According to Velleius, it was the ordinary soldiers, not the generals, who deserved the credit this day, and many legionaries would have been subsequently decorated by their commanders.[39]

Once Caecina and Plautius regained control of their army, cremated their dead, and patched up their wounded, they moved up the Sava Valley and joined Tiberius at Siscia. A Roman army of ten legions now occupied the sprawling Siscia camp, together with seventy auxiliary cohorts and three wings of cavalry, numbering roughly 100,000 men. But now an odd thing occurred. According to Velleius, even though the rebels still outnumbered the Romans two to one, Tiberius considered this combined army too large and unwieldy. After allowing the five legions of Caecina and Plautius several days to recover from their long march and recent desperate battle, he ordered them to return to the provinces from which they'd come.[40]

It is more likely that Tiberius had a bitter disagreement with Caecina and Plautius over the strategy to be employed against the two Batos. Tiberius was against pitched battles. Instead, he had decided to attack enemy supply lines and deprive the rebels of food, to wear them down and force their eventual capitulation while preventing them from entering Italy. Tiberius seemed to be more interested in keeping Roman casualties low than in rapidly defeating the rebels—which he probably thought was an impossibility anyway, considering their vast numbers and the mountainous country they occupied. He even provided his own portable hot bath for the use of Roman wounded, and a horse-drawn ambulance and his own slave-borne litter for the transfer of wounded Romans to the care of doctors in the rear. Velleius Paterculus would be wounded in this war and would be one of the officers to take advantage of this provision by Tiberius.

Caecina and Plautius, both extremely experienced generals, would have taken the opposite approach. After the near disaster at the Volcae Marshes, they would have been keen to draw the rebels into a huge battle and slaughter them wholesale, to satisfy their men's desire for vengeance. This would also allow them to quickly terminate the revolt and return to their provinces, whose defenses had been depleted by the removal of troops for this campaign. The two seasoned generals, both older men than Tiberius, seem to have insisted on rapid action.

Tiberius had supreme command, but he didn't have the authority to remove Caecina or Plautius from their posts; only Augustus could do that. Tiberius did, however, send the two generals and their troops back to where they'd come from, under the pretext that he didn't need them. To ensure they complied, Tiberius marched with Caecina, Plautius, and their five legions, with much of his own force, all the way to the border with Moesia.

When Augustus, in Rome, learned that his stepson had sent away

five legions and was actively avoiding full-scale battles with the Pannonian and Dalmatian rebels, his blood boiled. That autumn, taking elements of the Praetorian Guard and his German Guard bodyguard with
him, Augustus went up the Flaminian Way, a highway he had opened
in 27 BC, to Arminium, today's city of Rimini, on the northeast coast
of Italy. There, he based himself temporarily. Ostensibly, this would be
closer to the campaign in Pannonia, but in reality it was a veiled threat
to Tiberius: if he didn't deliver results soon, Augustus would arrive in
Pannonia and personally take charge.

The winter of AD 7–8 was particularly severe and prevented action by either side, but once the snow and ice had cleared from the
narrow mountain passes and rivers, Tiberius launched measured operations in Pannonia, ignoring Dalmatia for the time being. Then he—
and Rome—had a stroke of luck. By the summer, the two Batos had
fallen out. Bato the Pannonian, suspecting that his Dalmatian allies
lacked the determination to keep fighting, made unexpected visits to
Dalmatian outposts, seizing Dalmatian nobles and taking them back
to Pannonia as hostages against surrender to Rome. This infuriated
the Dalmatian Bato, but he was cunning enough to conceal his anger. Instead, he invited his Pannonian counterpart to a meeting to discuss tactics. Once the Pannonian Bato was in Dalmatian territory, his
namesake's troops fell on his bodyguards and killed them. Bato of the
Breuci was captured alive, and Bato of the Daesitiates summoned his
troops to a mass assembly. In front of them all, he put the Pannonian
Bato to death.

In doing this, the surviving Bato did Rome a service—and his
cause of freedom no good at all. The now leaderless Pannonians sent
messages to Tiberius, seeking to surrender. By year's end, tens of thousands of Pannonian rebels had come to the bank of the Bathinus River,
today's Bosna, which divided the territories of the Breuci and their relatives the Osseriates. Laying down their arms, the Pannonians pros-
trated themselves before Tiberius and surrendered unconditionally.

Augustus placed Marcus Lepidus in charge of restoring Roman

control throughout Pannonia, using the bulk of Tiberius's army, and recalled Tiberius to Italy. Lepidus, whom Augustus had made consul in AD 6, was distantly related to the Marcus Lepidus who'd attempted to overthrow Octavian/Augustus following the defeat of Sextus Pompey in Italy. Despite this, Augustus trusted implicitly in his ability and loyalty.

To deal with Dalmatia, a much larger territory than Pannonia, and track down and eliminate rebels led by the surviving Bato, Augustus ordered Germanicus to lead the 20th Legion, auxiliaries, and German cavalry in assaulting one Dalmatian rebel stronghold after another. In laborious, time-consuming sieges, Germanicus subsequently subdued the Mazaei tribe and took numerous Dalmatian towns, including Raetinum—which the locals burned, trapping some of Germanicus's troops inside—and Seretium, which Tiberius had previously failed to capture. Another hill town, Splonum, was particularly well-fortified, and Germanicus's siege equipment and battering rams proved useless. But a German cavalryman named Pusio threw a stone at a section of the wall, causing the parapet, and the rebel fighter leaning on it, to fall away. Dalmatian defenders, convinced that Germanicus had magical powers, surrendered.

Termination of the revolt was progressing much too slowly for Augustus, so in the summer of AD 9 he sent Tiberius to take command in Dalmatia. When Tiberius arrived from Rome, he brought with him Velleius Paterculus, who had just achieved the quaestorship. With his promotion, Velleius had been offered a post with a provincial governor, but when he said he preferred service under his patron Tiberius in Dalmatia, he was promoted to the Senate and appointed a legate in command of a legion in Dalmatia.

Another young man to journey to Dalmatia with Tiberius was Ornospades, a Parthian noble who'd been living in Rome as an exile from his homeland. Ornospades took charge of Tiberius's cavalry and rendered conspicuous service, for which he was granted Roman citizenship. He would later reconcile with the Parthian king, who would appoint him governor of Parthian Mesopotamia.

Marcus Lepidus, ordered to join Tiberius on the Dalmatian coast, was harassed all the way from Siscia by rebels who'd materialized from mountain strongholds and attempted to prevent the Roman forces from joining up. Lepidus's long, hellish march, with heavy casualties, would result in Lepidus arriving too late to help Tiberius.

Tiberius, forced to commence operations with the troops he had, sent Germanicus against rebel Dalmatian towns while he himself drove Bato ahead of him, bottling him up in the hill town of Andetrium, near today's Split. While Tiberius besieged the town, Dalmatian rebels appeared in his rear and struck his supply lines, making the Romans feel that they were the ones under siege. Eventually, Bato sent envoys seeking peace. The terms that Tiberius dictated required Bato to guarantee that all Dalmatian rebels would disarm. Roman deserters who had joined Bato, knowing they would be executed if they fell into Tiberius's hands, convinced him to hold out.

Breaking off negotiations, Tiberius commenced an assault on Andetrium. As Roman troops advanced up the slope in front of the town in a tightly packed square formation, rebels emerged from the city gates and gleefully rolled wagons, wheels, and the round wooden chests that were the specialty of the region down at them. But a second Roman force Tiberius had sent around the hill came up behind these men, caught them in the open, and slaughtered them. That night, Bato slipped away with some followers, and when daylight came Andetrium surrendered to Tiberius.

Meanwhile, Germanicus was besieging the coastal town of Arduba. Townsmen wanted to surrender, but German auxiliary deserters from the Roman army joined with the women of Arduba in urging the men not to give in. When their pleas fell on deaf ears, those women set fire to the city, then, clutching their children to them, threw themselves into the flames or made suicidal jumps from the city wall into the raging river below. Germanicus accepted the surrender of the living residents of Arduba, and soon representatives of other towns were coming to him seeking to capitulate.

By September AD 9, Bato was running out of places to hide. He sent his son Sceuas to Tiberius seeking new terms for his own surrender, including full pardons for himself and those family members and friends who remained with him. Tiberius agreed, and Bato was smuggled into his camp at night so Roman soldiers wouldn't recognize him and raise their swords against him. The next morning, when Bato was brought before Tiberius, the Roman prince asked why he had gone to war with Rome.

Bato replied, "We are your flocks, but you didn't send shepherds to look after us, you sent wolves."[41]

There, the fighting and the dying ended. The conflict has been described by Roman historians as two wars, the Pannonian and the Dalmatian, though in reality it was one, characterized by the Roman biographer Suetonius as "the most bitterly fought of all foreign wars· since Rome defeated Carthage."[42] Roman casualties had been high, but the war had proved catastrophic for the Dalmatians. According to Velleius, the Desiadates and Perustae tribes of Dalmatia "were almost entirely exterminated."[43]

Bato of the Daesitiates, his family members, and others pardoned with him were sent to the Roman naval base of Ravenna, on Italy's northeastern coast. There, with servants, and guards at the door, Bato lived out the rest of his life under house arrest. In AD 10, the year following the three-year war's termination, Illyricum was divided by Augustus into two provinces, Pannonia and Dalmatia, with legions stationed in each. By the reign of the emperor Claudius, two legions would be based in Dalmatia, at separate bases.

A number of Dalmatian tribes were forcibly resettled following the revolt, some to other parts of the Balkans, others as far away as modern Austria. Never again would there be a revolt in Pannonia or Dalmatia. On the contrary, the people of the region would embrace Roman culture. Numerous Roman emperors would be born in Pannonia, with five born in Sirmium alone, and the Dalmatian-born Roman emperor Diocletian would retire to a palace in Split.

Tiberius would celebrate a Triumph for ending the Dalmatian and Pannonian revolts, while generals of consular rank who'd participated in the war were granted Triumphal Decorations—all the bling of a Triumph without the heady excitement of the public parade through the cheering crowds of Rome.

Technically, Germanicus wasn't qualified to share these rewards because he had not yet become a consul; he was only of quaestor rank and not yet even of senatorial age. By law, a senator couldn't become a consul before the age of forty-two. Nonetheless, Augustus appointed Germanicus, his adoptive grandson, a consul in AD 12, when the young man was just twenty-six. This allowed Germanicus to also be awarded Triumphal Decorations and participate in Tiberius's Triumph parade when he celebrated it that same year.

Because of an emergency in September AD 9, just as the Dalmatian revolt was wrapping up, the Roman citizens whose freedmen servants had been seized by the army to combat the Pannonian and Dalmatian rebels never had them returned. The special units raised in Italy in AD 6 would be sorely needed as Rome suffered a shocking loss in Germany, and these freedmen units would be thrown into gaps in Roman defenses on the frontiers.

Römische Büste eines Germanen, nach der Tradition Arminius.
Im Kapitolinischen Museum zu Rom.

Roman bust of German prince and rebel leader Arminius, aka Hermann.
© *Look and Learn/Bridgeman Images.*

VII. ARMINIUS

GERMAN PRINCE, ROMAN OFFICER, FREEDOM FIGHTER. GERMANY, AD 9–21

O ne evening in September AD 9, while Tiberius and his nephew and adopted son Germanicus Caesar were wrapping up the long Pannonian-Dalmatian revolt, the Roman governor of Lower Germany, Publius Quinctilius Varus, was enjoying a fine dinner with friends and colleagues east of the Rhine in a vast, tented Roman military camp outside Mattium, capital of the German Chatti tribe. Varus, a man in his sixties, was a long way from home. This town of mud and timber huts sat in today's German state of Hesse on the Fulda River, just above the Eder, southern boundary of the Chatti, who had enjoyed allied status with Rome for several years.

Roman officer Velleius Paterculus, who was serving in Dalmatia with Tiberius at this time, knew the governor well. "Varus," he writes in his *Compendium*, "descended from a famous rather than a high-born family, was a man of mild character and of a quiet disposition, somewhat slow in mind as he was in body, and more accustomed to the leisure of the camp than to actual service in war." Yet, Varus had acted promptly when he served as governor of Syria in 4 BC. After rioting broke out in Jerusalem with the death of King Herod the Great, Varus had marched into Judea from Syria with one of his legions, crucified two thousand Jewish rioters, and restored order. That prompt action would have given Augustus the confidence to appoint Varus to govern the province of Lower Germany while Tiberius was occupied in the Balkans.

Besides, Varus's new area of command was considered a peaceful backwater by the time he arrived at his provincial capital of Cologne on the Lower Rhine in AD 5. Over more than a decade, Tiberius and his elder brother Drusus before him had subjected the German tribes immediately east of the Rhine to a series of campaigns, using up to thirteen legions at a time. To secure peace with Rome, Segimerus, king of the Cherusci Germans, who occupied an area of plain and forest near present-day Hanover, had given over his two sons to Rome as hostages when they were youths. The boys had been educated as Romans. One had taken the Roman name of Flavus, which is Latin for "yellow," suggesting that Flavus had strikingly fair hair. We don't know his German name. His brother's German name was Hermann, which meant "Man of War." Hermann's Roman name, Arminius, had similar military connotations, being a reference to weapons. A Roman bust depicts him as a frowning young man, clean-shaven in the Roman fashion, but with long, German-style hair, thick and wavy, covering his ears.

Both Flavus and Arminius had gone through Roman military training and been made members of the Equestrian Order. Appointed prefects, they'd been given command of German auxiliary units in the Roman army. In September AD 6, Flavus was with his unit, a cavalry wing then part of the Army of the Upper Rhine, at Mainz, west of the Rhine. Flavus had lost an eye in battle, probably while fighting the two Batos under Tiberius in Pannonia and Dalmatia.

Twenty-five-year-old Arminius was serving with Varus's army, and was there in the Roman camp as one of Varus's dinner guests. Arminius was married, and his father-in-law, Segestes, king of the Chatti, reclined on Varus's right during the dinner.

Tacitus, who, for this period of his *Annals*, consulted the now lost *German Wars*, a twenty-volume work by Pliny the Elder, writes that Segestes despised Arminius, and had been warning Varus for months not to trust the youth. Pliny, who commenced writing his book when serving as a prefect of auxiliaries at Mainz in AD 41–42, would have spoken with Germans who attended this banquet, in particular King

Segestes's son Segimundus, who survived the chaotic years of war that lay ahead to become a priest at Cologne. The king's daughter Thusnelda had been betrothed to a Chattian noble, but in the best traditions of romantic fiction she and Arminius had fallen in love and eloped. Segestes had never forgiven Arminius for this, but, counseled by Varus to keep relations between the Chatti and Cherusci on an even keel, he had kept his contempt for the youth in check—until the night of this banquet.

According to Tacitus's *Annals*, Varus's army was by this point "officerless," meaning that they were without the officers of legate rank who normally commanded the legions. Varus, who was lingering longer than was necessary as summer ended, enjoying the hospitality of the Germans, had sent the three senators commanding his legions back to Rome. When they set off with an auxiliary cavalry escort, these generals had left their second-in-commands, their "broad stripe" military tribunes, in charge of bringing their legions back to the winter camp west of the great river once Varus decided to end his excursion.

During the day of the banquet, word had reached Varus of unrest by German tribesmen to the north, beyond Cherusci territory—trouble that threatened the Cherusci, who were Roman allies. Reluctantly, Varus had ordered his army to prepare to march for the trouble spot the following morning. This dinner was his farewell to Segestes and his people.

As the dinner proceeded, Arminius volunteered to go on ahead of Varus's main force the next morning with a mounted detachment, to scout the way and organize support from his own people. Varus liked the young man, and trusted him implicitly, as a father trusts a favorite son. He quickly agreed to Arminius's idea. This was when King Segestes finally lost his composure. Rising up, he addressed Varus.

"From the time that Augustus Caesar gave me Roman citizenship," Tacitus writes that the king began, "I have chosen my friends and my enemies with an eye to Rome's advantage, not from hatred of my fatherland. I believe that Romans and Germans have the same interests, that peace is better than war. I'm no traitor. Traitors are hated even by those they love, and I am not hated by my people. But there are those here who are traitors, to Rome, to Germany, and to the peace." Turning to young Arminius and stabbing a finger in his direction, he declared, "This man is a traitor! Just as he violated my daughter, he's planning to violate the peace with Rome, and bring misery to us all!"

Arminius merely responded with a mocking smile.

This only annoyed King Segestes all the more. "Arrest myself and Arminius, here, now," he challenged Varus. "Arrest all the leading men of the tribes. I assure you, the German people will do nothing without their leaders." (Even as early as AD 6, the Germans had a strong leader ethic.) "Then you'll have the opportunity to sift the accusations and to determine the innocent and the guilty."

Several of the Roman officers at the dinner, tribunes of the legions and prefects of auxiliary units, backed Segestes's warning. Clearly, they didn't trust Arminius either, and hadn't for some time. Varus, annoyed by the whole affair, and irritated that officers in their twenties should deign to support the German king, turned to Arminius and demanded to know if there was any truth in Segestes's accusation. Arminius replied by scoffing at any suggestion that he was in the least disloyal to Rome.

Varus accepted Arminius's declaration of innocence without any further questions. Turning on Segestes and his own officers, he raged, "I will not have you slandering my friends!"[44]

King Segestes, who, Tacitus reports, secretly considered Varus a dilatory general who put off important decisions and proceeded without due diligence, stormed from Varus's pavilion, and out of the Roman camp. Back in Mattium, he decided to take matters into his own hands. When Arminius eventually left the banquet and returned to Mattium to rejoin his wife at the royal quarters, Segestes was waiting in the dark for him, with his most powerful warriors. Seized, bound, and gagged, Arminius was thrown into solitary confinement. But members of Segestes's own entourage sympathized with Arminius, and they alerted Arminius's Cheruscan bodyguards. These men came at the run and freed him, then chained Segestes in his place. All this occurred with the Romans in the nearby camp totally oblivious to what had transpired.

When, at dawn next day, Arminius and his cavalrymen rode off, supposedly to prepare the way for the march, the Roman general Varus had no idea that his ally King Segestes was a prisoner in his own capital. By mid-morning, a long Roman column trailed away from Mattium in marching order. In that column were the 17th, 18th, and 19th Legions, units that originated in Cisalpine Gaul, today's northern Italy. They were accompanied by six auxiliary cohorts and three auxiliary cavalry wings.

Several German nobles who'd accompanied Varus through the summer and been present at the previous evening's dinner rode with the Roman general, planning to return to their people once Varus had crossed the Rhine. One was twenty-six-year-old Boioculus, of the Ampsivari, a tribe residing northwest of the Cherusci, around the River Ems. Boioculus was prefect of Ampsivari auxiliaries who'd already gone to winter quarters, but to demonstrate his loyalty to Varus and to Rome he'd chosen to remain with Varus until he left German territory.

Normally, the Army of the Lower Rhine consisted of four legions, up to thirty-two auxiliary cohorts, and eight cavalry wings. Like Prefect Boioculus's men, some of the auxiliary cohorts that marched with Varus had already gone into winter camp east of the Rhine among allied German tribes. Others, including a cohort of archers from the East, had been detached to garrison forts previously built by Tiberius and his brother Drusus east of the Rhine. More auxiliaries had been transferred from the Rhine to participate in Tiberius's campaign to terminate the Pannonian and Dalmatian Revolt, which had been raging since AD 6.

Still, Varus's army was no mean force, containing 18,000 to 20,000 fighting men. They were followed by thousands of noncombatants, muleteers handling thousands of pack mules and scores of carts of the army's baggage train, as well as the slaves and freedmen servants of Roman officers, and traders and pimps who made a living from the legions. There were even women and children—prostitutes and their young, and, trailing their men from camp to camp, the de facto wives and illegitimate children of some Roman soldiers. Legionaries were then not permitted to marry while serving in the army; this regulation would only change late in the second century.

We know the identities of only a few of Varus's Roman officers. One was Numonius Vala, commander of one of Varus's three remaining cavalry wings. He was the son or grandson of a Gaius Numonius Vala, who was celebrated for storming the wall of an enemy fortification in an earlier war. According to Velleius, who was acquainted with him, Vala was an inoffensive and honorable man.

Another officer we know to have been serving with Varus was Caelius Caldus, an eighteen-year-old officer cadet of noble birth serving his six-month semester as a tribune of the thin stripe. Five "thin stripers" served with each legion, carrying out mostly administrative duties, with one or two also on the personal staff of the army commander. There could have been as many as sixteen or seventeen of these officer cadets marching with Varus. An ancestor of Caelius Caldus with the same name had been a consul, governed in Spain, and unsuccessfully fought Pompey the Great, on the side of Marius in the civil war that made Sulla dictator. From a later reference by Seneca we know that several of Caldus's fellow thin stripe tribunes came from similarly illustrious Roman families.

Velleius tells us that there were only two camp prefects in Varus's column. Every legion in the Roman army had a single camp prefect, normally a legion's third-in-command after its legate and its broad stripe tribune. The camp prefect would have been a former centurion, the highest-ranking enlisted man in a legion and the equivalent rank of a major in a modern army. He would usually lead large vexillations of several cohorts when they were detached from a legion for service elsewhere.

Varus's third camp prefect, Lucius Caedicius, was commanding a vexillation from one of Varus's legions stationed at Aliso, a fort originally built by Germanicus Caesar's father, Drusus, east of the Rhine on the Lippe River. This means that one of the legions with Varus was under strength by several cohorts. One of the two camp prefects now marching with Varus's legions was, we know, a Lucius Eggius.

Centurions were the lieutenants and captains of the Roman army, and by the first century they were always enlisted men promoted through legion ranks. Among the scores of centurions in Varus's force was fifty-three-year-old Marcus Caelius—no relation to the Caelius above. He was a first-rank centurion with the 18th Legion, and, having put in a full term with the army, was serving an extended enlistment; when Augustus first became emperor he required his legionaries to serve sixteen-year enlistments, but between 4 BC and AD 11 he summarily increased the term to twenty years, legion by legion. In addition, centurions and legionaries could volunteer for further enlistments, and some did. One centurion in Africa in the first century was still serving when aged in his seventies.

We know that Centurion Caelius had been born in March 44 BC, around the time of Julius Caesar's assassination, that his father's name was Titus, and his hometown was Bononia, today's Bologna in northern Italy, then in the province of Cisalpine Gaul. Caelius was a burly, curly-headed man who had garnered numerous bravery decorations, including a Civic Crown for saving a fellow Roman citizen's life and two golden torques and bracelets for valor in battle. Later events suggest his freedmen Privatus and Thiaminus were marching with the baggage train in Varus's column.[45]

Varus's course took him north, through tracts of flat countryside. A road-making detachment always preceded the legions, smoothing the way, and in these circumstances a legion might march eighteen miles in a day. Several days into the march, messengers from Arminius arrived at the gallop. They informed Varus that Arminius and his Cherusci were under attack from other hostile German tribesmen farther north, and offered to guide the Roman army via a shortcut through the Teutoburg Forest so that Varus could rescue Arminius.

Varus now told the German nobles riding with him to hurry away to their own people to collect reinforcements, and ordered his own troops to quicken the pace of their march as he hurried to save his young friend Arminius. Just the same, he kept his baggage train with him. Roman army baggage trains, called *impedimenta*, were indeed impediments to rapid movement, because the speed of a marching army was dictated by the speed of its slowest baggage vehicles. Had he left the baggage behind, Varus would have had to forgo the comforts of his furniture, silver dinnerware, and good wine.

The prospect of imminent action caused a number of the army's civilian camp followers to leave the column and head for the Rhine. Their aim was to cross the bridge of boats at Cologne by which the army had entered Greater Germany several months before. As these camp followers peeled away from the column, the German nobles rode away to do Varus's bidding. Prefect Boioculus of the Ampsivari was one of them. He had not gone far on his mission when he was met by mounted Cheruscan warriors. Surrounding him, they put him in chains. Boioculus was lodged in a hut in a German village, but soon managed to escape in the night. He would succeed in reaching and crossing the Rhine, and reporting to Roman officials. Varus must be warned, he would tell them—he and his army were marching into a trap! But by the time Boioculus raised the alarm, it would be too late. Varus would already be dead.

A trap had indeed been laid by Arminius and a host of German tribes. The previous winter, Arminius had secretly attended a council of tribal leaders to discuss joining forces in a war against Rome and driving the Romans out of Germany. Of all the German kings, princes, and nobles invited to this conference, only King Maroboduus of the Marcomanni had declined to attend. In 9 BC, under Roman pressure, the Marcomanni had relocated from the Main River Valley to Bohemia in today's Czech Republic, and in AD 6 Maroboduus had sealed a peace treaty with Augustus, a treaty he intended to honor.

At the council meeting, every tribal leader but one had spoken for going to war. The exception was King Segestes of the Chatti, who had vehemently opposed it. When a vote was taken, Segestes had been the lone voice to call "No!" When Arminius was elected to lead the tribes to war, Segestes had again voted against the proposition. Even his own son Segimerus and the other members of the Chattian delegation had voted in favor of war. So, when Segestes spoke against Arminius at the dinner with Varus, he knew firsthand that Arminius was about to revolt and was trying to prevent the Roman general from falling into his trap. He was also trying to protect his son Segimerus; if Segestes had revealed what had transpired at the tribal council meeting, about the vote and the plan to go to war, Varus would surely have arrested Segimerus and the other Chattian nobles on the spot.

At this point, Segestes was still a prisoner in his own capital, and his son Segimerus was leading thousands of Chattian warriors on the war path to join Arminius. Among the Chattian nobles taking their clans to war behind Segimerus were Catumerus, whose daughter had married Arminius's elder brother Flavus, as well as Arpus and Adgandestrius. All three of these men would later be kings of the Chatti. Trailing Varus's army, the Chattian warriors would position themselves to attack the Romans from the rear once Arminius sprang his trap.

As Varus's unsuspecting army neared the Weser Hills in today's German state of Lower Saxony, tens of thousands of German warriors were gathering ahead of the Romans in the Teutoburg Forest, having had nine months to arm, train, and reach the agreed-upon location for the ambush of the Roman army. Apart from the Cherusci and the Chatti, the tribes represented in a German army thought to have numbered in excess of twenty thousand warriors included the Marsi and the Fossi, near neighbors of the Cherusci and Chatti. From well to the south in today's Switzerland came the Chauci. The Bructeri from north of the Lippe River were there, as were the Usipetes and the Tubantes. Other tribes likely to have supplied fighting men were the Chamavi, the Angrivarii, the Sugambri, the Mattiaci, and perhaps Boioculus's

Ampsivari. Some of these tribes had Roman auxiliaries quartered among them for the winter, and before the tribal war parties set out for the Teutoburg, those auxiliaries were taken by surprise and massacred by their hosts. In addition to the men gathering at the Teutoburg, some tribesmen were assembling between the Weser Hills and the Rhine, to intercept and kill any Romans who escaped the ambush and fled west.

On average, German warriors were taller, broader men than the Romans, living on a diet of meat and dairy produce, as opposed to the Roman staples of bread and olive oil, with only a little meat added to the legionary diet. To daunt the Romans, Arminius would put his tallest fighters in the front ranks. The Germans were bearded, long-haired men, and before they set off to fight, every man had gone to his tribe's most sacred grove and made a vow to his gods not to cut his hair or beard until he had killed a Roman. Some German tribesmen even dyed their hair red when they went to war.

German arms varied by tribe and warrior status. Nobles usually carried a broadsword or Roman-style short sword and a knife, and wore Roman-style armor, helmets, and moccasin footwear. Their subjects frequently went barefoot and often fought naked to the waist apart from a fur cloak, without any armored protection. Most German warriors were only armed with a twelve-foot-long spear, as well as shorter javelins for both jabbing and throwing. All tribes carried wooden shields. The shield of the Chatti was small and square; that of the Chauci was four feet long.

The Roman troops in Varus's army were far better armed, trained, and disciplined than the Germans. Velleius describes the 17th, 18th, and 19th Legions as among the best of Rome's twenty-eight legions then in existence, although all three had ill-starred pasts. Fighting alongside each other for Julius Caesar, the 17th and 18th had been wiped out in 49 BC in Africa, at the start of the civil war launched by Caesar, and the legions had to be reformed with new recruits. The 19th Legion, meanwhile, had in 36 BC been forced to surrender after marching for Sextus Pompey when he was rebel governor of Sicily.

By AD 9, the men of all three of these legions were highly experienced. Since their mass enlistment these legionaries from northern Italy had spent a decade together, marched thousands of miles, fought and won countless battles, and amassed plenty of booty to finance their planned retirement. Most were in their late twenties or early thirties, and were tough and fit, and after years of shared dangers and triumphs had a tight bond with the comrades of their eight-man squads.

Varus's army entered the Teutoburg Forest in a strung-out column that was miles long. Not expecting to be attacked, Varus failed to post scouts. His troops proceeded in marching order, with helmets slung around their necks, shields on their left shoulders and heavily-laden baggage poles on their right. Arminius had the benefit of Roman military training, and he knew that on flat, clear ground, a Roman legion in battle formation with cavalry support was a machine that could drive over the top of its opponents. He had chosen the forest for his ambush because the trees made Roman cavalry next to useless, provided the Germans with cover, and made the usual Roman infantry defensive formations next to impossible.

The weather was also on the Germans' side. As the Roman army entered the forest, the sky swiftly blackened and a storm began to rage around the Roman troops, lashing them with rain, making the ground slippery and bogging heavily laden carts. The powerful wind wrenched limbs from trees and sent them crashing down on the column, sending pack animals bolting.

There, in the midst of the storm, Arminius launched his attack. From both sides, the column was assailed by flying missiles. Yelling Germans dashed in to attack horsemen and drag away defenseless non-combatants. Rather than put up a concerted defense, Varus ordered his troops to protect themselves with their shields and keep moving. He was convinced these Germans had been sent to prevent him reaching his friend Arminius. As Germanicus Caesar would later discover, the army's marching camp for the first night in the forest was textbook in layout and construction. It featured neat streets for thousands of leather tents and was surrounded by a deep trench and high earthen wall topped by the wooden stakes that each legionary carried bound to his baggage pole. Wooden gates and guard towers added to the protection.

On day two, the rain continued to lash down throughout the morning. Varus and his troops remained behind their camp walls, with the camp watched by Germans hidden in the trees. Once the sun shone through the clouds in the afternoon Varus kept his position to allow the way ahead to dry out a little. Arminius refrained from attacking the camp. He was waiting for more tribesmen to join him. Besides, he had the Romans where he wanted them.

That night, Varus and his officers held a council of war. Still certain that he must push on to relieve Arminius, Varus wanted the column to move out before dawn next day, but his officers convinced him their baggage was slowing them down and must be abandoned. Most of their pack mules would be taken with them, but the bells around the mules' necks would be stuffed with straw to silence them, so as not to alert the Germans to the army's movements. In darkness the next morning, the Roman column moved out. With the dawn, the rearguard set fire to the camp's gates and towers, and to the abandoned carts carrying everything from Varus's bed to the hundreds of legion catapults. Once the last Romans were out of sight, German tribesmen appeared from the trees and surged into the camp, attempting to salvage whatever they could.

The column proceeded over open country for part of the day, but, as it was being led by the Cherusci Arminius had sent to guide Varus, in the afternoon it again entered thick forest. There, the Germans were waiting, reinforced and rearmed. They mounted attacks so fierce that the column became bogged down, ceased to move, and became surrounded. Under constant assault, part of the army attempted to dig trenches and throw up walls for a fresh overnight camp.

It appears that at this point cavalry prefect Numonius Vala panicked. Taking all the surviving Roman cavalry with him, he plunged from the German encirclement and tried to drive through tribesmen who attempted to stop them, intent on heading west for the Rhine. In doing so he left Varus and the infantry to their fate and made a mockery of his family's name of Vala, awarded to an ancestor for valor in battle. "But [the goddess] Fortuna avenged his act," Velleius writes, "for, he didn't survive those whom he abandoned, but died in the act of deserting them."[46]

Tacitus writes that only the shattered remnant of a Roman army made a last stand at the partially built camp, with many of the surviving troops wounded. The exact location of this last stand is disputed by modern historians and archaeologists, but most agree that a site first identified in 1716 at Kalkriese just to the northeast of Osnabruck in today's Lower Saxony is the likely place. Archaeological digs at the forest site since the 1980s have unearthed the remains of trenches and four thousand Roman artifacts including Roman silver coins, the bones of a pack mule with a bell around its neck stuffed with straw, lead slingstones, and, most tellingly of all, a *dolabra*, the Roman entrenching tool carried by every legionary, inscribed with the name of the 19th Legion.

Nightfall brought a respite for the harried Roman army, but then the rain returned. Unable to erect their tents or light fires, Varus and his men spent a cold, wet, hungry night. When Varus sent out an advance guard the next morning to try to find a way out of the forest, they couldn't even keep their footing in the rain. Hemmed in by marshes on one side and Germans on the other, they retraced their steps and rejoined their colleagues. The Roman position was hopeless. Varus was trapped, and both sides knew it.

The tribesmen now launched an all-out assault. In search of some sort of cover, many Romans had resorted to lying in the shallow trench they had dug around the camp. The Germans swept into this trench and crossed it, employing wooden hurdles, and using rough scaling ladders climbed the low camp wall and went against the Romans manning the wall. Soon, tribesmen were inside the camp. Varus, perceiving that defeat was inevitable, fell on his sword, taking his life the way his father had done at the 42 BC Battle of Philippi in Greece, as a general in the army of Cassius and Brutus defeated by Octavian and Mark Antony. The remaining senior officers, the broad stripe tribunes, followed Varus's example and died by suicide.

This left Camp Prefect Lucius Eggius as the most senior Roman officer still living, and he called on his men to throw down their weapons and surrender to the Germans, "preferring," Velleius writes, "to die by torture at the hands of the enemy than in battle." Velleius thought this a noble act, although his emperor Augustus would have railed against any Roman soldier who surrendered to barbarians. What remained of Varus's army followed Eggius's lead, and suddenly there was a victorious roar from the tribes as they realized the battle was won.[47]

At least thirteen thousand Roman troops died in this three-day battle. The badly wounded were quickly dispatched by Germans following the surrender. Eggius and surviving junior tribunes and centurions were quickly bound in heavy chains the tribes had brought for this purpose, as the Roman rank and file were separated from their officers and made to dig large pits, which became their temporary prisons. In adjacent groves, large wicker baskets were suspended over fires by the tribesmen and the chained Roman officers were bundled into the baskets. Slowly, painfully, they were roasted, as an offering to the German gods. Their captured troops were forced to listen to their torture.

The body of Varus, stripped of armor and clothing, was reported to have been partially burned, suggesting either that his own men had tried to burn his body before it fell into German hands, or it was burned in a suspended basket by the tribesmen. The corpse was laid out on the ground by the Germans, and we are told that the son of Segimerus insulted the body, probably with a knife. Segimerus pulled him away. Then a powerful warrior with a broadsword stood over the body and swung his blade, severing Varus's head. Placed on the end of a spear, the head was paraded around the cheering German tribes. Arminius sent Varus's severed head to King Maroboduus of the Marcomanni, who would in turn send it to Augustus at Rome. Augustus would allow it to be interred in the Varus family vault.

Huddled among the Roman prisoners, Caelius Caldus, the teenage officer cadet, raised his chains above his head and crashed them down on his skull, braining himself and dying instantly. Other surviving Roman officers had longer, more agonizing deaths, with the centurions particularly despised for their past rough treatment of German allies. After their roasting, they were decapitated, with their skulls nailed to tree trunks.

Like the Roman pack animals and noncombatants, the captive rank-and-file Roman soldiers were led away to be shared among the tribes, in this case as slave labor. The captured standards of the legions were retained by the tribes that had won them—we know the Bructeri secured at least one legionary eagle, and the Chauci another. These standards would be deposited at shrines to the German gods in the tribes' sacred groves.

Meanwhile, other German tribesmen were falling on the Roman forts along the eastern Rhine, taking them by surprise and massacring their auxiliary garrisons. Just a lone Roman outpost, Fort Aliso, held out. Its commander, Camp Prefect Caedicius, had the advantage of advance warning, and in addition to at least a thousand legionaries his garrison included a cohort of archers from the East, who made short work of a large force of Germans that attacked the fort's walls. Noncombatants from the Varus column were sheltering at Fort Aliso, and once the Germans had been driven off these civilians were led from the fort at night by Caedicius and his men, and ushered back across the Rhine bridge at Cologne. Behind them, German warriors flooded into the abandoned fort and destroyed it.

When word of the massacre in the Teutoburg reached Varus's nephew Lucius Nonius Asprenas, governor of Upper Germany, he hurried from Mainz to Cologne with two legions, to strengthen the wavering allegiance of Germans who lived in the province of Lower Germany, and to defend against what he feared would be a trans-Rhine

German invasion. His first act upon reaching Cologne was to destroy the bridge of boats that stretched across the river.

In Rome, there was panic, led by the emperor himself, as people pictured barbaric German hordes invading Gaul and swarming into Italy. "Quinctilius Varus, give me back my legions!" Augustus famously wailed.[48]

So distrustful of Germans did Augustus suddenly become, that he sent the thousands of Batavians and Raetians of the German Guard, his personal bodyguard, to Italian islands, although he later welcomed them back once the panic subsided. He also urgently drafted every available Roman citizen of military age in Italy into service, executing any who tried to avoid the recruiting officers' summons. These levies were formed into so-called volunteer units, although few were genuine volunteers. Augustus sent them to Tiberius, who had orders to hurry back to western Germany with six legions to stem the Germanic tide.

Once it became clear that the intent of Arminius and the other tribal leaders was to eliminate all Roman influence from their fatherland east of the Rhine, but not to invade Roman territory, Augustus set the Rhine as the northwestern boundary of his empire. Stationing eight legions permanently west of the Rhine in Upper and Lower Germany, he warily watched the tribes east of the Rhine from across the river. As for Varus's three legions, Augustus never reformed them and forbade their numbers to ever be used again. Those legionaries in the cohorts of Camp Prefect Caedicius who escaped from Fort Aliso would have been distributed among existing legions that had lost men in Dalmatia and Pannonia.

Instead of creating new legions, Augustus left the army at twenty-five legions and used auxiliary units and the Italian "volunteers" to fill gaps on the frontiers. Three decades later, the emperor Nero would briefly raise a new legion and call it the 18th, but it proved an unlucky unit and the emperor Vespasian abolished it after it had been in existence for less than two years. To avoid the ill fortune of Varus's legions, it also became habit of the Palatium at Rome to never again put legions with three consecutive numbers in the same army.

Romans at the time called the battle in the Teutoburg Forest and what followed the Varian War. Velleius, who lived through this period and was serving with Tiberius, called it a disaster. As with the loss of Crassus's legions at the 53 BC Battle of Carrhae in Parthia, Romans would remember Varus's crushing defeat with a shudder. Half a century later, the Roman philosopher Seneca, who served as the emperor Nero's tutor and chief secretary, wrote to a friend: "Remember the Varus Disaster? Many a man of the most distinguished ancestry, who was doing his military service as the first step on the road to a seat in the Senate, was brought low by Fortune."[49]

The men of the legions stationed on the Rhine certainly didn't forget the Varus Disaster, or the humiliation of Roman arms that it represented, as became obvious just five years after the event. In AD 13, Germanicus Caesar was posted to the Rhine as commander in chief of Upper and Lower Germany and Gaul, basing himself at Cologne with his wife, Agrippina the Elder, and infant son Gaius, who picked up the nickname Caligula, or "Little Boot," from Germanicus's legionaries because of the little military sandals he wore. In August the following year, while Germanicus was in Gaul supervising the annual tax collection, the emperor Augustus died in Italy. On the Rhine, the legions rioted, killing some of their more brutal centurions and booting out others, and putting their generals under veritable siege.

After Germanicus rushed back to Cologne he discovered that among the legions' grievances were the lengthened enlistments that Augustus had imposed on them. Germanicus promised to let those men who had served sixteen years or were infirm go into immediate retirement. But the troops had other demands. Tiberius was Augustus's stepson and heir, but he hadn't stepped up to claim the throne, and unlike Tiberius, Germanicus was universally popular. To Germanicus's horror, his men now called on him to take the throne, and swore to back him with their swords. Declaring his loyalty to his adoptive father, Tiberius, Germanicus played his last card in a bid to regain control of his legions, promising to lead them across the Rhine to punish the Germans for the Varus Disaster.

This immediately won the legions' approval, and after Germanicus hurried along the Rhine to make the same promise to the four legions based at Mainz, he ordered preparations for a trans-Rhine operation in October, when Rome's legions usually went into camp for the winter. This surprise operation, involving twelve thousand men from four legions plus twenty-six auxiliary cohorts and eight wings of cavalry, crossed the river via a new bridge of boats and struck at the Marsi tribe between the Lippe and Ruhr Rivers. The Marsi were celebrating a religious festival and caught completely unawares. After inflicting thousands of casualties, the Roman army withdrew to the Rhine. Warriors from the Bructeri, Tubantes, and Usipetes tribes surged after them, only to be swatted away by the waiting 20th Legion rearguard.

News of this punishing operation was received with joy in Rome, where Tiberius had finally accepted the throne on September 17. The Senate voted Germanicus a Triumph. The young general had only just begun. He ordered preparations for another invasion of Germany in the spring, but when reports arrived that Cherusci warriors were attacking Arminius's father-in-law Segestes in Chattian territory in early AD 15, Germanicus launched a two-pronged attack across the Rhine with eight legions as soon as the winter ice melted. Marching rapidly to the Eder and reaching Mattium, the Chattian capital, Germanicus found that Segestes had taken refuge in a stronghold in the hills with his daughter Thusnelda, Arminius's wife, and was under siege from the Cherusci.

After burning Mattium, Germanicus marched on the Chattian stronghold, drove off the Cherusci, and secured Segestes and his entourage, including Thusnelda, who, it turned out, was pregnant. With his prize prisoners, Germanicus withdrew across the Rhine. Segestes was housed at Mainz, but Thusnelda was sent to live under house arrest at Ravenna in northeastern Italy, where she would give birth to a son named Thumelicus. To keep Thusnelda company, Germanicus also sent her (unnamed) sister-in-law, the wife of Arminius's brother Flavus, to Ravenna, where she would also raise a son, Italicus. With his wife and son virtual hostages at Ravenna, this also served to ensure the loyalty of Flavus.

That summer, Germanicus and his legions again crossed the Rhine, this time in a three-pronged operation that saw him personally drive deep into Germany, going up the Ems River using ships of the Rhine Fleet. There, the two other Roman columns, traveling overland, linked up with him, putting eighty thousand Roman troops in the heart of German territory. From the Ems, Germanicus marched to the site of the battle in the Teutoburg Forest, where his troops heaped mounds of earth over the whitened bones of Varus's thousands of Roman dead, men whose bodies had been left by the Germans to rot where they fell. A number of Germanicus's legionaries were from Cisalpine Gaul, and, as Tacitus writes, Germanicus's men labored "in grief and anger . . . not a soldier knowing whether he was interring the remains of a relative or a stranger."[50]

But the return to the legions' bases west of the Rhine was no easy matter. Aulus Caecina Severus, governor of Moesia during the Pannonian Revolt, was the new governor of Lower Germany and commander of one of Germanicus's columns. The route Caecina and his four legions took back to the Rhine at Cologne included an elevated road called Long Bridges, one that passed through marshland. Here, Arminius and thousands of German tribesmen were waiting in the surrounding hills, and they struck as Caecina's column straggled along the narrow causeway.

"Behold a Varus!" Arminius exclaimed to his men. "And legions entangled in Varus's fate."[51]

The Battle of Long Bridges lasted several days as the Roman army struggled along the road. Thousands of Roman troops were killed and wounded; at one point Caecina's horse was killed under him and men of the 1st Legion had to save him from falling into German hands. The 1st Legion would subsequently be awarded the *Germanica* title for valiant service in Germany under Germanicus, becoming the 1st Germanica Legion. By the last night of the battle, Caecina's legions had succeeded in making camp on an island in the marshes. The next morning, Arminius, persuaded against his better judgment by his uncle Inguiomerus, led an attack on the camp, only for Caecina to permit the leading German party to enter the camp and swing troops behind them, trapping them inside.

Arminius and his seriously wounded uncle only just managed to escape the Roman trap, and Caecina's four battered, bloody legions, having abandoned their baggage, were able to make a rapid march to the Rhine. When the Cologne garrison panicked at a rumor that Caecina's army had been wiped out by Arminius, Germanicus's wife, Agrippina, took it upon herself to prevent the troops from destroying the bridge. Only then were the legions able to cross the bridge to safety.

As Germanicus himself was making his return to the Rhine, he had sent four thousand cavalry sweeping through Bructeri territory, destroying everything in their path. In a sacred grove of the tribe, Germanicus's cavalry commander Lucius Stertinius discovered the eagle standard of the 19th Legion. News of its recovery caused rejoicing at Rome, and this, along with the reverential treatment Germanicus had given the Roman soldiers' remains at the Teutoburg, meant that Germanicus's popularity with the Roman people reached a new high.

Alas, his adoptive father, the emperor Tiberius, was not so impressed, railing against the fact that Germanicus had conducted gladiatorial games in the Teutoburg as a funeral rite, when Germanicus, as a member of the highest Roman priestly order, was not supposed to pollute his hands with the dead. Tiberius also complained about the way Germanicus's wife, Agrippina, had interfered with matters at the Cologne bridge, declaring that this was not women's business—even though her intervention had allowed Caecina's army to use the bridge to escape Germany.

Tiberius also did more than complain. He moved to keep in check the nephew Augustus had forced him to adopt, whom he never really liked. Motivated by Sejanus, his manipulative prefect of the Praetorian Guard—who reminded Tiberius that Germanicus's legions had previously offered to make him emperor in preference to Tiberius—the emperor ordered two cohorts of the Praetorian Guard to march from Rome to join Germanicus's army on the Rhine. Officially, these two thousand men were going to "assist" Germanicus. In reality, they were sent to keep an eye on him, and to act against him if there was any indication that Germanicus might decide to take the throne for himself.

Thirty-one-year-old Germanicus launched a new campaign in Germany in the summer of AD 16 at the head of 28,000 legionaries, 30,000 auxiliaries, 6,000 men from allied German tribes, 8,000 cavalry including 2,000 horse archers, and the newly arrived 2,000 Praetorian guardsmen. Having expected Germanicus to return, his thirty-three-year-old adversary Arminius convinced the German tribes they must stand and fight. When Germanicus made camp in the territory of the Angrivarii, he learned that, persuaded by Arminius, the Angrivars had torn up their treaty with Rome. Germanicus immediately dispatched his cavalry under Lucius Stertinius to convince the Angrivars to return to that treaty, using fire and sword.

Among Stertinius's mounted units was a wing commanded by Flavus, Arminius's brother. After the Roman cavalry had swept all the way to the Angrivarii capital on the Weser River and brought the tribe back to the treaty table, Stertinius was astonished to be told that Arminius was nearby and wished to speak with Flavus. Arminius had based himself in Angrivar territory, at the Angrivar Barrier, a massive earthwork built by the Angrivarii as a barrier against the Cherusci when the two tribes had been at war. Stertinius, on the southern bank of the Weser, found Arminius standing on the northern bank with other German leaders and their bodyguards, and a yelled conference across the water followed. Tacitus reports their conversation word-for-word.

"Has Germanicus Caesar arrived?" Arminius called.

"Caesar has come," Stertinius replied.

"Good, we have been expecting him. Is my brother with you?"

When Stertinius confirmed that Flavus was indeed accompanying him, Arminius went on to explain that it was some years since the brothers had seen each other, and, having heard that Flavus had been injured in action, he had promised their mother he would try to determine whether Flavus was in good health.

Stertinius agreed to the pair conversing, as long as both were unarmed and spoke in Latin. Arminius, for his part, stipulated that Stertinius's horse archers be withdrawn well back from the river. Calling Flavus forward, Stertinius told the Cheruscan to convince Arminius to surrender, assuring him that Germanicus would pardon the rebel leader if he did so. He then stood to one side, to listen in.

Arminius began by asking about his brother's very obvious facial wound. When Flavus told his brother where and when he had lost his eye, Arminius asked, "And what reward did you receive?"

"A golden crown, golden torque and other decorations, and a salary increase," Flavus replied.

"The Romans buy their slaves cheaply these days," Arminius scoffed.

Flavus, trying to keep his cool, urged his brother to surrender, assuring him that Germanicus would pardon him, that Arminius could not defeat Rome with its infinite resources, and that Arminius was destined to lose the war if he didn't give up now.

Arminius in turn accused Flavus of betraying his own people, and urged him to come over to the German side. "What mother deserves a traitor for a son?" he added.

Flavus responded by informing Arminius that he now had a son, born to Thusnelda at Ravenna, who would be raised a Roman. This hit a sore spot with Arminius, who suddenly accused Flavus of cowardice. At this, Flavus lost his temper, and, determined to show his brother he was no coward, called for his weapons. Stertinius, seeing this was going nowhere, pulled Flavus away, and the conference ended with both sides departing.[52]

Germanicus split his cavalry into three divisions and deployed them to seek out Arminius and his army. One of these forces was made up of wings of Batavian horsemen led by Chariovalda, the king of the

Batavi. Chariovalda and his men encountered Cheruscan warriors by the Weser River, and eagerly gave chase when they turned and fled— only to ride into a trap set by Arminius. Chariovalda was among numerous Batavians killed before the remainder could fight their way out of the ambush. News of this savaging of the Roman mounted column spread like wildfire through the German tribes, as Arminius boasted that Germanicus Caesar had been given a bloody nose.

Departing the Angrivar Barrier, leaving in charge his uncle Inguiomerus, who was still recovering from his Long Bridges wounds, Arminius brought the tribes together to confront Germanicus as he advanced along the Weser. When Germanicus's army of 74,000 men came marching down the Weser River Plain, which the Romans called Idistaviso, 50,000 German tribesmen formed battle lines in their path. Arminius chose the high ground, a bare hillock beside the river, and was so confident of victory that he'd brought thousands of chains with which to bind his expected Roman prisoners. Yet, oddly, while Arminius, a proven master strategist, could call on thousands of mounted warriors, he came to this battle solely with foot soldiers, a tactical error.

Facing the Germans, Germanicus formed his army up in two battle lines on the flat beside the river, with his auxiliaries and allied tribesmen in the front line, the legions behind, and cavalry on the landward flank.

"Look, Caesar!" one of his aides cried, pointing to the exceptional sight of eight eagles flying past in formation, one for each of Germanicus's legions, heading in the direction of the German army.

Germanicus grinned. "Follow the Roman birds, the true deities of our legions!" he called, before ordering the frontline auxiliaries to charge.[53]

Trumpets blared, and 36,000 auxiliaries from around the empire, along with allied Germans, went forward with a clamor of national war cries, surging up the hill. At the same time, the air filled with arrows from the two thousand mounted Roman archers, which coursed overhead toward the Germans in a cloud. With a pounding of hooves,

Stertinius and the cavalry charged along the landward wing to outflank the German position.

Emitting a fierce roar, the German tribes charged down the hill without waiting for orders from Arminius, giving away the advantage of higher ground. Arminius had no alternative but to kick his horse forward and join the charge. With the river on one side, and Roman cavalry cutting off escape on the other wing before turning into their rear, the tribesmen were smashed in front by the auxiliaries and allied tribesmen. As survivors staggered back, they were compressed between the frontal attackers and the cavalry.

As fighting continued, Arminius, on horseback, received a head wound from a Roman missile. He saw tribesmen being cut down all around him in their thousands, and other Germans drowning in the Weser as they attempted to escape slashing Roman cavalry broadswords. When he heard Roman trumpets blare as Germanicus sent his legions into the fray to finish off the Germans, Arminius realized the battle was lost. Smearing his own blood over his face, he drove his horse through the struggling German infantry, reached the trees, and escaped with a few companions. The Battle of Idistavisus, as the Romans called it, was over almost as soon as it began. "It was a great victory," Tacitus writes, "and without bloodshed to us."[54]

In the days following this crushing defeat, Arminius, gathering survivors from the Weser battle, plus new tribal recruits and thousands of cavalry, rejoined his uncle at the Angrivar Barrier. Here, he planned a trap for Germanicus, who, he guessed, would be in hot pursuit. Placing his thousands of mounted warriors in a forest, Arminius intended to draw Germanicus into an attack on his infantry on the earthwork. When this occurred, the German cavalry in the forest was to emerge and assault the Roman rear, trapping Germanicus between two German forces and marshy ground on the flanks.

Unfortunately for the Germans, Arminius's plan was leaked to Germanicus by a German deserter. As a result, while advancing with his infantry, the Roman general sent his cavalry via another route, now led by Seius Tubero, a senator who was a close friend of Tiberius and who had been sent to Germanicus by the emperor along with the Praetorian guardsmen. Germanicus gave Tubero express orders to surprise and destroy the German cavalry waiting in the forest, while Germanicus led a frontal assault on the Angrivar Barrier.

Knowing full well why Tiberius had sent the two Praetorian cohorts to him, Germanicus personally led the haughty Italian guardsmen in the charge to and up the barrier, first removing his helmet to fight bareheaded—to ensure that no Praetorian would kill him in the battle with the excuse that he hadn't recognized the general. With Germanicus at their head, tens of thousands of yelling Roman infantrymen flooded to the barrier then climbed it with scaling ladders, under sustained German missile fire all the way.

With overwhelming numbers, the Romans drove the Germans from the position and chased them to the nearby swamps. Once again, Arminius and his uncle escaped, but masses of German warriors were cut down at the barrier, with others perishing in the swamps while trying to flee. Germanicus's greatest regret was that while Tubero and his cavalry prevented the German riders from engaging him in his rear, Tubero didn't stop them from making their escape. It was almost as if this had been Tubero's intention, to rob Germanicus of an even greater victory.

As Germanicus was returning from this campaign by water, a number of his ships were wrecked in a storm. So that the Germans would not take heart from this, Germanicus almost immediately led another incursion across the Rhine, returning from this raid with another of Varus's three lost eagle standards. That winter, as Germanicus was again being hailed the conquering hero at Rome, the young general was preparing for one last German campaign in AD 17, a campaign to finally snare Arminius and put an end to the German threat to Rome.

But jealous Tiberius couldn't stomach the public glorification of Germanicus. Ordering him home to Rome, Tiberius told his adopted son to take his Triumph in May AD 17 then head to the East to become Roman commander in chief there. Germanicus had no choice but comply, and after he left the Rhine no more major Roman campaigns in Germany were authorized by Tiberius.

Arminius was never captured by the Romans, and he never surrendered. Nor did he ever lead another German army against Rome. His repeated defeats at the hands of Germanicus had lost him the confidence of the German tribes, and in AD 21 he was murdered by fellow Germans amid struggles for power within the tribes. His son Thumelicus was raised at Ravenna, where, as a youth, he was sent to train as a gladiator, but he died before reaching the age of twenty. When Arminius's nephew Italicus grew to manhood he was sent by Rome to his own people beyond the Rhine, in the hope that he would be accepted by the Germans and be made their king—a pro-Roman king. But the young man failed to impress the tribes.

During the reign of the emperor Claudius, a Roman army campaigning in Germany seized the last missing eagle standard from Varus's lost legions, which was being held by the Chauci tribe. This army also freed a number of former legionaries of Varus, who had been enslaved by the Germans for four decades. These old men returned to Roman territory west of the Rhine, but, as they'd surrendered to Arminius, Claudius decreed that they could never set foot in Italy, under pain of death.

In the nineteenth century, Arminius, aka Hermann, became a symbol of German nationalism. A massive statue of Arminius, the *Hermannsdenkmal*, was unveiled in 1875 outside Detmold in Germany's Lippe district. Standing 173 feet tall, the statue depicts him with raised sword and wearing a fanciful winged helmet. In 1897, a similar statue, entitled *Hermann the German*, was erected in the United States by German immigrants at New Ulm, Minnesota. Seventy feet high, it is the third-largest copper statue in the United States.

No such massive statues to Arminius's nemesis Germanicus Caesar survive to this day, although triumphal Roman arches dedicated to Germanicus still stand in the ruins of Pompeii, Italy, and in Orange and Saintes, France, and a life-size bronze statue of Germanicus was unearthed in 1963 at the Italian hill village of Amelia in Umbria, where it can be seen today.

Ruins of Carthage, capital of Roman Africa, headquarters of efforts to defeat the rebel Tacfarinas. *Bridgeman Images*.

VIII. TACFARINAS

NUMIDIAN SOLDIER TURNED REVOLUTIONARY. NORTH AFRICA, AD 16–24

By the year AD 17, the year that Germanicus Caesar was celebrating a Triumph in Rome for his crushing victories over the rebel Arminius and his German allies, Rome had a major problem on its hands in North Africa.

A deserter from the Roman army named Tacfarinas, a native Berber—the traditional inhabitants of North Africa from Egypt to the Atlantic—had launched a revolt in Rome's province of Africa. This province produced half the grain consumed across the Roman world, with just six wealthy senators at Rome owning half the grain-producing land in the province. In expanding its landholdings across the fertile Tunisian Plateau, Rome had pushed the nomadic native tribes into the North African desert. Tacfarinas wanted his country back.

We know very little about the man—neither his age nor his appearance. As a Berber, he would have been swarthy, dark-haired, and bearded. As tattoos are known to have been traditional among Berber chiefs, he may have had those as well. Almost certainly a member of the nomadic Musulami tribe of Numidia, Tacfarinas had served with a Roman army auxiliary unit in Africa for some years. Why he deserted, we don't know. Perhaps he was escaping punishment for some infraction of Roman army regulations.

At first, Tacfarinas and the small band he led were mere bandits, raiding Roman farms in southern Tunisia. The fact that he was able to quickly attract and coalesce large numbers of fellow tribesmen into an army around him suggests he may have been the relative of a Musulami noble, perhaps the son of a chief. Further, because he trained his army in Roman army tactics, splitting his men into units with officers and serving behind standards, it's possible that, rather than being a rank-and-file auxiliary, he'd been an officer, perhaps the prefect commanding an auxiliary cohort. It was this ability to organize, train, and command his men that set Tacfarinas apart from earlier Berber leaders. In a previous century, hundreds of thousands of Berber warriors had attempted to resist the Carthaginians in North Africa, only to fail through lack of cohesion and coordination.

As Tacfarinas and his army terrorized Roman farms, towns, and highways throughout the North African interior, they attracted more deserters from the Roman army, and, led by a chieftain named Mazippa, were joined by thousands of dark-skinned, curly-headed members of the Mauri tribe from Morocco. The Moors, as they became known, were famously skillful horsemen, riding without saddles, and the Moorish warriors who joined Tacfarinas with their steeds gave him the ability to strike far and fast. By AD 17, Tacfarinas had thirty thousand men marching and riding for him.

To counter this uprising, the Roman governor of Africa, Furius Camillus, a former consul but an inexperienced military commander, had a force made up of the five thousand men of the resident 3rd Augusta Legion, the Lions (the lion was the legion's emblem), plus a similar number of auxiliaries. At the outbreak of the revolt, the 3rd Augusta was based inland at Ammaedra, today's Haida in Tunisia. It was later moved to Theveste, today's Tebessa in Algeria. In the spring of AD 17, Camillus marched his army over the African plain toward Tacfarinas to do battle, and the rebel commander, whose forces outnumbered the Romans three to one, obliged by lining up his army of excited tribesmen eager for combat.

Once Camillus calmly formed his army, with his Lions in the middle of his line, auxiliaries on their flanks and cavalry on the wings, the native army charged en masse into a solid wall of Roman shields.

The rebels learned that day that tackling the Roman army on its own terms was a recipe for disaster. Thousands of warriors were slaughtered, although Tacfarinas and his lieutenants escaped to fight another day.

When news of Camillus's victory reached Rome, the Senate awarded him Triumphal Decorations—prematurely, as it would turn out. Tacfarinas regrouped and recommenced raiding the following year. By the autumn of AD 19 the emperor Tiberius had ordered a legion from Pannonia to transfer to Africa to help the 3rd Augusta Legion and the new governor, Lucius Apronius, a personal friend of Tiberius, eliminate the rebels. That legion was the 9th Hispana, and in December it marched from its home at Siscia, today's Sisak in Croatia, through Italy and Sicily, finally crossing the sea to Africa by troopship.

Lucius Apronius, who had proved useless while serving under Germanicus Caesar on the Rhine, broke up the 9th Hispana's cohorts and distributed them around border forts. By the spring of AD 20, while the legionaries sat isolated in their forts, Tacfarinas took control of the roads. When Tacfarinas struck near one fort, Centurion Decrius, commanding a 9th Hispana cohort of new recruits, led his men in pursuit, only to be confronted by a massive rebel force. Under missile attack, Decrius's men turned and ran, while Decrius himself, surrounded, stood his ground and fought to the death. Governor Apronius was furious at the cowardice of Decrius's men, and ordered the cohort decimated, with every tenth man flogged to death. Ironically, the last time a Roman legion was recorded to have suffered decimation, in 49 BC at the orders of Julius Caesar, it had been this very same ill-starred 9th Legion.

When Apronius learned that Tacfarinas had camped with his booty near the Mediterranean coast, he gave his son Caesianus a thousand legionaries, cavalry and auxiliaries, and orders to attack at once. Unlike the Romans, Tacfarinas never fortified his camps, and Caesianus, a prefect in his twenties, succeeded in making a surprise dawn attack. Tacfarinas and most of his men escaped, but Apronius's son captured the camp and the loot it contained. For this, the Senate awarded Triumphal Decorations to Governor Apronius—again, somewhat prematurely. Apronius and his son returned to Rome, and in AD 21 a new governor arrived, Junius Blaesus, uncle of Sejanus, Tiberius's manipulative prefect of the Praetorian Guard.

At the same time, Tacfarinas cheekily sent envoys to Tiberius at Rome, offering peace in Africa in return for money and land for Tacfarinas and his men. If his offer was not accepted, he said, he would wage interminable war on Rome. Tiberius was beside himself with fury. Not even during the devastating Spartacus Revolt, he declared, had Spartacus been offered amnesty by Rome, and Tacfarinas could expect nothing from him. The emperor ordered Blaesus to offer pardons to Tacfarinas's followers, but to spare no effort in hunting down the rebel chief himself.[55]

Some rebels did take advantage of this pardon offer, but Tacfarinas withdrew to the interior and recruited new followers from the Garamantes tribe, with promises of Roman booty. With his rebuilt army he began raiding the peaceful Leptitani tribe—which had remained loyal to Rome—in the southeast. Dividing his force into several detachments, he would strike quickly then dash away, often ambushing Roman forces that attempted to pursue him, using a waiting second force.

To counter the revitalized rebel, Governor Blaesus divided his forces as well, creating three divisions made up of the 3rd Augusta Legion under his own command, the 9th Hispana Legion under its legate Cornelius Lentulus Scipio, and auxiliary cohorts led by Blaesus's son, a prefect. The 9th Hispana focused on the left flank, Leptitanian territory, aiming to cut off Tacfarinas's retreat to the Garamantes homeland. Prefect Blaesus took the right flank, driving west to protect the city of Cirta, modern Constantine, the capital of Numidia. The governor himself pushed up the center of the advance.

All three Roman task forces linked up deep inside southern Tunisia, where they built a series of forts. Instead of withdrawing to their major bases for the winter as they usually did, the Roman forces stayed put. Emerging from these forts, detachments under first-rank centuri-ons went on search-and-destroy missions, chasing rebel bands across sandy wastes. One of these parties returned with Tacfarinas's captured brother, but, frustratingly for Blaesus, Tacfarinas himself remained at large.

In the spring of AD 22, the governor's year-long posting ended and he returned to Rome, where Tiberius not only awarded Blaesus Triumphal Decorations, he had him hailed *imperator* for his so-called victory over the rebels. As Tacitus was to note, however, while the stat-ues of three former governors of Africa standing in Rome each now ludicrously bore the laurel wreath of a *triumphator* for triumphing over the rebels, Tacfarinas had yet to be defeated. To make things worse, Tiberius ordered the 9th Hispana Legion back to its home base in Pannonia, leaving the new governor, Publius Dolabella, fewer forces to combat the continuing threat.[56]

Encouraged by this, Tacfarinas emerged from hiding in AD 23, his new rebel force greatly enlarged by tribesmen who believed the rebel's claim that he had sent one Roman legion running from Africa and would soon drive all Romans from their homeland. When Tacfarinas now boldly lay siege to the town of Thubuscum, governor Dolabella gathered every soldier he could lay his hands on and marched to the town's relief. Tacfarinas withdrew ahead of the Roman relief force, so Dolabella took a leaf from Blaesus's book, dividing his army into four divisions to pursue the rebels from different directions. In addition, possessing a wing of Moorish cavalry that had remained loyal to Rome, Dolabella handpicked men from this unit and sent them galloping to the rebels' rear to cut off their escape route.

Before long, Dolabella learned, possibly from an informant, that Tacfarinas had encamped at the partly ruined fortress of Auzea. At forced march, Dolabella and his troops closed in on the rebels from four directions. Having failed to learn from earlier experience, the over-confident Tacfarinas had not built a defensive wall around his camp, had not posted pickets, and allowed his horses to graze in the open. In the early hours of the morning, "with the sound of trumpets and fierce shouts," Roman legionaries surged into the undefended camp "in close array." Thousands of Numidians and Moors were roused from their sleep only to be slaughtered at the end of Roman swords, "like cattle," in the words of Tacitus.[57]

In the light of the dawn, Tacfarinas himself was cornered and surrounded with his young son and a few bodyguards. Those bodyguards were felled around the rebel leader by the Romans, and his son was snatched from him alive. Dolabella had given orders for Tacfarinas himself to be taken alive, but Tacfarinas knew that, if captured, he would be paraded through the streets of Rome, past hooting Roman crowds, before being garroted at the end of a Triumph. Rather than face that humiliation, he made a suicidal charge at his attackers, and died fighting. His seven-year revolt died with him.

Dolabella took Tacfarinas's son and surviving lieutenants with him when he returned to Rome—yet Tiberius failed to award Triumphal Decorations to Dolabella for terminating the revolt. Praetorian Prefect Sejanus felt that it would diminish the glory of his uncle Blaesus— not that his glory would last long. Soon, both Blaesus and his nephew would be dead, after Sejanus was found by Tiberius to be plotting the emperor's overthrow.

Bronze head of Germanicus Caesar, heir to emperor Tiberius's throne, whom Piso was accused of murdering. *Bridgeman Images.*

IX. PISO

REVOLTING TO ESCAPE A MURDER
CHARGE. CILICIA, AD 19–20

In October AD 19, a small fleet of Roman warships put into the Greek island of Cos, today's Kos in the southern Agean. The ships were carrying the recently dismissed governor of the Roman province of Syria, as well as his wife, son, and retinue including hundreds of personal slaves. That former governor was Gnaeus Calpurnius Piso. A man in his early sixties, former consul, and onetime governor of Africa and Nearer Spain, Piso had been fired from his post as proconsul of Syria, the highest-paid and most powerful gubernatorial job in the Roman Empire. The man who'd fired him was thirty-three-year-old Germanicus Caesar, a man inferior in age to Piso but superior in rank as Roman commander in chief for the East, and nephew, adopted son, and heir of the emperor Tiberius.

Germanicus, after falling seriously ill in his palace at Daphne, outside Antioch, the Syrian capital, had accused Piso and his wife, Plancina, of poisoning him. After an ugly, heated confrontation, in which Piso had raised his voice and perhaps also his fist to Germanicus, the normally calm, cool, and collected Germanicus had formally ended their friendship in writing and ordered the hotheaded Piso back to Rome.

Once Piso had set sail from Syria, Germanicus had again fallen gravely ill, and Piso decided to linger at Cos to see what news came out of Syria about the ailing prince. Cos was a wealthy and productive little island. Home to famous wine, and factories where female slaves produced exquisite silk garments, Cos had an extensive public library that had been financed in part by the emperor Tiberius's personal physician Gaius Stertinius Xenophon, a native of the island. While awaiting news from Syria, Piso and his party moved into several of the island's many richly decorated villas. Before long, several centurions loyal to Piso arrived by sea from Syria. Apparently from the 6th Ferrata Legion, one of the four legions based in Syria, the centurions came aboard a ship from Laodicea, the port of Antioch. Germanicus, the centurions announced, had died in Daphne on October 10.

Germanicus, hero of the Roman people, who as a young man had helped Tiberius terminate the Pannonian Revolt—and who, in his twenties, had defeated the German armies of the rebel Arminius, recapturing lost Roman standards, restoring Roman control on the Rhine, and giving Romans back their pride—would never again lead a Roman army to victory. Germanicus, who had just annexed Commagene as a Roman province, and who had marched into Armenia with a handful of men and installed a Rome-backed king on the Armenian throne right under the noses of the Parthians, would never again alter the political map of the Roman world.

"His death was lamented by all men everywhere," writes Jewish historian Josephus. "Everybody grieved at his death, as if they had lost someone close to them." Roman biographer Suetonius would record that barbarian nations then at war with Rome immediately made peace on hearing of Germanicus's death. "It was as if a personal tragedy had afflicted the entire world," he said. Later, the Roman historian Cassius Dio would write, "While he was the bravest of men against the enemy, he was the most gentle of men with his fellow countrymen." According to first-century historian Tacitus, had Germanicus lived to become ruler of Rome, he would surely have outdone the achievements of Alexander the Great.[58]

When the news of Germanicus's death reached Rome in the second half of October, the city came to a standstill. Shops closed, public business ceased, streets emptied. Then, shock turned to anger. Tens of thousands of Romans ran riot, stoning temples, upsetting altars, and throwing the statues of their household gods into the street as they blamed the gods for taking their hero from them. Soon, this anger would be directed against the emperor Tiberius. It was widely believed that he was jealous of Germanicus, while his mother, Livia, actively hated Germanicus's wife, Agrippina. It was even suggested that Tiberius had posted the famously obstreperous Piso to Syria to make life difficult for Germanicus, or even to murder him there.

On the island of Cos, in the quarters of Gnaeus Piso and his wife, Plancina Munatia, there were celebrations. Piso even made offerings of thanks at the island's temple of Apollo and other temples on Cos. His wife, who had been wearing black in mourning for her recently departed sister, threw off her mourning gown and donned brightly colored garments in celebration of the death of the prince.

The centurions who had delivered the news to Piso urged him to return to Syria and reclaim governorship of the province, assuring him that the legions stationed in Syria would follow him. One of Germanicus's clients, the former consul Gnaeus Sentius, who had been at Germanicus's bedside when the prince died, had assumed the post of governor of Syria. But, said the centurions, Sentius had no authority from Rome to do so.

On the other hand, Piso's youngest son, Marcus, who was aged around thirty and had served as his father's quaestor, or adjutant, in Syria, argued that it would be far wiser to continue the journey home to Rome. Although he'd said nothing at the time, Marcus had not approved of the disrespectful, insubordinate way his father had acted toward Germanicus over the past eighteen months. He couldn't stand by and let his parent court disaster.

"So far," Marcus told his father, "you haven't done anything that would suggest you are guilty of murder. And vague rumors are nothing to worry about. Perhaps your confrontation with Germanicus deserves public detestation, but it doesn't deserve your punishment. But if you return to Syria, and Sentius resists you with force, it will mean that you have launched into civil war. In that case, you won't retain the support of the centurions or the soldiers, who will be powerfully influenced by the memory of their general [Germanicus] and their deep-rooted affection for the Caesar family."[59]

But Marcus's was a lone voice. Other sycophantic members of his father's entourage, led by Piso's client and intimate friend, the senator and former legion commander Domitius Celer, reminded Piso that he had been appointed governor of Syria by the emperor Tiberius. In Celer's opinion, until the emperor himself terminated his appointment, Piso should act as if he still was governor.

This was just what Piso wanted to hear. As Tacitus would write, Piso had an inflated opinion of his own importance. From the same family line as Julius Caesar's third wife, Calpurnia, he was aware that the emperor Augustus had once named him as one of three senators, apart from Augustus's family members, that he considered qualified to succeed him. At Rome, Piso had even acted in a haughty manner toward Tiberius. Now the arrogant, conceited Piso quickly dictated a letter to Tiberius, accusing the late Germanicus of luxury and arrogance and assuring the emperor that he was retaking control of the legions in Syria in the spirit of loyalty to Tiberius.[60]

Piso then sent Domitius Celer ahead to Laodicea in his fastest ship, via the most direct route, with orders to take command of the legions in Syria and bring them to meet Piso when he arrived back in the province. As Celer sailed for Syria with the centurions who had brought the news of Germanicus's death, Piso and the rest of his party boarded their ships and set sail, following the coast of modern-day Turkey northeast toward Laodicea.

En route, Piso's little fleet encountered a fleet of ships coming the other way, carrying Germanicus's thirty-two-year-old widow, Agrippina the Elder, and the ashes of her husband, as the shattered Agrippina returned to Rome. She was accompanied by a number of friends and clients of Germanicus, headed by Vibius Marsus, a former consul. In Syria, Marsus had joined acting governor Sentius in conducting an inquiry into Germanicus's death. They had found damning evidence against Piso and Plancina which, to their minds, proved the couple had wanted Germanicus dead. More than that, they had arrested a Syrian woman, Martina, who was infamous for making and providing poisons, and who, according to the testimony of slaves at the governor's palace in Antioch, had visited Plancina prior to Germanicus's death. Martina the poison-maker was at that very moment below deck aboard Marsus's ship, in chains, to be produced as a witness against Piso and Plancina at a murder trial in Rome.

As they drew nearer, each fleet prepared for action against the other, but sensible heads eventually prevailed on both sides. The two flagships came so close that, from the prow of the flagship of Agrippina's fleet, Marsus was able to yell across the calm water to Piso.

"You are going the wrong way, Gnaeus Piso," called Marsus. "You must go to Rome and defend yourself there."

"I'll be there," Piso called back, with a laugh in his voice, "as soon as the praetor who tries poisoning cases fixes a date for the trial."[61]

The two fleets parted. Agrippina would cross the sea to Corfu, and from there to Brindisi on the boot of Italy, where she would land in front of thousands of silent, grieving locals. Behind the ashes of Germanicus, carried from Brindisi on a bier by tribunes and centurions of the Praetorian Guard and escorted by two thousand troops of the Guard, Agrippina would solemnly walk all the way to the capital. Along the way, the people of southern Italy would line the route, in mourning black and often in tears, to pay their respects to Germanicus and Agrippina, this charismatic couple who had been the JFK and Jackie Kennedy of their era.

Piso had been alarmed by the chance meeting with Marsus. Worried by the possibility that Celer might not be able to turn the Syrian legions away from Sentius's command after all, he decided to put into the nearest safe anchorage, on the coast of the province of Cilicia, northwest of Syria. At Celenderis in Cilicia there was a formidable coastal fortress, a castle, standing on a point with water on three sides, and Piso and his party went ashore there and occupied the fortress.

From Celenderis, Piso sent out messages to the Roman governors of the region and the allied kings of the Middle East, claiming that he was still governor of Syria and calling on them to send him military support. Only the governor of Cilicia obeyed, sending a contingent of auxiliary light infantry to Celenderis, to which Piso added his slaves and those of his wife. In addition, a small number of men from the legions in Syria who hoped to earn large rewards from Piso deserted their units and hurried to join him.

Naturally, word of Piso's occupation of Celenderis soon reached the ears of Governor Sentius in Antioch. Sentius sent a messenger galloping to Piso in Cilicia, informing him that when Domitius Celer reached the base of the 6th Ferrata Legion at Zeugma on the Euphrates River, he had been arrested by the legion's commanding general, Pacuvius. At this moment, Celer and the centurions who had traveled with him were in chains. Sentius also warned Piso against any further attempts to interfere with the legions of the region, as the units would remain faithful to Sentius and the memory of Germanicus. Piso had made his bed, and now he needed to lie in it.

As it happened, several thousand new legion recruits were at that time passing through Cilicia. Piso's son Marcus, as his father's quaestor, had been in charge of army recruiting in Antioch, so he was aware that these men would be on their way to Syria at this time. Against his better judgment, Marcus Piso hurried to intercept these troops and commandeer them for his father. The recruits, Roman citizens between the ages of eighteen and forty-six, were bound for the 4th Scythica Legion and 6th Ferrata Legion in Syria, units that would be undergoing their twenty-year discharge and reenlistment in the new year.

None of these men were armed. They were due to receive their armor, helmets, shields, and weapons once they reached their legions' Syrian bases, where they would commence an intense three-month training period; they were to be ready to march with their legions once the AD 20 campaigning season opened in March. Piso quickly snaffled these untrained recruits and armed them by sending them out to confiscate the scythes and pitchforks of farmers of the district. He then took them to Celenderis.

Governor Sentius hadn't been idle, either. Accompanied by the officers from the Syrian legions who were most loyal to Germanicus, he loaded Pacuvius's 6th Ferrata Legion plus detachments from Syria's three other legions aboard ships at Laodicea, and sailed along the coast to Celenderis. Arriving at the cove of Celenderis, Sentius landed his force of ten thousand men along with their siege equipment. When Sentius lined up his troops in battle order at the bottom of the slope on the landward side of the Celenderis fortress, Piso marched his motley force of some five thousand men out to face them from the rocky heights above. From the fortress wall, Piso then addressed his force.

"Merely stand in battle order," he assured his men, "and the soldiers [of Sentius] will not fight when they see that Piso, whom they themselves once called 'father,' is the stronger—if right is to decide. And if arms are to decide, he is far from powerless."[62]

As Piso's men nervously stood their ground, they took in the sight of the legionaries below in their tight-packed ranks, with several cohorts being held back in reserve behind them by Sentius on the narrow front. Many of Sentius's legionaries were veterans with close to twenty years' service under their belts, and were tough and experienced killers. Their opponents were mostly farmers and laborers. Tacitus would later write that, while one side had the advantage of a formidable position, the other had the advantage of a formidable soldiery, and recognizing this, Piso's men had "neither heart nor hope."[63]

Sentius ordered his front ranks to charge. Trumpets blared and the legionaries ran forward. While Sentius's troops struggled up the steep slope under a rain of missiles from Piso's men, it briefly looked as if Piso might prevail. But, with shields raised and legs pumping, the legionaries mounted the slope, and Piso's men turned from the brink and ran back into the fortress, slamming the gates shut behind them. Sentius then ordered preparations made for an assault on the castle, with catapults and scaling ladders brought up.

Taking advantage of this lull, Piso left the castle and joined his fleet of ships in the cove, then ordered them to launch a sortie against Sentius's ships, which were anchored in the bay. But these vessels were all from the same battle fleet, and Piso's seamen and marines refused to go against their comrades. Boiling with anger, Piso returned to the castle, and from the walls, called down to the legionaries working below as they prepared to storm the fortification. He knew a number of these men by name, or was provided with their names by his staff. Pounding his chest with emotion, he called on men individually to come over to his side, proclaiming the right of his cause and promising money and other rewards for all who joined him.

A *signifer*, or standard-bearer, of the 6th Ferrata Legion, carrying his silver open-hand standard of one of the legion's maniples, was won over by Piso and dashed forward to join the rebel governor, with the castle gate opening to admit him. For a brief moment Piso thought he might have inspired a mass mutiny, but no other legionary followed the standard-bearer's example.

Governor Sentius, meanwhile, acted quickly to ensure there would be no further desertion from his ranks. His personal trumpeter sounded "Prepare to Attack," which the legion trumpets quickly repeated, and the men of the legions took up their scaling ladders and moved to their starting positions for an assault on the castle wall. At the scores of catapults that had been set up behind the assault line, steel-tipped bolts and flaming arrows were loaded into Scorpion anti-personnel artillery, and larger catapults were armed with round stone balls.

"Wait!" cried Piso. From the castle wall, he now offered to disarm his men. He begged Sentius to allow him to remain at Celenderis while the emperor was consulted in Rome as to who was the rightful governor of Syria. Sentius refused the offer point-blank, and countered with an offer of his own: if Piso surrendered, he would be given several ships and a small military escort that would take him to Rome to stand trial.

Piso agreed to this. His troops lay down their arms and deserters were arrested. The legion recruits were assimilated into Sentius's force, which soon returned to Syria, and Piso was sent on his way to Italy. His son Marcus went on ahead to Rome to attempt to win the emperor's support for his father. Once Piso was in the Adriatic he landed in Dalmatia and paid a visit to the provincial capital Burnum, where the governor was Tiberius's natural son and new heir, Drusus. Married to Germanicus's sister Livilla, Drusus had been close to his half-brother Germanicus. Yet, Drusus assured Piso he preferred to believe that the charges being leveled against him were groundless—doing so on the orders of Tiberius in the view of historian Tacitus.[64]

Sailing due west across the Adriatic, Piso and his party landed at Ancona on Italy's mid-east coast, then set off for Rome by road. On the Flaminian Way they fell in with the column of the 9th Hispana Legion, which was being transferred by the Palatium from its regular base at Sisak in Pannonia to join the renewed fight against the rebel Tacfarinas in Africa. The legion would march all the way across Italy to take ship for Sicily en route to Carthage. The tribune commanding the legion on the march welcomed the former consul into the column, and Piso and Plancina were carried in litters at its head all the way to Narnia. There, they left the column and traveled by boat down the Tiber to Rome and their palatial home on the Palatine Hill, home of the emperors.

After the huge public outcry at Rome for Germanicus's death to be avenged, Tiberius agreed to a trial of Piso and Plancina in the Senate, for the murder of Germanicus and the insurrection in Cilicia. Three leading senators, close friends of Germanicus who had been with him in the East—including Quintus Vitellius, uncle of the future emperor Vitellius—conducted the prosecution, which was given two days by Tiberius to put its case. The hugely unpopular Piso could find no advocates for his defense other than his sons, Gnaeus Jr. and Marcus, and they were allocated three Senate sitting days for the task. Then, sensationally, Piso's wife, Plancina, disassociated herself from her husband and his defense.

With all of Rome hanging on every word of the proceedings, Tiberius opened the trial of Piso with a speech to the packed Senate benches in which he attempted to appear even-handed, although he rebuked the prosecutors for what he described as their unrestricted zeal. To the senators, Tiberius said of Piso, "It is for you to determine, with unbiased minds, whether he provoked the young prince there through rivalry and willful opposition, whether he rejoiced at his death, whether he wickedly ended his life... Also consider this. Did Piso deal with the legions in a seditious, revolutionary manner? Did he seek popularity with the troops by underhand means? Did he attempt to retake the province of Syria using armed force? Or are these all fabrications put about by his accusers?"[65]

The trial started badly for the prosecutors. They had kept their key witness, Martina the poison-maker, under guard at Brindisi, intending to bring her to Rome at the last moment to testify. But someone sympathetic to Piso had gotten to her; Martina was found dead in her room at Brindisi. So, the three prosecutors spoke of what they had personally seen and heard in the months, weeks, and days leading up to and immediately following Germanicus's death. Their testimony was eloquent, but circumstantial, and hardly damning. As the trial adjourned for six days before the defense advocates were to launch their case, there was a broad public fear that, although Piso was likely to face banishment on the insurrection charges, he might actually be acquitted of the murder charge.

That night after the prosecution wrapped up its case, Piso, at home on the Palatine, wrote and sealed a letter addressed to Tiberius, then calmly ate dinner and retired to his bedroom as usual. The following morning, Piso was found dead in his bedroom, his throat cut and a sword beside him. Later that day, Tiberius informed a stunned Senate of Piso's death, then read aloud the letter that, he said, Piso had written the previous evening.

"Crushed by a conspiracy of my enemies and the hatred attracted by a false charge," Piso had begun, "since my truth and innocence find no place here I call on the immortal gods to witness that toward you, Caesar, I have acted loyally, with similar respect for your mother." This reference to Tiberius's mother, Livia, who had despised the family of Germanicus and been a close friend of Piso's wife, Plancina—even conducting a covert meeting with Plancina prior to her departure for the East with her husband—would be seen as incriminating of Livia, with many Romans suggesting that Livia had put Plancina up to poisoning Germanicus. In his note, Piso also begged the emperor to spare his sons from any punishment, in particular his youngest boy. "Marcus Piso strove to persuade me not to return to Syria," he wrote. "I wish that I had given in to my young son, rather than to his aged father."[66]

This was hardly a confession, and not even a suicide note, according to Tacitus, who in his youth had spoken to senators who'd assured him they knew for a fact that someone had been sent to slit Piso's throat that night, and make it look like suicide.[67]

But Piso's death enabled Tiberius to wrap up the trial, recommending that Marcus Piso be spared punishment for following his father's orders. The presiding consul, Aurelius Cotta, declaring Piso guilty on all charges, suggested a range of punishments, but recommended that, in the light of the intercession of Tiberius's mother, Livia, Plancina be spared. It would later emerge that Tiberius had circulated a letter to senators at the request of his mother, in which he called for Plancina to be absolved of all charges.

The Senate duly voted to absolve Plancina, pardon Marcus Piso, remove Gnaeus Piso Sr.'s name from all public records, and confiscate half of Piso's immense estate, with the other half going to his eldest son, Gnaeus. There, this "mockery of a trial," as Tacitus calls it, came to an end.[68]

There would be one postscript. Four years after Tiberius's mother, Livia, had passed away in 29 AD, Tiberius reinstated the charge of Germanicus's murder against Plancina. Before the case could come to trial, Plancina, too, took her own life. Whether she and Piso had truly been involved in Germanicus's death was never indisputably established.

Germanicus Caesar would be fondly remembered for generations, with a day in June devoted to offerings in his name. His son Gaius (Caligula) and grandson Nero would both be extremely popular with ordinary Romans at the outset of their imperial reigns, because they were descendants of the revered Germanicus.

GALLIC CAVALRY.

Gallic cavalry in Roman service at the time of Sacrovir's revolt. © *Look and Learn/Bridgeman Images*.

X. SACROVIR

LEADING THE GAULS AGAINST TIBERIUS.
GAUL, AD 21

By AD 21, Tiberius Caesar had been emperor of Rome for seven years. Under his rule, scores of Gaul's tribal states vied with each other to build ever grander public works in their territories, to emulate Rome's glory and advertise their loyalty to Rome, and provincial nobles borrowed heavily to live the lifestyle of the Roman rich. Leading Romans loaned provincials money at extortionate rates of interest, then called in the loans and seized the property of those who couldn't pay. A number of Gallic nobles were ruined by this practice, and resentment against Rome began to simmer in their provinces. One man, Julius Sacrovir, a noble of the Aedui tribe in the central east of today's France, decided to capitalize on this resentment by raising a revolt against Rome.

Sacrovir's father or grandfather had been granted Roman citizenship, most likely by Augustus, around the time the emperor founded a new capital for the Aedui, giving it his name, Augustodunum, or Augustus's Fortress, which became over time today's Autun. Sacrovir himself had achieved membership in Rome's Equestrian Order and was a prefect commanding a cohort of Aeduian auxiliaries in Rome's army of the Lower Rhine, based at Cologne. To achieve and maintain Equestrian status, it was necessary to have a net worth of 400,000 sesterces. While Sacrovir was not personally affected by the scandalous Roman loans practice, he knew plenty of men back home who were.

Sacrovir shared his seditious thoughts with a fellow soldier, Julius Florus, a member of the Treveri—a tribe of Belgic Gaul that occupied the Moselle River valley in today's western Germany. Florus was a prefect commanding a wing of Treveran cavalry attached to the Army of the Lower Rhine. Before they left Cologne to go on furlough over the winter of AD 20–21, the pair agreed to foment revolt among their own people back home. Sacrovir would talk to the Aedui and their neighbors, while Florus spoke to leaders in Belgic Gaul, with both urging the secret manufacture of arms for an uprising in the spring.

They spoke to small groups and before the popular assemblies of Romanized Gallic cities, deprecating the oppressive loans that cities and individuals were struggling to repay and reminding their listeners of the cruelty and arrogance of their provincial governors. They also hinted that, since the recent murder of Germanicus Caesar—heir to the Roman throne and nephew and adopted son of Tiberius—legionaries on the Rhine had been discontented with Tiberius, with many blaming Tiberius for Germanicus's death.

By the time that Sacrovir and Florus returned to their units on the Lower Rhine for the commencement of the Roman Army's campaigning season in March AD 21, several Gallic tribes were ripe for revolt. The first to throw off Roman control were the Andecavi, who lived between the Seine and Loire Rivers on the Atlantic Coast, and their neighbors the Turoni, of today's Touraine region in central northwest France. Sacrovir had incited both tribes, but the Turoni had long harbored rebellious sentiments and needed little prodding. Theirs had been the first tribe to join Vercingetorix's Arverni when they rose against Julius Caesar the previous century.

Alerted to seditious activity in the territory of the Andecavi, the governor of Gallia Lugdunensis, based in Lugdunum, today's French city of Lyon, sent a Roman officer named Manius Acillius Aviola to investigate. Almost certainly, Aviola, whose father was a senator who would become a consul three years later, was either a tribune on the governor's staff or the tribune commanding the 18th Cohort of Rome's City Guard, which was stationed permanently in Lyon to guard the imperial mint located in the city.

On realizing the Andecavi were preparing to rise in revolt, Aviola, an officer in his twenties, summoned the City Guard cohort from Lugdunum. The only Roman military unit based in the province, this cohort numbered 1,500 men. All were freedmen, former imperial slaves, originating from a variety of countries around the Roman world. As the cohort marched from Lyon to join Aviola, his superior the governor sent urgently for reinforcements from the governor of Lower Germany, who commanded an army of four legions and numerous auxiliary cohorts and cavalry wings.

As it turned out, the reinforcements were not needed against the Andecavi, because the City Guard cohort from Lugdunum, led by Aviola, swiftly and savagely put down the disorganized Andecavian unrest. Nonetheless, the governor of Lower Germany, Lucius Visellius Varro, reacted quickly to the request for help from his colleague in Lyon. He sent a legion detachment led by a tribune or camp prefect, plus a cohort of Gallic auxiliaries led by none other than Sacrovir, the covert rebel. Governor Varro also wrote to Gallic chieftains whose loyalty he trusted implicitly, calling on them to lead their people in support of the troops he was sending into Gaul.

Aviola the tribune took command of the force that assembled in Lyon—the Rhine legionaries and auxiliaries, and Gallic militiamen sent by their tribes—then marched into northwest Gaul to deal with the Turoni, who massed their young men to oppose him. A short, sharp battle followed. After an exchange of missiles by both sides, the Roman force charged and the rebels were easily dispersed, with their poorly armed foot soldiers fleeing, and their leaders captured.

In this contest, Sacrovir removed his helmet and fought bareheaded against his fellow Gauls. This was to show his bravery, or so he assured Aviola afterward. But several of the Gallic prisoners declared to the tribune that it was Sacrovir who had come and spoken to them of revolt over the winter. Under questioning, they suggested that Sacrovir had removed his helmet to be recognized by the Turoni and avoid being targeted by them as he waited to see which way the fortunes of war went. If the Gauls had looked to be gaining the upper hand, they said, Sacrovir would have changed sides. Aviola sent a report of this testimony to the emperor Tiberius at Rome, but Tiberius was disdainful, and Sacrovir was allowed to return to the Army of the Lower Rhine with his troops.

Meanwhile, Sacrovir's accomplice in revolt, Florus, had attempted to convince his own Treveran cavalry unit to desert with him and form the nucleus of a rebel Belgic army, but only a handful of the troopers accompanied him when he set off from the Rhine to gather Belgic recruits. Varro, governor of Lower Germany, and Gaius Silius, his counterpart in Upper Germany, quickly sent legionary detachments to oppose Florus. Heading west, the Treveran rebel succeeded in gathering a motley band of Belgic Gauls and was heading for the Ardennes Forest in today's Belgium when he was tracked down by a cavalry *ala* (wing) sent on in advance of Silius's legion detachments.

This wing was commanded by the prefect Julius Indus, a fellow Treveran who had a longstanding personal feud with Florus and was determined to eradicate him. Indus was apparently quite a wealthy man; at the outbreak of rebellion in Gaul, to prove his loyalty to Rome he had recruited this wing of 480 troopers at his own expense, selecting each man personally. As a consequence, the unit was called the Ala Indiana Gallorum, or Indus's Gallic Wing.[69]

With a charge, Indus's enthusiastic Gallic cavalry shattered the disorganized rabble led by Florus, and Florus himself fled. After being hounded from one forest hiding place to another by searching Roman troops, Florus found his last escape route blocked, and took his own life. The swift death of Florus put an end to unrest among the Treveri, Turoni, and other Belgic Gauls, but Sacrovir had in the meantime committed to rebellion among his own people. Realizing that he had narrowly escaped arrest following the battle with the Turoni, he talked the Gauls of his own auxiliary cohort and those of another into joining him in deserting the Roman army—apparently while en route back to the Rhine. Sacrovir then led these men to his home city, Autun.

Sacrovir's own people, the Aedui, had been covertly manufacturing weapons for a revolt since he'd first raised the subject with their leading men, and now the tribe rose up behind him. Young Gauls studying in Autun, which, for centuries, was a center of learning in Gaul, quickly flooded to his banner, driven by the idealism of youth and a thirst for adventure. At the same time, from throughout the territory of the Aedui and the neighboring Sequani, tens of thousands of recruits hurried to join Sacrovir in a bid to free their land from their Roman overlords.

When news of this gathering at Autun reached Rome, it would be rumored that as many as sixty-four Gallic states were now involved in the uprising, with wild German tribes expected to flood across the Rhine and join the rebels. It was even said that Spain was ready to rise up against Rome. Tiberius, however, seemed unperturbed, and showed no inclination to personally lead a force to Gaul to put down the revolt. Instead, expecting his Rhine commanders to handle the situation, he said nothing, and did nothing. But, while recognizing that this latest threat was much greater than any posed so far in the stuttering Gallic revolt, Varro and Silius, the governors of Lower and Upper Germany, argued about who should personally lead their legions against Sacrovir's rebels. The two men had long been rivals and were never friends. Varro was in fact jealous of Silius, who had been a client and close friend of Germanicus Caesar. Silius had marched with Germanicus against the rebel German Arminius and been awarded Triumphal Decorations, the next best thing to a Triumph, for the victories against Arminius's Germans. While both generals wanted the glory of terminating this revolt, Varro eventually yielded to the advice of subordinates who argued that he, an old and infirm man, should yield to the younger, more energetic Silius.

So it was Silius who personally led two full legions from Mainz to deal with Sacrovir. Those legions amounted to some ten thousand men, but, in this era, legions didn't march without at least two wings of supporting cavalry each, and rarely marched without eight to ten auxiliary cohorts attached to each legion. These auxiliary units effectively doubled the strength of a legion, so Silius would have led a force into Gaul totaling approximately nineteen thousand foot soldiers and a thousand cavalry.

Slowed by the lumbering pace of his baggage train, Silius sent his auxiliary light infantry on in advance of the main column, and as they entered the territory of the Sequani, the upper river basin of the Saone to the foot of the Jura Mountains, the auxiliaries ravaged every village in their path. As Silius brought his legions to the territory of the Aedui, his junior officers and rank and file vied with each other to set the quickest pace so they could swiftly come to grips with the rebels.

Twelve miles from Autun, the now-reunited Roman force found Sacrovir and a rebel army of 40,000 men formed up on the plain, waiting to do battle. Of those 40,000 Gauls, 8,000 were armed and equipped like legionaries, with armored vests and shields. The remainder were without armor and carried only rudimentary weapons—hatchets, axes, knives, and rough pikes, which were basically a pole with a pointed end. In addition, a company of some forty burly gladiators, all of them slaves, had been recruited by Sacrovir from a gladiatorial school in Autun. These men were trained to fight as *crupellarii*, a class of gladiator that originated in Gaul and wore segmented armor from head to toe, inclusive of a fully enclosed helmet with slits for eyeholes.

As Sacrovir placed the gladiators and his best armed men in the center of his line, with the lightly armed men on his wings, Silius's troops eagerly took their assigned places in the Roman battle line. The two legions occupied the center, with auxiliaries on the outside and a cavalry wing on each flank of the battle line.

Riding up and down his front line on a splendid charger, Sacrovir urged his countrymen on, reminding them of past victories by Gallic armies over the Romans and painting a picture of the life of freedom that victory would bring. Silius also addressed his troops, telling them that the Aedui were too accustomed to wealth and luxury under the Romans to be fighters. But, with a view to the future reincorporation of the tribe into Rome's provincial administration, he added, "Spare them when they flee!"[70]

There came a deafening roar from Silius's twenty thousand men, and then the trumpets sounded "Charge!" As the Roman cavalry thundered across the plain to attack each flank of the Gallic army, Silius's foot soldiers charged Sacrovir's center. The forty thousand untrained and untried Gauls stood, stupefied and terrified, as the Romans came sweeping toward them, and then the cavalry was slashing into the Gallic flanks. Little resistance was offered by the unarmored Gauls on the wings. Soon, these men were throwing away their weapons and running. The Roman cavalry let them go, turning to attack the Gallic center just as the legions crashed into Sacrovir's best men.

Only the gladiators put up solid resistance, creating an immovable wall in the path of the attackers. With javelins and swords glancing off the thick gladiatorial armor, the Romans resorted to using discarded Gallic weapons against the gladiators, hacking away with hatchets and axes. In the end, the Romans overcame the gladiators by pushing them over with the Gauls' own pikes, leaving them on their backs, flailing like overturned cockroaches.

Sacrovir, seeing the inevitability of defeat, turned and galloped away, accompanied by his most loyal followers. They returned to Autun, but elements of the Roman army soon reached the city, and the rebel leaders fled to a farmhouse outside Autun. When the farmhouse was surrounded, Sacrovir took his own life. His companions killed each other. The last man standing took a brand from the fire and set the building's thatched roof alight, and the bodies were consumed by the burning building.

With the revolt snuffed out, the Aedui and Sequani once more submitted to Roman rule as the idealistic young men from their motley army were restored to them; no doubt the traditional privileges to the tribes were reduced, at least in the short term. In Rome, Tiberius would finally inform the Senate by letter that there had been a revolt in Gaul, adding that it had been swiftly put down by his loyal generals.

The Gallic cavalry unit raised by Julius Indus, which had performed so well for Rome in the revolt, was soon transferred to Britain.

Aviola, the tribune who led the initial response to the revolt, would rise through the Roman military and civil service ranks to join the Senate. Later, in the AD 50s, he would become a consul.

By the end of the year of the revolt, the general who had terminated it, Gaius Silius, retired from his governorship of Upper Germany after seven years in the post and returned to Rome a hero. Varro, the governor of Lower Germany, also returned to Rome, and in late AD 23 was appointed one of the two consuls for the coming year.

On January 1, AD 24, the first day of Varro's consulship (his fellow consul was Cornelius Cethegus), the priests of Rome led the traditional prayers to the gods for the health of the emperor. They added prayers for the health of Tiberius's natural son Drusus and grandsons Nero Germanicus and Drusus Germanicus, the sons of Germanicus, who were first, second, and third in line for the throne when Tiberius died.

This celebration of Germanicus's sons incensed Tiberius, who summoned the priests to the Palatium and admonished them. According to Tacitus, Tiberius "was never friendly to the house of Germanicus," including Germanicus's widow, Agrippina, and his sons, and was "vexed beyond endurance at [the sons'] youth being honored equally with his declining years." At the same time, Lucius Sejanus, Tiberius's prefect of the Praetorian Guard, called for action against the most enterprising leaders of what he called "the party of Agrippina," the friends of Germanicus and his family.[71] Not only was Gaius Silius, the hero of the Sacrovir Revolt, a former friend and client of Agrippina's late husband, Germanicus, but Silius's wife, Sosia Galla, was Agrippina's cousin and confidant. Sejanus decided that Silius and his wife would be the first friends of Agrippina to be made an example of. The man he and Tiberius chose for the job was Varro, the current consul and Silius's old rival.

In the Senate, Varro charged Silius with treason, accusing him of having been in sympathy with Sacrovir and, in not acting early against the rebels—as he, Varro had done—of actively supporting Sacrovir's uprising. Varro further charged that Silius and his wife had extorted large amounts from provincials during his years governing Upper Germany. Because Varro, the prosecutor in the case, would also be giving evidence, Silius asked that the matter be held over until after Varro's consulship ended, but Tiberius refused the request and ordered the Senate trial to proceed.

Evidence was produced that Silius's wife had indeed extorted money from provincials, but the treason charge against Silius relied entirely on Varro's word. Still, Silius could see that Tiberius was intent on destroying him. To save his family, he took his own life. Sosia was subsequently sent into exile, and Silius's estate was sold off to make up for the money he had supposedly accrued illegally—although not a single provincial came forward to make a claim against his estate. In the end, one fourth of his wife's estate went to the prosecutors, with the balance going to her children. Only then, as Sejanus set out to destroy more family and friends of Germanicus, was the Sacrovir Revolt forgotten.

Bust of the emperor Claudius, object of Scribonianus's revolt. *Tarker/Bridgeman Images.*

XI. SCRIBONIANUS

LEADING HIS LEGIONS AGAINST
CLAUDIUS. DALMATIA, AD 42

The story of the military revolt by Lucius Arruntius Camillus Scribonianus against the emperor Claudius begins with a friend of Scribonianus, the senator Lucius Annius Vinicianus. In AD 40, just after he had served as consul, Vinicianus had become leader of the plot formed by officers of the Praetorian Guard and German Guard that resulted in the January AD 41 assassination of the young emperor Gaius, better known by his family nickname of Caligula.

A member of a noted Roman family, Vinicianus was the nephew of Marcus Vinicius, husband of Caligula's youngest sister, Livilla. He had also been a close friend of Marcus Lepidus, husband of Caligula's favorite sister, Drusilla, until Caligula had Lepidus executed for plotting against him. Jewish historian Josephus writes that Vinicianus had a double motive for participating in the plot against Caligula—revenge for the killing of Lepidus, and self-preservation, as he feared that, as an associate of Lepidus, his head might be next on the chopping block. There was also a third motivating factor: ambition. Vinicianus himself desired to replace Caligula on the Roman throne.[72]

In the nighttime hours following the stabbing of Caligula backstage at a temporary theater on the Palatine Hill, the alarmed Senate had met in emergency session as it attempted to determine a way forward, to restore order and calm to Rome as soon as possible. Several names of noted senators were put forward as potential replacements for Caligula, among them Vinicianus, Decimus Valerius Asiaticus, and

Lucius Arruntius Camillus Scribonianus—referred to as both Camillus and Scribonianus by historians.

There was great sympathy for Asiaticus among his fellow senators—once at a dinner party, Caligula had taken the senator's attractive wife to another room and raped her, and Asiaticus had to grin and bear it. Despite this sympathy, Vinicianus put up a strong argument against Asiaticus being chosen by the Senate to take the throne. But the two days of Senate debate became moot when it was learned that the Praetorian Guard and German Guard had hailed Caligula's uncle Claudius as the new emperor, and the Senate bowed to the will of the troops and followed suit.

For a year, Vinicianus tolerated the new emperor. But Claudius had a stutter and walked with a limp, and while he was well-read and had himself written several books, Claudius had no military experience whatsoever, was personally timid, and was easily flattered by women. As far as Vinicianus was concerned, these were not the qualities of a Roman emperor, and he worried that if he didn't take steps to replace Claudius, others would, and he would be left out in the cold.

The biggest problem facing Vinicianus was that he had no military backing. The Praetorian and German Guard officers who had taken leading parts in Caligula's assassination had all been executed by order of the Senate, without implicating Vinicianus and other senators who had supported the plot. The officers and men of the Guard were now firmly loyal to Claudius, who paid them well for their loyalty. So, Vinicianus came up with a plan.

While Vinicianus had no troops to call upon, his friend Lucius Scribonianus did. Scribonianus was governor of the Roman province of Dalmatia, just across the Adriatic Sea from Italy, where he had two legions under his command. If Vinicianus could persuade Scribonianus to march on Rome with his legions to depose Claudius, he could then convince the weak-kneed but well-intentioned Claudius to step down in Scribonianus's favor, to avoid bloodshed.

There seems to have been a secret part B to Vinicianus's plan—once Claudius had stepped down, and Scribonianus was marching for Italy, Vinicianus would put himself forward as the savior of Rome, and, with the support of the Praetorians and German Guard, seize the vacant throne for himself and win over Scribonianus's troops.

So, in the late winter of AD 41–42, Vinicianus sent covert messages to Scribonianus, promising him the throne if he led his legions on Rome. Scribonianus was older than Vinicianus and had been a consul ten years earlier. Not only was he a descendant of Pompey the Great, but his father Camillus had been awarded Triumphal Decorations for his successful AD 17 campaign in Africa against the rebel Tacfarinas—quite possibly, Scribonianus had been in Africa with his father at the time. Scribonianus clearly had no trouble envisioning himself as an emperor of Rome, and at the beginning of the third week in March AD 42, he called a general assembly of his troops at the Dalmatian provincial capital, Burnum, today's Kistanje in Croatia.

Of the two legions then stationed in Dalmatia, the 11th Legion had its winter base at Burnum, while the 7th Legion was based not far away at Tilurium, near today's Croatian city of Split, farther down the Dalmatian coast. The entire 11th Legion would have been present for this special assembly, while senior centurions and the standard-bearers of the 7th Legion would have been summoned to also join the assembly. Standard-bearers, while only roughly the equivalent of corporals in today's military, had great influence with the legions' rank and file, as they were chosen to watch over both their sacred standards and the legionaries' savings held in legion banks.

The troops would have been preparing for the lustration exercise, the religious ceremony that commenced the Roman army's annual campaigning season on March 19, but this early assembly turned out to be something very different. Scribonianus astounded his soldiers by announcing that he intended to dethrone their emperor Claudius. But, says Roman historian Cassius Dio, to his troops he "held out the hope" that, once Claudius was out of the way, he would restore the Roman

Republic that had existed during the time of his ancestor Pompey the Great.[73] Many Romans of the lower classes and even some members of the Senatorial Order secretly harbored a fondness for the memory of Pompey and hankered for a return of the democratic Republic of old, with the elimination of the imperial system.

What Scribonianus didn't tell his troops was that, on reaching Rome, he expected that the Senate, led by his good friend Vinicianus, would offer him the throne—and he would feel compelled to take it, for the good of all. Scribonianus ordered his legions to prepare to march on Rome to depose Claudius as soon as the lustration's religious ceremonies ended on March 23. At the same time, he sent Claudius an "impudent, threatening and insulting" letter calling on him to step down.[74]

Claudius, highly alarmed, called a meeting of the advisers he trusted most, his Praetorian commanders and the freedmen who ran his government for him, and canvassed the idea of abdicating and going into retirement. As word of Scribonianus's letter spread throughout Rome, Vinicianus made known his support for Scribonianus's call for Claudius's abdication, and senators and equites flocked to his door to throw their support behind him. But the meeting at the Palatium didn't go as either Vinicianus or Scribonianus had hoped. Claudius's advisers were firm in their belief that he should stay on the throne, believing that either Scribonianus was bluffing, or the Praetorian Guard would deal with him.

In Dalmatia, too, Scribonianus's plan was unraveling. On March 19, the eagle-bearers of the 7th and 11th Legions went to take their golden eagle standards from the ground in their camp shrines. This was for the lustration exercise, when priests would anoint the eagles with perfumes and dress them with garlands. But the eagles would not budge, or so said the two eagle-bearers. News of this flooded through the legion camps, and suddenly thousands of normally very brave but very superstitious Roman legionaries were afraid. Neither Scribonianus nor his senior officers had the gumption to stride to the shrines and personally pull the standards from the ground, in case the gods truly were conspiring against them.

Centurions and rank-and-file soldiers now gathered in conspiratorial clusters in camp, and agreeing to act immediately, they returned to their quarters, strapped on their swords, then strode to the *praetoriums* of the commanders of their two legions, who had stood with Scribonianus when he announced he was deposing the emperor, and killed them on the spot.

When word of this reached Scribonianus at his gubernatorial palace in Burnum, he panicked, and fled the city. Riding to the coast, he took a boat to the pretty little Dalmatian island of Issa, today's Vis. There, realizing he would be arrested and executed for treason, with his family deprived of his estate, he took his own life, preserving his children's inheritance. As soon as it was learned at Rome that the Scribonianus Revolt had collapsed and Scribonianus himself was dead, Vinicianus followed his friend's example and slit his wrists. From beginning to bloody end, the Scribonianus Revolt had lasted just five days.

Claudius was grateful and relieved. So much so that he pardoned and promoted the men who had killed their own officers to terminate Scribonianus's short-lived rebellion. He granted the two legions involved the honorific title *Claudia Pia Fidelis*, meaning "Claudius's Loyal and Patriotic." They would become commonly known as the 7th Claudia Legion and 11th Claudia Legion thereafter. Claudius also dispatched Lucius Otho, a leading senator, former governor of Africa, and father of future emperor Otho, to take Scribonianus's place as governor of Dalmatia.

Otho was a famously strict disciplinarian. Ignoring his emperor's soft approach and the pardon extended by Claudius, he executed every soldier who had taken part in the murder of their own officers, even though those men had acted for Claudius, not against him. This earned Otho the disapproval of Claudius, who gave him no new appointments thereafter, but it didn't save the loyal legionaries who were beheaded in front of Otho.

Finally, just to be on the safe side and ensure the two legions never acted in concert again, the Palatium separated them, transferring the 7th Claudia Legion to a new permanent station in the province of Moesia, on the Danube.

British resistance leader King Caratacus is handed over to the Romans by Venutius's wife, Queen Cartimandua of the Brigantes. © *Look and Learn/ Bridgeman Images*.

XII. VENUTIUS

LEADING THE BRIGANTIC REVOLTS.
BRITAIN, AD 52 AND 69–80

S ometime between AD 43 and 48, Britain's first known queen took
the throne. Her name was Cartimandua, or Pony Chaser, and she
was queen of the Brigantes, a large, powerful Celtic tribe centered
around the Pennine Hills in today's Yorkshire, northern England, who
controlled more territory than any other British tribe. The name *Brigantes* literally means "high ones," and this has been interpreted by some
to mean hill dwellers, while others have taken it literally, feeling the
Brigantes considered themselves superior to all other British tribes.

Cartimandua apparently inherited her throne from her late grandfather King Bellinorix when she was only in her twenties or thirties.
Her husband, ruling at her side, was Venutius, who is described by
Tacitus as "pre-eminent in military skills" and "long loyal to Rome."[75]
Intermarriage between nobilities of different tribes was a common way
of cementing intertribal alliances, and later events tell us that Venutius was not a Brigant but a noble of one of the tribes that bordered
Brigantia—some suggest the Carveti, who lived to Brigantia's immediate northwest. Cartimandua, described by Tacitus as being lustful
and possessing a savage temper, and Venutius, whom Tacitus says was
"high spirited," seem to have enjoyed a long and happy marriage until
they quarreled over the fate of Caratacus, a fellow British noble.[76]

Following the AD 43 Roman invasion of Britain, Caratacus, the
then thirty-year-old king of the Catuvellauni tribe of southern England, had fled west after two devastating defeats at the hands of the

legions, one at the Medway River, the other at the Thames. In Wales, the Silures, the fiercest of the Celtic tribes, welcomed Caratacus and made him their war leader.

For the next seven years, Caratacus led the Welsh tribes in resisting Roman attempts to push into their mountainous lands. He employed hit-and-run tactics to harass Roman supply lines and attack outlying camps and legion columns on the march, using the locals' knowledge of rivers, ravines, and mountain paths in often heavily wooded country to strike from cover before melting away into the difficult Welsh terrain.

But when Publius Ostorius, the Roman governor of Britain for the past two years, commenced a concerted push into north Wales in the late spring of AD 50 with 22,000 troops, the tribes seem to have grown impatient with their war leader. They demanded that Caratacus deliver them a major victory via a set-piece battle, and drive the Romans out of Wales. Caratacus assembled as many as thirty thousand warriors from at least five Welsh tribes, and using skirmishers to harass the Roman force, lured it to a prepared battle site in the Severn River Valley, thought by some historians to be near the present-day town of Llanidloes.

A stone wall had been built around the foot of surrounding hills in the shape of a *U*, and Caratacus's plan was to lure the Roman troops into the *U*, then seal off the end and trap them there. Ostorius took the bait, but unfortunately for Caratacus the legionaries and the Batavian auxiliary cohorts with them charged the wall, mounted it, and massacred thousands of Welsh defenders in desperate hand-to-hand fighting. Gaius Civilis, the Batavian cohort commander who would later rebel against Rome (and whose story is told later in this book), is believed to have lost an eye in this battle, fighting on the Roman side.

Caratacus's wife, daughter, and two younger brothers were all captured by Ostorius, but Caratacus himself escaped and went into hiding. For many months he avoided capture until, in late AD 51 or early AD 52, he turned up in the territory of the Brigantes and sought sanctuary with Queen Cartimandua at her tribal capital. This mud hut capital is believed to have been located at the Iron Age Stanwick hill fort site in today's Yorkshire, a little north of Richmond. A horse and chariot stables and training area located by archaeologists at Melsonby half a mile away was probably part of the royal complex.

But Caratacus was out of luck. Cartimandua clapped him in chains and sent him south to Governor Ostorius, who sent him to Rome in AD 52 chained to a centurion. In Rome, forty-two-year-old Caratacus gave an impressive speech before emperor Claudius and his empress, Agrippina the Younger, which convinced Claudius to spare his life. Caratacus was permitted to live in Rome with his family for the rest of his days, under permanent house arrest. The large house he occupied is thought to have been the Palatium Britannicum on the Via Urbana, site of the later Basilica of St. Pudenziana.

Governor Ostorius would be awarded Triumphal Decorations by the Senate for his Welsh victory, while the emperor Claudius celebrated a Triumph as if he had personally defeated the Welsh. Ostorius, usually a meek man, was satisfied with his award and sat on his laurels thereafter, failing to initiate any more military campaigns in Britain, which allowed the Welsh tribes to rebuild. Rome's loyal ally Queen Cartimandua, meanwhile, was richly rewarded with treasure and privileges for her part in Caratacus's downfall, which Tacitus brands as nothing less than "treachery."[77]

The queen's husband and co-ruler Venutius seems to have agreed with Tacitus, for he violently disagreed with his wife. Disgusted by her betrayal of a fellow British royal, he argued bitterly with her. Cartimandua, a strong woman, promptly divorced Venutius, and, to add insult to injury, married his armor-bearer Vellocatus—apparently a handsome and well-built fellow, but not a member of the royal class— making him "partner of her bed and throne."[78]

Venutius instantly went to war with his wife, but she outsmarted him by "cunning stratagems" by which she captured his brothers and other family members. This enraged the other tribes allied to the

Brigantes, "who were stung with the shame at the prospect of falling under the dominion of a woman," says Tacitus.[79] Rome's newest governor of Britannia, Aulus Didius Gallus, foreseeing that this wasn't going to end well, sent several cohorts of auxiliaries to Brigantia to bolster the queen's bodyguard.

Sure enough, Venutius was welcomed by nearby tribes, who sympathized with him for the way he'd been treated by Cartimandua, and with Venutius at their head, they went to war with her. "The flower of their youth, picked out for war, invaded her kingdom," Tacitus reports. "A sharp contest followed, which was at first doubtful, but had a satisfactory termination" for Cartimandua and Rome.[80]

The auxiliary cohorts stationed in Brigantia and subsequently the 9th Hispana Legion under the legate Caesius Nasica were involved in the campaign to put down Venutius's revolt. We are given no details of the fighting or how, where, and when it was terminated, but we know that Venutius survived to reenter Roman history seventeen years later. Perhaps a peace treaty was negotiated. Cartimandua retained her throne, and Venutius remained a free man, apparently living with his own tribe.

In AD 69, the name of Venutius again brought grave concern to the Romans. At that time, Rome's empire was wracked by a civil war that had followed the death of Nero. The Roman garrison in Britannia had been reduced to three legions in AD 66, with the withdrawal of the 14th Gemina Legion (later the 14th Gemina Martia Victrix Legion) to mainland Europe and the troops of the remaining legions redistributed around Britain. In AD 69, Vitellius, the third emperor to succeed Nero, further weakened the Roman garrison in Britain by withdrawing cohorts from the remaining legions to support his overthrow of his predecessor Otho. The reduced state of Roman forces in AD 69 encouraged Venutius to ignite a new rebellion.

The 9th Hispana, the northernmost of the legions that remained in Britain, had since AD 48 been spread over three fortresses, two on the border between Britannia and Brigantia in today's Lincolnshire, territory of the recently subjected Coritani tribe. One of these forts was a forty-one-acre site at Lindum, present-day Lincoln, where four cohorts and supporting auxiliaries were based. Two more 9th Hispana cohorts and auxiliaries were located just ten miles to Lincoln's west, at a thirty-acre fort at Newton on Trent, guarding a crossing of the River Trent. Lincoln sat at the junction of two major Roman roads, Fosse Way from the southwest and Ermine Street from the south, with a lesser road branching off west from Lincoln to Newton.

Fifty miles back down Ermine Street, a twenty-seven-acre fort had been in existence at Longthorpe, just south of today's Peterborough in Cambridgeshire, ever since a brief AD 44 uprising of the Iceni tribe of Norfolk that had been quickly put down by auxiliaries. Here, by AD 60, the four remaining cohorts of the 9th Hispana and a wing of cavalry were also stationed, a day's march from Iceni territory and two-and-a-half-days' march from Lincoln.

The largest 9th Hispana fortress, at Lincoln, appears to have contained the legion commander's headquarters. This fortress occupied a hill overlooking the Fosse Way and Ermine Street road junction and a lake that provided freshwater. This Lincoln base seems to have been one of the starting points for Venutius's new rebellion. Archaeological evidence tells us the Lincoln fortress was burned to the ground during this period, while Tacitus records that "Venutius collected some auxiliaries" and attacked both Cartimandua and her Roman protectors.[81]

At least one cohort of Roman auxiliaries, probably more, went over to Venutius and his rebels, apparently motivated by Venutius's promises of booty and independence from Rome. No exclusively British auxiliary units existed in this period, so the auxiliaries who joined Venutius were from outside Britain and were almost certainly stationed at Lincoln, the nearest Roman base to the territory of the Brigantes. Tacitus makes no mention of any Roman casualties at this AD 69 outbreak of rebel hostilities, which suggests that, with the usual 9th Hispana Legion cohorts that occupied Lincoln away fighting for Vitellius in Europe, the auxiliaries were sole occupants of the fortress. Rising up and looting and burning their own fortress, they joined Venutius, who brought the Brigantes into his uprising and attacked his ex-wife at her capital. His new revolt "brought Cartimandua into the utmost peril," Tacitus records.[82]

Venutius had the sympathy of the Brigantes, and with her own people now against her, the queen sent a desperate request to the Roman governor for help. He responded by rushing auxiliary infantry and cavalry to her aid. With Lincoln destroyed and Newton abandoned, the Roman rescue force risked being cut off in rebel Brigantia. Unable to hold the Brigantic capital, the Roman auxiliaries withdrew, evacuating Cartimandua and her retinue southwest to the Roman base of Deva Victrix, today's town of Chester, roughly due west of Longthorpe.

In a remote location on today's Welsh border, Chester was home to the 20th Valeria Victrix Legion. But the Roman governor, probably spooked by Venutius's swift success, withdrew half the legion south to new headquarters at Viroconium, today's Wroxter on the Severn River, previously home to the 14th Gemina Legion.

In the wake of Cartimandua's flight, the entire Brigantic nation went over to Venutius, who assumed the mantle of their king. "Venutius retained the kingdom," says Tacitus, "and we had war on our hands."[83] The war for Brigantia would last for years. Although Venutius made no attempt to invade Roman Britannia to his south, he was fiercely determined to keep his own lands free, and he united tribes of the north in resisting further Roman expansion. A Celtic tribal grouping name from this era, the Corion Toutas, or People's Army, may well refer to the allied force Venutius brought together.

In AD 71, a new governor, Quintus Petilius Cerialis, arrived with orders from Rome's latest emperor, Vespasian, to deal with Venutius and conquer the Brigantes. Cerialis's track record was uneven. As commander of the 9th Hispana Legion in AD 60, Cerialis had lost two thousand men to Boudicca's rebels. In December AD 69, he'd failed to rescue Vespasian's brother Sabinus when the Capitol at Rome was stormed by emperor Vitellius's supporters—an event eerily similar to the January 6, 2021, storming of the US Capitol in Washington, DC. But Vespasian, who was related to Cerialis by marriage, gave him the opportunity to redeem himself, when Cerialis led the campaign to put down the Civilis Revolt on the Rhine in AD 70, which he'd successfully carried out.

Buoyed by this success, Cerialis arrived in Britain ready for war. He was accompanied by the relatively new 2nd Adiutrix Legion, which had served him faithfully on the Rhine, plus a large number of newly raised auxiliary units, both infantry and cavalry, including nine Batavian cohorts partly made up of Batavians who had fought for the rebel Civilis.[84]

Advancing with an army of twenty thousand men to Lincoln in the summer of AD 71, Cerialis divided the 2nd Adiutrix's cohorts. Half the legion rebuilt and occupied the Lincoln fortress. The remainder went to Chester, to share that base with elements of the 20th Valeria Victrix Legion. Using Lincoln as his jumping-off point, by the winter of AD 71–72 Cerialis had advanced fifty-five miles north as the crow flies, to Eboracum, a flat site near the junction of the Ouse and Foss Rivers that became today's city of York.

The 9th Hispana Legion built a new base there, which Cerialis used as his headquarters for operations against Venutius over the next three years. He reinforced the 9th Hispana with cohorts of the 20th Valeria Victrix Legion led by its commander Gnaeus Agricola, about whom his son-in-law Tacitus would write: "At first it was merely hard work and danger that Cerialis shared with him [Agricola]. The glory came later. Several times he was entrusted with a detachment of the army to test his ability. Eventually, when he had passed the test, he was entrusted with larger forces. Yet he never sought to glorify himself by bragging of his achievements. It was his chief, he said, who planned all his successful operations."[85]

Those successful operations meant that, when Cerialis went home and was replaced by Sextus Frontinus in AD 74, Britannia was secure, but the Brigantic War was still being fought on its northern border, albeit on a limited search and destroy basis. Frontinus focused on defeating the Silures in Wales, which he achieved by the end of his four-year posting, after which the 2nd Adiutrix was stationed in South Wales. Agricola returned to Britain in AD 78, this time as governor, and he appears to have finally snuffed out all Brigantic resistance within a year or two, because, by the AD 80s he was campaigning as far north as today's Inverness in Scotland. In the second century there was some reported Brigantic resistance, but this amounted to little, and from the third century York became the capital of what was by then the very Romanized province of Britannia Inferior, which included the former kingdom of Brigantia.

Of Venutius and Queen Cartimandua we never hear another thing. The unpopular Cartimandua never regained her throne. Presumably she lived out her days in a comfortable Roman villa outside Chester. Venutius never surrendered. Neither was he killed or captured by the Romans. The presumption is that he fought a guerrilla war against the Roman advance into Brigantia until he died in old age, perhaps during Agricola's tenure as governor when first-century Brigantic resistance finally died.

Having fought the Romans for forty years and never falling to the invaders, Venutius was arguably the most successful of all the rebels against Rome, even if he didn't free his people.

Romantic nineteenth-century statue of Boudicca and her daughters by R. A. Artlett. © *Look and Learn/Bridgeman Images*.

XIII. BOUDICCA

WAR QUEEN AND REVOLT LEADER.
BRITAIN, AD 59-61

O ne day in the winter of AD 59–60, in the remote, watery expanse of the Fens in the east of England, a tall, tawny-haired woman in her thirties stood on a grassy bank with a large hare in her hands. Around her clustered Druid priests and the leaders of several Celtic British tribes who, under the pretense of a religious ceremony, had just elected the woman their war leader. She was the widow of Prasutagus, the late king of the Iceni tribe in today's Norfolk. Her Celtic name was Boudicca, or Victory. The Roman occupiers of Britain called her Boadicea.

The hare, to the Celts, was a sacred animal. Representing rebirth in the spring, it was believed to possess spiritual powers and be capable of predicting the future. Those at this gathering fervently believed that, when Boudicca released this hare from her grasp, it would foretell their future fate. If the hare jumped in one direction, it meant they would be victorious if they went to war the following spring. If it jumped in the opposite direction, they would fail, and should therefore not go to war. When Boudicca released the hare, it jumped in the direction of war with Rome and the rebirth of British independence.

"We have no fear of the Romans!" Boudicca declared, according to Cassius Dio. "We'll show them that they are hares and foxes trying to rule over dogs and wolves!"[86]

From the Fens, the tribal leaders hurried back to their people and prepared for a spring uprising. Boudicca and her Iceni had multiple grievances against Rome. After her husband's death (from natural causes), Decianus Catus, the Roman procurator, or financial administrator, had sent his slaves from Londinium, today's London, a city the Romans had founded by the Thames River. The slaves' job was to collect death duties on the king's estate. Those tax collectors had beaten Boudicca with rods. They also arrested all Prasutagus's male relatives and hauled them away to slavery, eliminating a male heir to the Iceni throne. Other Iceni nobles were robbed of their valuables, and Prasutagus's villa was stripped of everything portable. When Boudicca's two teenage daughters protested, the tax collectors had beaten and raped them. One legend, little believed by historians, says the girls subsequently cut off their own breasts. Certainly, under tribal custom, defiled as they were, they could no longer marry or suckle their own children.

By May of AD 60, the Iceni, their southern neighbors the Trinovantes, and other tribes of southern Britain had covertly made weapons, ammunition, and war chariots. Two other factors had influenced the tribes' decision to go to war at this time. Several of the four legions stationed in Britain were sending thousands of their men into retirement after twenty years' service. New recruits from Europe and the East were not expected to arrive until late in the year. In the interim, those legions were understrength. Additionally, the tribes knew that the Roman governor of Britain, Gaius Suetonius Paulinus, would be campaigning in the spring, in yet-to-be-conquered Wales.

The revolt exploded to life when the tribes gathered to celebrate their annual Celtic fertility festival in May, knowing that, in April, Paulinus had left his provincial capital of Camulodunum, today's Colchester in Essex, and was now far away in North Wales with the entire 14th Gemina Legion, several cohorts of the 2nd Augusta Legion, eight cohorts of Batavian auxiliaries, and one thousand cavalrymen.

Led by Boudicca, in hundreds of war chariots and on foot, the Iceni and Trinovantes tribes converged on Colchester. This former mud-hut Celtic town had been Romanized since the AD 43 Roman invasion, with brick and stone buildings including the massive Temple of Claudius and a central forum. With the town granted favored *colonia* status, thousands of retired legionaries had settled here, especially those from the 14th Gemina Legion. Some veterans occupied land parcels confiscated from the Celts, others had sold their land grants and gone into business in the town.

The day before the rebels attacked Colchester, a statue of Venus in the town forum had fallen to the ground, probably toppled by rebel sympathizers. On the day of the attack, townspeople were alerted that something was amiss by smoke rising from burning farm buildings around Colchester. The Romans had never built a wall around Colchester, considering southern Britannia pacified, but there was a walled fort on the western side of the town. Originally comprising fifty acres and large enough to accommodate 12,500 men, the fort had been reduced and now contained a small garrison of perhaps an auxiliary cohort and several cavalry squadrons. While some rebels surrounded and sealed off the fort, Boudicca and thousands of her fighters flooded unimpeded into the town, killing and looting indiscriminately.

Retired legionaries had just enough time to dash with their families to the Temple of Claudius, where their old standards were kept. With family members crowded into the basement—today the basement of Colchester's Norman castle, which was built over the temple site—the old soldiers barricaded the temple and fought off swarming attackers.

The rebels unsuccessfully besieged the temple and fort for two days, until they gained entry to the temple via its basement, probably admitted by Celtic boys forced by Rome to train as priests of Claudius. Prior to the Roman invasion, the sons of British nobles had trained as Druid priests. Having infiltrated the temple from below, the rebels overran it, taking thousands of prisoners. Boudicca's followers then spent days torturing captive men, women, and children, both Romans and Romanized Britons, before impaling some on long stakes and burning others to death. The Roman troops trapped in the fort witnessed this. But one night, while the rebels were busy celebrating, a cavalry troop slipped from the fort. Some troopers galloped for the nearest legion base, today's Longthorpe in Cambridgeshire, to raise the alarm. Others rode for Wales, to warn the governor of the disaster.

After razing temple and town, the Britons abandoned efforts to take the fort and spread through Essex, looting and burning. West of Colchester, four cohorts of the 9th Hispana Legion and several squadrons of auxiliary cavalry from Longthorpe—led by the 9th Hispana's newly arrived commander Quintus Petilius Cerialis, hurrying to Colchester in response to the attack—blundered straight into a rebel ambush. Surrounded and overwhelmed by massive numbers, all two thousand legionaries were massacred. Cerialis and some cavalrymen cut their way free and rode to the comparative safety of the Colchester fort. The rebels were now between Cerialis and the remainder of his cohorts at their Lincolnshire bases, cutting them off.

Governor Paulinus had just successfully and bloodily invaded the Welsh island of Anglesey when he received word of the revolt. He garrisoned Anglesey with his 2nd Augusta cohorts, under the legion's commander and supported by four Batavian cohorts—including one commanded by Gaius Civilis, future rebel against Rome. Paulinus then headed southeast for London at forced march with his remaining troops. Ahead of him galloped mounted messengers. One went to the remaining 2nd Augusta Legion cohorts based at Issa, today's Exeter in Devon, ordering them to join him. Another went to the 20th Valeria Victrix Legion's commander at Wroxeter, on the Wales border, who had recently let thousands of his men go into rural retirement months before their replacements arrived. These veterans were ordered to arm and join Paulinus behind their Evocati militia standards. Legionaries at that time served twenty years in the legions, plus an additional five in the Evocati reserve following retirement.

When Paulinus and his army reached London, he decided the town, which at the time also had no protective wall, was indefensible. Withdrawing north up the Roman road, Watling Street, he took into his column those residents who chose to leave. Many Londoners remained, naively believing the rebels would not harm fellow Britons. North of London, Paulinus passed through the Roman *municipium* of Verulamium, near today's St. Albans in Hertfordshire, taking more refugees into his column as he awaited reinforcements. In the end, just two thousand retired legionaries of the 20th Valeria Victrix joined his army. The commander at Exeter, Camp Prefect Poenius Postumus, blatantly ignored the governor's order to bring his three thousand troops to Paulinus.

The rebel army, gathering more recruits as they went, was now 120,000 strong according to Dio. This force fell on London, which was even more defenseless than Colchester. Procurator Catus had already boarded a ship and fled to Gaul. In the coming days, after an orgy of looting, torture, killing, and burning, the rebels left London a smoking ruin and marched north, doing the same to Verulamium. Then, joined by their families driving booty-laden carts, the British rebels set off to overtake and destroy Paulinus and his small army.

A day's march short of Wales, Paulinus halted his retreat and carefully chose a location for a final stand. The most likely location is where Watling Street crossed the Anker River, near the later town of Mancetter, or "Place of the Chariots." Here, one morning in late May or June, Paulinus lined up his troops in a location approached by a narrow pass through the hills, with thick forest at their backs and open plain before them. The 14th Gemina legionaries and 20th Valeria Victrix veterans occupied the army's center, with the four Batavian cohorts beside them and a cavalry wing on each flank.

Governor Paulinus positioned himself in the center with his staff, which included eighteen-year-old Gnaeus Agricola, then a "thin-stripe" tribune, an officer cadet on a six-month assignment to Britain. Agricola's son-in-law Tacitus would later write that the situation for Agricola and his comrades was desperate: "Never before nor since has Britain been in a more disturbed or perilous state. Veterans had been massacred, colonies burned to the ground, armies cut off. They had to fight for their lives before they could think of victory."[87]

The Roman force totaled ten thousand men. Dio writes that 230,000 Britons flooded the plain in front of them. Joyously, the families lined the far end and flanks of the battlefield in their carts and prepared to watch the battle as if watching a sporting contest. With the massed tribes in their clan groups, several hundred British chariots formed up in front of their loosely grouped ranks. Paulinus now issued two orders, which were transmitted by trumpet calls: "Form wedges," then, "Close ranks." In the Roman center, the 14th Gemina shuffled into one large, closely packed wedge, point forward. On either side of them, the veterans and Batavians formed two smaller wedges, with the cavalry still on the wings.

The long-haired Boudicca, dressed in a multicolored tunic, with a cloak over her shoulder and golden necklace around her neck, was in a British chariot, accompanied by her daughters. Shaking the spear in her hand, she addressed her excited warriors.

"Forget that I am a woman or the member of a royal family," she called, in a long speech Dio attributes to her. "Now I am one of you, regaining my freedom, avenging my scourged body and the lost chastity of my daughters." The air filled with rebel cheers, chanting, and singing.[88]

Across the battlefield, Paulinus rode among his units, addressing them. "By conquering, do you want to avenge those who've been killed," he asked one group, "and at the same time set the rest of the world an example?" To another group, he said, "It would be better for us to fall fighting bravely than to be captured and impaled."[89]

With a signal from Boudicca the chariots surged forward, and in a massive wave the tribes charged behind them at the run, bellowing at the top of their lungs. As the chariots bore down on them, the Roman infantrymen stood their ground, shields raised. Once each chariot-borne warrior had launched his spears, his vehicle swung away. Many Britons didn't survive the charge, as thousands of javelins let fly by the stationary Romans impaled British ponies. On Paulinus's orders, every soldier retained a single javelin. When the chariot attack ended, another Roman trumpet call rang out: "Advance!"

As a thousand Roman cavalrymen charged down the wings, chasing chariots, the three infantry wedges moved forward together, one regimented step at a time. The Britons, pushed by the massive weight of numbers from behind, were compressed into the wedges. As the legionaries pumped javelins back and forth into British faces, the Roman force acted like a threshing machine. When a wounded tribesman fell, he was trampled to death or finished off as a wedge passed over him. Panic swiftly set in. While some tribesmen stood and fought, others turned and attempted to escape the wedges through their own tight ranks. Within minutes, despite their huge numerical advantage, the Britons had lost control of the battle.

In this Battle of Watling Street, to this day the largest battle ever fought on British soil and the largest home defeat ever suffered by British forces, Roman troops went on killing and chasing down rebels until sunset. There were a reported eight hundred Roman fatalities. But an estimated eighty thousand Britons died that day; a similar number of Roman troops, veterans, and civilians had been killed throughout the weeks of the revolt. With Boudicca apparently wounded, she and her daughters escaped and went into hiding. That year, or the next, they took their own lives, using poison, and the tribes gave her a costly funeral.

To bolster Paulinus's army, Rome sent thousands of troops from Europe in AD 61. An auxiliary fort was rapidly built in London. Nine years later, the prefect in charge of the London fort's construction, Treveran Julius Classicus, would join Julius Civilis in revolting on the Rhine. Into the winter of AD 60–61 the bitter governor Paulinus, who took the British revolt personally, unrelentingly hunted down fugitive rebel leaders and punished anyone who had helped them. The runaway procurator Catus was dismissed. When Catus's replacement Julius Classicanus complained to Paulinus that his methods were too severe, he was told to mind his own business. So, Classicanus wrote to the emperor saying the revolt couldn't be wrapped up while Paulinus was governor.

In response, Nero sent his secretary Polyclitus to Britain in the spring of AD 61. Polyclitus reported that Paulinus had everything under control. Almost immediately, it became clear that this was untrue when a rebel band massacred the crews of a squadron from Rome's Britannic Fleet lying in an English bay. Although the culprits were hunted down, Nero recalled Paulinus. His replacement as governor, Petronius Turpilianus, employed a more conciliatory approach, rebuilding British towns and relationships. That year, AD 61, the revolt was consigned to history.

Paulinus returned to Rome famous as the savior of Britannia. Nero hailed the men of the 14th Gemina Legion as his "most valuable troops," and they became both renowned and feared as Conquerors of Britain. Gnaeus Agricola survived the Battle of Watling Street to return to Britain twice, first as a legion commander and later as governor. As for the cowardly Camp Prefect Postumus at Exeter, when he learned of the Roman victory at Watling Street, he fell on his own sword.

In the nineteenth century, after Alfred Lord Tennyson eulogized her in a patriotic poem, Boudicca would be hailed as a British freedom fighter, and in 1902 a statue of Boudicca in her chariot, accompanied by her daughters, was unveiled on London's Thames Embankment. There is much that is historically wrong about this statue. Boudicca wears a Roman helmet and armor. The chariot is Roman, not British. Worse, it has solid wheels equipped with anachronistic scythes, and no reins. The horses are large thoroughbred cavalry mounts, not nimble British chariot ponies. Most ironically of all, the statue celebrates a woman who didn't save London; she destroyed it.

Spoils of the Jerusalem Temple carried in the Triumph of Vespasian and Titus, from Arch of Titus, Rome. © *Look and Learn/Bridgeman Images*.

XIV. MENAHEM, ELEAZAR, JOSEPHUS, JOHN, AND SIMON

FIRST JEWISH REVOLT. PALESTINE, AD 66–73

In June AD 66, ten thousand exultant Jews entered the city of Jerusalem brandishing weapons. Their leader was Menahem ben Judah from the Golan Heights, who for several years past had headed the Jewish nationalist group the Sicarii, or Daggermen. Until now, the Sicarii had restricted themselves to sabotage and assassinating Jews who collaborated with Rome. But Menahem and a band of several hundred Sicarii had just surprised and wiped out a cohort of Rome's 3rd Gallica Legion garrisoning the Herodian fortress of Masada, which overlooked the Dead Sea, southeast of Jerusalem. Arming themselves with Roman armor and weapons, and with seventy thousand weapons stashed at Masada by King Herod, they marched on Jerusalem, one hundred miles away by road, attracting thousands of Jewish recruits en route.

Menahem's objective was to throw the Romans out of Judea, then a Roman sub-province whose governor answered to the governor of Syria. Other Jews had the same idea, and by the time the Sicarii entered Jerusalem the Roman garrison there was under siege from the Zealots, another anti-Roman group, led by Eleazar ben Ananius, son of a former Jewish high priest. Menahem forcibly took charge of rebel efforts, and murdered Eleazar's father, who had gone over to the Romans. He then naively accepted an invitation from Eleazar to worship at the Temple, which the Zealots controlled. When the unarmed Sicarii entered the Temple, the Zealots fell on them. Menahem and his lieutenants were killed. Some Sicarii fled to Masada; others remained, accepting Eleazar as their new leader.

The Zealots soon wiped out the 3rd Gallica Legion cohort garrisoning Jerusalem by promising to let them depart as long as they disarmed. As soon as the Romans were defenseless, the Zealots butchered them. Only their commanding centurion was spared, after he vowed to convert to Judaism. When the Jewish cavalry wing of King Herod Agrippa II stationed in the city was soon after permitted to leave unmolested, the rebels controlled Jerusalem. Swiftly, rebel bands also captured the outlying Roman-held fortresses of Cypros and Machaerus. Only one Roman outpost held out: the coastal city of Ashkelon, held by a single 3rd Gallica cohort and a cavalry detachment, which inflicted thousands of Jewish casualties when repulsing rebel attacks.

At Jerusalem the rebels elected a governing council, which appointed commanders for different regions. To command in Galilee, they appointed thirty-year-old rabbi Yoseph ben Matthias, who would later take the Roman name Flavius Josephus.

The revolt had been sparked by the brutal acts of the arrogant Roman procurator of Judea, Gessius Florus, but Jewish discontent with their Roman overlords was rife throughout the Roman world. Once word of the Judean uprising spread, Jews across the Middle East rebelled, but with very different results. In the Egyptian capital of Alexandria, the Roman governor Tiberius Alexander, himself a Jew, used his 12,000 legionaries to brutally suppress the uprising, killing 50,000 Jews. In Damascus, Syria, the Roman authorities put the city's 10,000 Jewish residents into a holding camp, only to later kill them all.

The timid governor of Syria, Cestius Gallus, was slow to react to the Judean uprising, even though 1,500 Roman legionaries had been massacred. He began by sending a tribune from his capital, Antioch, to conduct an inquiry, before begrudgingly assembling a thirty-thousand-man army of legionaries, auxiliaries, and troops from Roman allies in the East. In October, Gallus's force moved out of Ptolemais on the Mediterranean coast. While Gallus did send mobile detachments ranging through Galilee in search of rebels, his objective was Jerusalem, and in late October his column came up through the dry hills from the coast. The Roman army was attacked as it made camp nine miles north of Jerusalem, while its baggage train, strung out back down the narrow road, was looted of much of its artillery by rebels under the peasant leader Simon bar Giora.

Gallus moved to Mount Scopus within sight of Jerusalem, and on November 1, commenced assaults on the city's formidable walls. Just six days later, Gallus's mid-ranking officers talked him into abandoning the assault—with what argument, we don't know. As the Roman army pulled out and retraced its steps toward the coast, the rebels harried it all the way. The general commanding the 6th Ferrata Legion was killed, as were tribunes and centurions, with the sacred golden eagle standard of the 12th Fulminata Legion carried away by rebels.

Trapped in the Beth-Horon Valley, Gallus left behind four hundred men who volunteered for a suicide mission—delay the Jews while he snuck away with the rest of the army in the night. By the time Gallus had returned to Antioch, his mission was a failure—he had lost 5,680 men, for nothing. The Jews still held Judea and Galilee. Gallus died there at Antioch that December, probably from a heart attack, although some said he died from shame.

In February AD 67, the twenty-nine-year-old emperor Nero, then in Greece, called in one of his best generals, Titus Flavius Vespasianus—Vespasian, as we know him—giving him total authority in the East and the brief to terminate the Judean Revolt. Vespasian hurried to put together a 32,000-man army based around four legions, making his twenty-nine-year-old son, Titus, then just a tribune, his deputy.

Over the next eighteen months Vespasian methodically eliminated rebel resistance in Galilee, holding off an assault on Jerusalem until his rear was secure. When the Galilean town of Jotapata fell, its rebel commander, the future Josephus, tricked his fellow Jews and surrendered himself to Vespasian. By predicting that Vespasian and his son would both become emperors of Rome, Josephus saved his own life. More than that, he became one of Vespasian's advisers.

In June AD 68, Vespasian learned that Nero was dead, apparently by his own hand. Now Vespasian stalled major operations until he received fresh orders from a new emperor. As the throne changed hands three times over the next year, he launched few major operations. When his own legions hailed Vespasian emperor in July AD 69, he turned his attention to taking the throne from incumbent emperor Vitellius, giving his son Titus the job of conquering rebel Jerusalem.

By the time Titus and his army arrived outside Jerusalem in May AD 70, head-spinning power struggles within the Jewish leadership had seen factional infighting that cost thousands of Jewish lives. Two new rivals to Eleazar's Zealots had emerged: a band led by John of Gischala and a religious faction led by former high priest Ananus ben Ananus. A fourth faction, led by Simon bar Giora, had been driven away, taking refuge with the Sicarii at Masada. But Simon had built his forces and taken much of Idumea from the Zealots by force. When Eleazar kidnapped Simon's wife, Simon countered by marching against Jerusalem, forcing Eleazar to return her.

The religious faction in Jerusalem then had the bright idea of letting Simon and his men into Jerusalem to deal with the Zealots. Once inside, Simon allied with the Zealots, who invited in yet another faction, the Idumeans, and with their help overwhelmed and slaughtered the religious faction. The Idumeans then departed, leaving Jerusalem divided between Eleazar's Zealots, Simon bar Giora's band, and John of Gischala's followers.

This was the situation when Titus commenced operations against Jerusalem. Of the million Jewish people then trapped in the city, only thirty thousand were armed rebels. With those rebels defying several calls from Josephus for surrender in return for a pardon, Titus gave his four legions different operational sectors, where they slowly built earth ramps. The three Jewish factional leaders had agreed to cooperate, only for John to launch a surprise attack on the Zealots, killing many and forcing Eleazar and his surviving men to accept John's leadership.

Over three bloody months, Roman troops breached the outer wall and occupied part of the Antonia Fortress beside the Temple Mount, frequently fighting off damaging Jewish counterattacks, with Titus often personally leading his troops. Once Titus encircled the city with entrenchments in the summer its fate was sealed. Hundreds of thousands of Jewish civilians died from starvation, as the rebel fighters kept what food there was for themselves. Josephus's parents were among those who died.

In August, the Romans launched an assault on the Temple. Titus wanted to spare the grand edifice, but his overenthusiastic troops set fire to it. On August 6, or August 30—the date is disputed—the Second Temple, which had been built on the ruins of the Temple of Solomon when Jerusalem was controlled by the Persians, was burned to the ground.

The last Jewish defenders, holding the Upper City, were killed in the following weeks. Survivors went underground, hiding in tunnels beneath the burning, corpse-ridden city. After the fighting ended on September 26, Titus ordered the almost total destruction of Jerusalem. Only part of the Palace of Herod remained, incorporated into a new legion base built on the site, as did the western wall of the Temple Mount. Ninety-seven thousand Jewish prisoners were taken—men, women, and children. Resistance leaders, once identified, were crucified. The fittest young Jewish men were singled out to fight in Roman amphitheaters, with eight hundred taking part in the parade of the Triumph that Titus and his father would celebrate at Rome. The remaining prisoners were sold into slavery. Three years later, the last rebel bastion, Masada, would fall to the 10th Fretensis Legion.

The rebel leader Eleazar disappeared in the last weeks of the fighting in Jerusalem, either killed or having starved to death. John of Gischala surrendered when he was offered his life. Simon bar Giora remained in hiding until October, when he emerged from beneath Temple Mount ruins and surrendered unconditionally. John was permitted to live, apparently in permanent house arrest in Rome. Simon, after being led through Rome's streets in the conquerors' Triumph, was ceremonially garroted in the Forum before a large crowd.

Josephus was able to save several relatives from crucifixion by appealing to Titus, but he lost a farm in Judea when it was confiscated to become a Roman guard post. In compensation, Vespasian gave him another Judean estate. "He also honored me with the privileges of a Roman citizen," Josephus would later write, "and gave me an annual pension."[90]

Despised as a traitor by fellow Jews, Josephus lived at Rome, writing his biography and several important histories for Roman consumption, including his *Jewish War*, a firsthand account and our best source on the Jewish Revolt, and a history of the Jewish people.

As for the Jewish people, banned from the environs of Jerusalem, it was inevitable that they would again venture into rebellion against Rome. The Second Jewish Revolt would erupt a little more than a half century later.

Coin produced by Vindex at the Lyon mint during his revolt. *Werner Forman/ UIG/Bridgeman Images.*

XV. VINDEX

LEADING THE GAULS AGAINST NERO.
GAUL, AD 68

Gaius Julius Vindex was a Gaul who rose to the highest levels of office available to provincials in the first century. Born in the province of Aquitania around AD 25 during the reign of the emperor Tiberius, he was the son, grandson, or great-grandson of an Aquitanian noble, almost certainly of the powerful and warlike Arverni tribe, who was granted Roman citizenship by Julius Caesar or the emperor Augustus. Highly intelligent, handsome, and a fine soldier, Vindex had been made a member of the Senate in Rome by the emperor Claudius, a rare honor for a Gaul. After that he would have commanded a legion and possibly also achieved the rank of praetor, a senior judge of Rome. Vindex appears to have been a client of the daughter of Germanicus, Agrippina the Younger, and through her influence was appointed by her son, the emperor Nero, to the post of governor of the province of Gallia Lugdunensis, which bordered Aquitania, a post he held for some years.

Following Nero's murder of Agrippina in AD 59, Vindex had retained Nero's favor, and his governorship. But by AD 67 he had tired of Nero's increasingly erratic rule and focus on the Roman East. Nero was planning a military operation at the Caspian Gates against the Parthians in AD 68–69, while at the same time plunging into an invasion of Ethiopia south from Egypt. He intended to base himself in Alexandria for months or even years while his generals did the soldiering. That summer of AD 67, as the young emperor headed east, he went first to Greece to compete in four public games, including the Olympic Games, as a charioteer, actor, and singer. It was Nero's appearances on stage that annoyed Vindex most of all.

"I have often heard him sing, play the herald and act in tragedies," Vindex complained to friends and allies. "I have seen him in chains, hustled about as a criminal, heavy with child; yes, in the labors of childbirth—in short, imitating all the situations of mythology."[91]

This, in the opinion of Vindex, was no way for an emperor of Rome to act. So, in the second half of the year, with Nero in Greece, Vindex wrote discreetly to other provincial governors around the empire, sounding them out on a proposal to remove Nero and replace him with a leading senator. While Vindex was described as an ambitious man, he demonstrated no ambition to make himself emperor, and by early AD 68 he had settled on seventy-year-old Servius Galba, governor of the province of Nearer Spain, as his choice to replace Nero. Galba was a highly experienced senator and a tough general who led his troops from the front, and he was well respected by the army and the Senate.

But Galba sat on the fence after Vindex wrote offering to place him on the throne, as did other governors, neither committing to an overthrow of Nero nor informing Nero that Vindex was agitating for his removal. Having gone this far, however, Vindex could not turn back. He himself would have to make the overthrow happen. In March of AD 68, Vindex sent messages to chieftains throughout Gaul seeking their support, and began speaking at public gatherings around his province, encouraging a popular uprising to remove Nero.

"Rise now at length against him," Vindex urged. "Succor yourselves and succor the Romans. Liberate the entire world!"[92]

But Vindex's talk of revolt in his own provincial capital didn't inspire mass support there. The people of Lyon were strongly for Nero and the Caesar family—both the late emperor Claudius Caesar and his elder brother, the famous general Germanicus Caesar, grandfather of Nero, had been born in the city. When Rome was ravaged by the Great Fire in AD 64, Lyon had raised four million sesterces and sent it to Nero for the capital's restoration fund. And when Lyon was itself victim of a serious fire over the winter of AD 64–65, Nero had reciprocated by returning the four million sesterces, for rebuilding. Another reason for Lyon to remain faithful to Nero was the fact that the 1,500 men of the 18th Cohort of the City Guard of Rome were permanently based in the city, guarding Lyon's imperial mint. As this unit had proven during the Sacrovir Revolt, its troops would not hesitate to brutally quash Gallic rebellion.

Other Gallic cities and tribal regions were less loyal to Nero. Some had fought Rome, on and off, for hundreds of years, with Vindex's own Arverni rebelling as recently as the Sacrovir Revolt, forty-seven years before. Vindex set out to exploit the widespread dissatisfaction by combining all discontents behind his standard.

The city that most quickly swung behind the plan was Vienna, today's city of Vienne. Just twenty-two miles south of Lyon on the Rhone River, the city was located across the provincial border, in Gallia Narbonensis. The previous century, Vienna's native Allobroges tribe had evicted Roman settlers, who had gone north to establish Lyon, and there had been no love lost between the two cities since. Because Lyon was for Nero, Vienne was against Nero, and, as later events indicate, Vienne armed at least ten thousand men to march with Vindex.

By the middle of May, Vindex was able to bring together fifty thousand men, many mere youths, to form an army he planned to lead into Italy to seize the throne for Galba, and Galba would have no choice but to accept it—or so Vindex believed. Apart from the Viennese, Tacitus indicates that the Arverni and Aedui, who had both risen under Sacrovir, were also in this army, but otherwise we know nothing of its makeup.

At mass assemblies, Vindex made all his recruits swear an oath to the Senate and people of Rome, and to promise that they would kill him should he do anything contrary to that oath. Producing money in Lyon's imperial mint to pay for arms and supplies, but still using the SPQR (Senate and People of Rome) motif, Vindex gave his troops little opportunity to train. To enter Italy before forces loyal to Nero attempted to intervene, Vindex set off to the south with his men that May, intent on crossing the Cottian Alps before summer, gathering more recruits as he went.

But word of Vindex's seditious activities had spread. It reached Nero in Greece, where he was already contending with a revolt by the Jews of Judea. In response, he ordered units assigned to his Caspian Gates and Egyptian campaigns to turn around wherever they were and hurry to Italy, while he himself sailed home. He also ordered units currently in Italy to march to block Vindex's path across the Alps, and commanded the governor of Upper Germany to lead troops against the rebel rear.

A senator especially loyal to Nero, Junius Blaesus, set off from northern Italy for the Cottian Alps passes with a unit only recently raised for Nero's Caspian Gates venture, called the Phalanx of Alexander. Every one of its five thousand men had to be Italian and six feet tall. Nero had intended this unit to emulate the Greek phalanxes of Alexander the Great, employing very long spears in closely packed ranks, but this unit reverted to normal legion arms and tactics, and before long it was renamed the 1st Italica Legion. Accompanying the unit was a renowned cavalry wing, the Taurine Horse, from today's Turin.

From Upper Germany, the governor Lucius Verginius Rufus, who would become a consul in AD 63, marched with at least ten thousand legionaries from his four legions, plus at least one auxiliary cohort from Belgic Gaul and two wings of Batavian auxiliary cavalry. In total, the force numbered around twenty thousand men. By late May, pushing south at forced march pace, Rufus was able to beat Vindex and his dawdling army to the Gallic city of Vesontio, today's Besancon in southeast France, which lay at the entrance to the alpine passes. When the Roman army arrived outside Vesontio, the city closed its gates in sympathy with Vindex. Incensed by this, Rufus ordered his army to surround the city and prepare a siege.

At this point, Vindex and his army arrived and camped close by, ready to support the people of Vesontio. Messengers rode back and forth between the two camps, and it was agreed between Vindex and Rufus, who would have known each other, that they would meet, alone, to discuss a peaceful resolution. Fifty-four-year-old Rufus was a literary man, not a military man. A noted author, he was guardian of the writer Pliny the Younger, and when Rufus died thirty years later his funeral oration would be delivered by the famous historian Tacitus.

According to later Roman historian Cassius Dio, Rufus actually sympathized with Vindex's cause and was happy to see Nero deposed. Dio conjectured that the pair came to an agreement against Nero, under which they would place Galba on the throne, with Rufus ruling all the Gauls and Vindex all of Spain. As part of their deal, Vindex's army would occupy Vesontio in preparation for crossing the Alps.[93]

Vindex rode back to his camp, told his men of the negotiated settlement, and ordered them to march into Vesontio. In good spirits, the Gauls set off for the city in loose marching order, carrying their baggage. But word had not yet reached the Roman troops from their commander Rufus that the Gauls were to be allowed to pass through their lines and enter Vesontio. Seeing an opportunity to catch the rebels on the march, two wings of Batavian auxiliary cavalry mounted up on their own initiative and charged the Gauls. According to Tacitus, the Batavians rode unprepared Gauls from the Aedui and Arverni tribes into the ground. As the cavalry massacred the Gauls, Rufus's legionaries rushed to join the slaughter.[94]

Vindex was unable to stop the carnage. Despairing that his noble cause had come to an ignoble end, he drew his sword and fell on it, taking his own life. Soon, Roman soldiers were flooding around his body, inflicting more wounds on it with their weapons and claiming a piece of the glory of his defeat. Rufus, meanwhile, was distraught, mourning the loss of Vindex, an honorable man, and the perception that he, Rufus, had dishonorably betrayed Vindex and his followers.

The revolt ended there and then, but not before Rufus refused the offer of Nero's throne from his own victorious troops. As Rufus led his men back to the Rhine, Gallic survivors of Vindex's army were escorted back to their homes by the troops from Italy led by Junius Blaesus, who had arrived after crossing the Alps. Basing themselves in Lyon, Blaesus and his troops restored order to the province, and Blaesus took over the governorship.

Several weeks later, the empire was shocked to learn that, on June 8, Nero had taken his own life in Rome, abandoned by his bodyguards and hunted by the Praetorian Guard's cavalry. Believing, erroneously, that Nero had fled for Egypt, the Senate had proclaimed Galba emperor. Once again, Rufus's troops on the Upper Rhine offered him the throne, and once again he refused it, bowing to the Senate's will. After Rufus died in AD 97 at the ripe age of eighty-two, his ward Pliny would record the inscription on his tombstone, dictated by Rufus himself: "Here lies Rufus, who after defeating Vindex, did not take power, but gave it to the fatherland."[95]

Once word of Nero's suicide reached Galba in Spain, he assembled an army and marched on Rome to accept the throne. Galba would acknowledge that he owed his throne to Vindex's actions, honoring Vindex's memory with several coin issues. Galba would be assassinated after just seven months as emperor, sparking a war for the throne.

Civilis incites his fellow Batavians to revolt, eighteenth-century engraving.
Universal History Archive/UIG/Bridgeman Images.

XVI. CIVILIS

FORMER ROMAN OFFICER, REVOLT LEADER. THE RHINE, AD 69–70

In a tent in a Balkans marching camp in the summer of AD 69, a junior Roman general dictated a letter to a secretary. The general was Marcus Antonius Primus, commander of the 7th Galbiana Legion, and his letter was addressed to Gaius Julius Civilis, a nobleman of the Batavi tribe.

Civilis, aged in his late forties, had been commander of a cohort of Batavian auxiliaries in the Roman army, commencing his service in Britain within a year or two of the AD 43 Roman invasion of Britain. He'd been stationed in Britain with his unit for many years, taking part in the campaigns that eventually subjugated Wales and the island of Anglesey. In Britain, Civilis had served alongside Titus Flavius Vespasianus, the future Roman emperor Vespasian, who was then the general commanding the 2nd Augusta Legion. Civilis had become the general's friend, and later also got to know Vespasian's son Titus when he was stationed in Britain as a tribune.

"My respect for Vespasian is longstanding," Civilis was to say in AD 70. "While he was a subject [of other emperors], we were called friends."[96]

Primus knew of that friendship, and his letter called on Civilis to do Vespasian a favor. Primus was leading an army that was marching on Rome. The previous year, the emperor Nero had died by his own hand. Since then, three emperors had briefly occupied the throne. The latest was Aulus Vitellius, whose troops had recently taken the throne by force from the emperor Otho at the April 14 Battle of Bedriacum, near Cremona in central Italy. Vespasian had been commanding the long, grinding campaign in Judea to end the First Jewish Revolt, but in July the legions in Judea, Egypt, and Syria had hailed him emperor, in opposition to Vitellius. Gaius Licinius Mucianus, governor of Syria, who was loyal to Vespasian, had soon set off for Italy, leading a legion and thirteen thousand retired legionaries recalled to their standards, aiming to dethrone Vitellius.

Meanwhile, six cohorts of the 3rd Gallica Legion had recently arrived on the Danube after being stationed in Judea. One of its cohorts was still back in Judea, serving in Vespasian's army. These 3rd Gallica men also hailed Vespasian emperor, and set off for Italy. As they marched, they picked up several other legions who swore for Vespasian, among them the 7th Galbiana. Marcus Primus of the 7th Galbiana, always an opportunist, had claimed leadership of this growing force as it headed for Italy. When Vespasian learned of this he wrote to Primus, urging him to wait until Mucianus arrived from Syria to take command of all anti-Vitellius forces. But Primus wanted the glory of taking Rome for himself, so he ignored Vespasian's letter, continued on his march to Italy, and wrote to Civilis.

In this letter, Primus asked Civilis to raise a rebellion among his fellow Batavians on the Rhine, as a distraction to Vitellius's troops there. For the past few years, Vitellius had been based at Cologne on the Rhine as Roman governor of Lower Germany. There, he had commanded four legions, amounting to some twenty thousand men, plus a similar number of auxiliary troops. That January, Vitellius's legions had hailed him emperor, swiftly followed by the four legions based in Upper Germany. To overthrow Otho, Vitellius had split seven of the eight Rhine legions in half. This force, led by Vitellius's deputy Aulus Caecina, had marched to Italy and defeated Otho and his army at Bedriacum. Vitellius had then joined his troops and advanced to occupy Rome.

As a result, the Rhine legions had been left significantly undermanned. Seven were at half strength with four to five cohorts each,

while the newly formed 18th Legion consisted of six cohorts; four Lib-
yan cohorts of the legion were in Egypt, where they had joined the
other legions of the East in hailing Vespasian emperor. Primus reck-
oned that a pro-Vespasian rebellion by the Batavians on their doorstep
would force these Rhine-based troops to remain where they were to
combat it, keeping Vitellianist troops off Primus's back as he pushed
on toward Rome.

Civilis readily agreed to stir up rebellion on the Rhine. But un-
beknownst to Primus, Civilis had no intention of rebelling for Vespasian. Primus's suggestion fanned a fire of independence that had been
smoldering in Civilis's breast for some time. Civilis was a relative of
Chariovalda, the last king of the Batavi tribe; by some accounts he was
the late king's grandson or nephew. Chariovalda had died in AD 16
while leading Batavian auxiliaries in support of Germanicus Caesar's
campaign to defeat the German tribes led by Arminius, another former
Roman officer who had rebelled against Rome. The emperor Tiberius
had subsequently prevented a new king from being installed to rule the
Batavi; instead, he absorbed their territory into the province of Lower
Germany under a Roman governor, while still recognizing the other
terms of the alliance with the Batavi, that dated back to Caesar.

The Batavian royal family had continued to be prominent in tribal
affairs. They had provided officers to command the auxiliary infantry
cohorts and cavalry wings supplied by the tribe to Rome's field armies and
to the German Guard, the personal bodyguard of the emperors. Under
the original alliance, the Batavi supplied approximately twenty thousand
men to the Roman army at any one time, but paid no taxes to Rome.
Other tribes that came under Roman rule, such as those in Britain, both
supplied auxiliaries and paid taxes in the form of grain and money.

The Batavi escaped taxation because their auxiliaries were the most
valued in the Roman army. The tribe was of German origin, originating east of the Rhine some centuries back, and their young men
offered Rome's emperors a Germanic fierceness and resilience that few
non-German tribes could match. Their cavalrymen even trained their

horses to swim rivers with their riders, while those riders were fully armored and armed. Time and again through Roman history, Roman generals used that unique Batavian river-crossing skill as a tactical advantage to surprise opponents from behind.

The Batavian royal family had held Roman citizenship since the days of Julius Caesar, as denoted by their three-part names and the middle name Julius. In addition, they held rank in Roman society. All prefects commanding auxiliary cohorts in the Roman army and tribunes in the German Guard had to be "equites," members of the Equestrian Order. As equites, they ranked between Rome's plebeians and members of the Senatorial Order. To be equites, too, they had to have assets worth at least 400,000 sesterces, meaning they were far from poor compared to the annual salary of a legionary at this time, which was nine hundred sesterces.

Civilis had lost an eye in battle in Britain, most likely during an AD 50 assault against a fortified position in the Severn River Valley held by the Silures tribe and their ally from eastern Britain, King Caratacus. The slashing sword wound had left him without an eye and with an ugly facial scar, but despite this Civilis was outgoing, popular, and confident, and he would put these qualities to work against Rome.

Civilis, you see, had been harboring a grievance against Rome for the past year. In AD 68, the eight Batavian auxiliary cohorts that had been attached to the 14th Gemina Martia Victrix Legion in Britain for decades were separated from the legion after both were transferred across the English Channel. They were being sent to Carnuntum in Pannonia in preparation for an AD 69 campaign the emperor Nero was planning against the Caspian Gates, a campaign that would be aborted because of the Jewish Revolt. But while they were passing through Lingone tribal territory in Gaul, the Batavians had brawled viciously with their longtime campmates of the 14th Gemina Legion, and both units were separated. While the 14th Gemina continued the march to Carnuntum, all eight Batavian cohorts were reassigned to the army of the Upper Rhine, based at Mogantiacum, today's city of Mainz, at the

confluence of the Rhine and Main Rivers. Civilis and his brother Claudius Julius Paulus, "scions of the royal family, ranked very high above
the rest of their nation," in the words of Tacitus, commanded two of
those Batavian cohorts.[97]

Shortly after their transfer to Mainz, the brothers were arrested by
the governor of Lower Germany, Fonteius Capito, on a false charge of
fomenting rebellion against the emperor Nero. Civilis's brother Paulus
was swiftly executed by decapitation, but Civilis was sent to Rome in
chains for an appeal to be heard by Nero. He was still in prison when
Nero died, and the next emperor, Galba, dismissed the charge and sent
him back to his unit. But when Vitellius took the throne, Civilis was
again arrested and imprisoned in Mainz, with Vitellius's troops on the
Rhine clamoring for his execution. Vitellius, who worried that Civilis's
death could cause the Batavian people to rise up against him in protest,
ordered Civilis's release, after which the Batavian returned yet again to
the command of his cohort.

Civilis was a free man, but his arrest and treatment in prison ran-
kled, and he would never forget or forgive the execution of his brother.
With Vitellius ordering the mass conscription of all military-age Batavian males to bolster his army now that he had Vespasian's approaching
armies to contend with, Civilis saw an opportunity to cement his people behind him, and against Rome. For, the Batavians had more than
fulfilled their obligations to Rome, and Civilis's countrymen were livid
at this across-the-board conscription order.

As the most senior surviving Batavian royal, Civilis called a religious banquet in a grove sacred to the Batavi outside Mainz, inviting
all the chiefs of his nation and the boldest of the Batavian lower class.
Once the feast had been well oiled by beer, a favorite drink of Germans,
Civilis arose and delivered a passionate speech.

He declared:

There is no alliance as there once was—we are treated as slaves.
Now the conscription is at hand, tearing, we may say, children

from their parents forever, and brothers from brothers. Never has the power of Rome been more weakened. In the winter quarters of the legions there is nothing but property to plunder and a few old men. Only dare to look up, and cease to tremble at the empty names of legions. For we have a vast force of horsemen and foot soldiers. We have the Germans, our kinsmen. We have the Gauls bent on the same goals. Even to the Roman people this war won't be displeasing. If defeated, we shall reckon it a service to Vespasian, and if successful—no account need be rendered![98]

That was all it took to convince his countrymen to rise up against Rome with him. As Civilis knew, the Batavians were already discontented over the looming Roman conscription, and they were ready to rise. Banquet attendees, led by Civilis, swore oaths by their gods to free their homeland. Civilis, the one-eyed, highly experienced military commander, was likened by his followers to the past one-eyed generals Hannibal the Carthaginian and Sertorius the rebel Roman governor of Spain, each of whom had, in his day, humiliated Rome. But, in their excitement for rebellion, what none of the banqueters chose to recall was that both Hannibal and Sertorius had eventually been defeated by Rome.

Now that he had his chief countrymen on his side, back at Mainz, Civilis spoke to the men of the eight Batavian cohorts and ten other auxiliary cohorts stationed at the city, cementing these nine thousand troops behind the banner of revolt.

When, in late October, as was the custom each year, Roman troops at Mainz were dispersing to camps along the Rhine to spend the winter, Civilis and his cohort were ordered to Novaesium, today's German city of Neuss. As they marched along beside the Rhine, Civilis sent a message to Brinno, a leader of the small Canninefates tribe, which, like the much more numerous Batavian people, lived on the "island" at the North Sea mouth of the Rhine. When the emperor Caligula had in

AD 39 massed legions on the Rhine and then made a brief incursion into Germany east of the great river, treating it as a game to amuse his friends, Brinno's father, then a Canninefates leader, had scoffed at the Roman emperor's expedition. Brinno now enthusiastically backed Civilis's plan for rising against Rome.

It was Brinno who launched the war, summoning the support of the Frisii, a German tribe from along the North Sea Frisian coast above the Rhine. The Frisii had long had an uneasy relationship with Rome; they paid their taxes but had risen in brief rebellion several times in the past. Using sturdy clinker-built Frisian ships, thousands of Canninefates and Frisians stealthily came up the Rhine to the fortified Roman base of Campus Vetera, or Old Camp, today the German city of Xanten. Home to Rome's Rhine fleet, this base could hold as many as ten thousand Roman troops. But with the withdrawal of legions to support Vitellius in Italy, aside from a few seamen and marines just two auxiliary cohorts currently occupied the base—one made up of Tungrian Germans, the other, Ubian Germans.

Both the Tungrians and Ubians at Xanten remained loyal to Rome, but their prefects could see it was pointless trying to hold such a large camp with less than a thousand men. So the prefects set fire to the base and ordered their men to withdraw west, to the island in the Batavian heartland. At the same time they ordered the twenty-four warships then docked at Xanten to shadow their two cohorts as they withdrew in good order. The prefects themselves—Romans in their late twenties who had previously served as tribunes with the legions but who were not yet old enough to qualify for Senate membership—deserted their men, mounting up and galloping off up the Rhine, supposedly to summon reinforcements.

The prefects left a centurion, Aquilius, in charge. From an archaeological discovery on the Rhine we know his full name was Gaius Aquilius Proculus. His last name, Proculus, indicates he was born when his father, another Aquilius, was away, probably on military service. In this era, apart from selected units such as those of the Batavians, the commanding officers of auxiliary cohorts were invariably Roman prefects, supported by a pair of centurions commanding the cohort's two maniples, or companies, with the most senior of the two serving as the cohort's second-in-command. These centurions were always highly experienced men transferred to auxiliary cohorts after lengthy legion service.

Gaius Aquilius Proculus had previously been one of the ten first-rank centurions of the 8th Augusta Legion, stationed on the Danube in the province of Moesia, taking part in the First Battle of Bedriacum on the emperor Otho's side. On the legion's surrender to Vitellius's forces, it had been sent back to Moesia. Most likely, Centurion Aquilius had been ardently for Otho, and, as the 8th Augusta was dispatched back to where it came from, Aquilius had been detached at Bedriacum by Vitellius's commanders and transferred to the German auxiliary unit on the Rhine, amid Vitellius's loyal legions, to separate a potential troublemaker from his fellows. Consequently, Aquilius had only been with his auxiliary unit a matter of months.

Civilis had only recently reached Neuss with his Batavian cohort, arriving ahead of the two legions assigned to winter at the same camp, when word arrived of the rising of the Canninefates and Frisii downstream. Immediately, Civilis sent a courier dashing to Mainz with a message for Hordeonius Flaccus, the old, lame Roman general Vitellius had left in charge of both Upper and Lower Germany. Telling Flaccus of the uprising and blaming the two Roman prefects for deserting their posts, Civilis assured the general that he and his Batavian cohort could easily put down the revolt. Flaccus, an indolent man who would never personally lead his troops into battle, quickly sent back word authorizing Civilis to do as he proposed. This allowed Civilis and his cohort to hurry away from Neuss and head for the Canninefates and Frisians.

As for Brinno and his German rebels, after looting the burning Roman fortress at Xanten and slaughtering Roman traders who lived outside it, they set off after the retreating auxiliaries, eventually trapping them beside the Rhine on the northern side of the "island." Centurion

Aquilius now ordered his men to form battle lines and instructed the squadron of warships that had been keeping pace with his two cohorts to form up along the riverbank behind his men, with their marines and onboard Scorpion catapults covering them.

There was soon a problem aboard the ships. Many of their paid oarsmen were Batavians, and they began to back water and even drive their ships stern-first into the opposite bank of the Rhine. Amid this chaos, the oarsmen rose up and overpowered the marines aboard. The ship masters and centurions commanding marines who hadn't agreed to go over to the rebel side were killed on the spot. In this way, Aquilius lost the support of the naval squadron. Things were about to get worse.

Civilis and his Batavian cohort arrived on the scene. Instead of going against the rebels, however, Civilis took charge of them, dividing his Batavians, Canninefates, and Frisians into three distinct divisions and facing off against Aquilius and his greatly outnumbered men. Battle commenced, with javelins flying through the air from both sides. At this point, Aquilius's Tungrian cohort went over to the rebels' side. This left Aquilius with just the 480 men of his Ubian cohort. The Ubii, natives of the region around today's Cologne, had been Rome's first German allies, and these men stayed with Centurion Aquilius, even though they knew it was highly unlikely any of them would survive. Civilis and his men charged. The battle was brief. Centurion Aquilius and his men were cut down.

As Civilis's men collected the weapons and equipment of the Ubian dead littering the battlefield to arm new recruits, they also looted their dead opponents of their clothing and valuables. Centurion Aquilius was stripped of his decorations including a silver medal for valor, issued to him when still with the 8th Augusta Legion. Centuries later, this medal would be unearthed at Krefeld, near today's Nijmegen in the Netherlands, at the site of a Roman auxiliary cavalry camp; it must have been buried there later in the revolt, by the rebel who had taken it from Aquilius's body.

Civilis found himself in command on the Lower Rhine, reinforced by the Tungrian German cohort and controlling the lower reaches of the river itself via his captured squadron of two dozen light warships. Even he would have been surprised by how quickly and easily this had been achieved.

Word spread like wildfire through Germany that Germans on the Rhine under Civilis, prince of the Batavians, had thrown off the Roman yoke, and numerous German tribes sent Civilis messages offering help. At the same time, Civilis wrote to tribal leaders throughout Gaul, urging them to follow his lead and revolt against Rome. He also sent word to Mainz, calling on the seven cohorts of Batavian auxiliaries stationed there to join him on the Lower Rhine. But before this message reached its destination these cohorts had set off with their ten fellow auxiliary cohorts on the start of a long march to Rome; they had been coincidentally summoned there by Vitellius himself, to bolster his forces now that the Vespasianist armies of Primus and Mucianus had entered Italy.

When word reached Governor Flaccus in Mainz that an important base on the Lower Rhine had been lost along with its troops and ships, Flaccus anxiously called in and briefed Munius Lupercus, the most senior of the two generals commanding the pair of legions assigned to winter quarters at Neuss. A senator of legate rank, the equivalent of a brigadier general today, Lupercus immediately went to work. At his disposal he had five cohorts from his own legion, the 15th Primigenia, and five cohorts from the 5th Alaudae Legion commanded by his colleague Numisius Rufus, plus a cohort of Ubian auxiliary foot soldiers, a wing of five hundred Treveran auxiliary cavalry from today's Trier in Germany, and a wing of Batavian cavalry.

At this point, while it was known that Civilis's Batavian cohort had rebelled, Roman commanders had no suspicions about the loyalty of all Batavian troops in the Roman army. Taking the Batavian cavalry with him didn't concern Lupercus. Besides, the Batavian prefect commanding this cavalry unit, Claudius Labeo, was a known rival and enemy of Civilis.

Lupercus left a thousand legionaries to garrison the Neuss legion base, then he and his deputy Rufus took the remainder of their troops across the Rhine, apparently via a bridge of boats. Lupercus and Rufus were intent on marching down the far bank of the river and catching the rebels by surprise. This Roman force numbered around five thousand legionaries, five hundred auxiliary light infantry, and a thousand cavalry. As this Roman column of some 6,500 men came down the Rhine, not far from the ruins of Campus Vetera, they found Civilis and his troops lined up in battle order, waiting for them.

The rebels had by this time been joined by their women and children, including Civilis's mother and sisters, and Civilis had these civilians form up in the rear of his force to encourage their men in battle. Civilis himself was surrounded by the Roman standards previously carried by his own men and the Ubians who had fallen with Centurion Aquilius. Now, these standards were his trophies. His men were still in their Roman-style units, but now they carried new standards featuring animals sacred to the Germans—the wild boar, the wolf, and the like.

As the two forces faced off, the Roman troops let out their customary war cry, but this was drowned out by the deep, swelling Germanic war song of the rebels and the shrieks of their women. The Roman commander Lupercus had stationed Claudius Labeo's Batavian cavalry unit on his left wing, while the Treveran cavalrymen were posted on the right wing. Lupercus's Ubian auxiliaries occupied the extremity of the Roman infantry line on the left, beside the two legions. But even before Lupercus could order "Charge," Labeo and his Batavian cavalry wheeled and rode away, then swung, reformed, and charged the now exposed auxiliaries on the extreme left of Lupercus's line.

This betrayal seems to have been orchestrated in advance, for Civilis then led his foot soldiers in falling on the Roman right, where the heavily outnumbered Treveran cavalry, usually rated the best in the Roman army apart from the Batavians, broke and galloped away across the flat landscape. The Ubian auxiliaries soon followed suit, throwing away their shields and running for it. This left the men of the 5th

Alaudae and 15th Primigenia Legions outnumbered, devoid of cavalry support and under assault from both left and right.

Lupercus's legionaries were holding their composure and their ground, however, and he gave instructions for an orderly withdrawal to Campus Vetera, where the Roman column's civilian muleteers, cart drivers, and other camp followers had already sought shelter. With the rebels snapping at their heels, but letting them retreat, the two legions gained the safety of the abandoned fortress. There, Lupercus had his men destroy the town buildings that had been built up to the camp's walls, to create a field of fire for his catapults.

The rebels surrounded this Roman base, which they had overrun at the outset of their uprising, but for the moment Civilis made no attempt to storm the camp. Within its walls, Lupercus prepared to withstand a lengthy siege. Civilis, in the meantime, was distrustful of Claudius Labeo, the prefect of the Batavian cavalry wing that had defected to him at the outset of the battle, and he sent Labeo under guard deep into the territory of the Frisii on the North Sea coast. Before long, Labeo would bribe his Frisian jailers and escape, going into hiding in today's Belgium.

While all this was occurring, Civilis's courier had overtaken the seven Batavian infantry cohorts on the highway to Gaul and passed on his message calling on them to join him. Halting their progress, the Batavians sent a message to Governor Flaccus at Mainz, demanding a cash bonus, double pay, and the allocation of more cavalry to their column before they continued their march to Rome. Flaccus didn't reply; he couldn't—all this would have to be authorized by Vitellius in Rome. This was all the excuse the Batavians needed. Within a day or two, all 3,500 men of the seven cohorts turned around and set off for the Lower Rhine to join Civilis.

When Flaccus learned of this, the governor called together all the tribunes and centurions who were at Mainz and asked for their opinions as to whether he should oppose the Batavian march with force. A number of his officers had become nervous about the loyalties of all the auxiliaries on the Rhine, and they advised him to confine all his troops to camp to prevent other auxiliary troops from emulating the Batavians. This was what Flaccus did, at first.

Before long, however, Flaccus changed his mind and sent a message to Herrenius Gallus, commander of the 1st Germanica Legion at Bonna, today's German city of Bonn on the Rhine. He ordered Gallus to place his troops in the path of the approaching Batavian force while he himself marched after them with troops from Mainz. This was a workable plan, one which, in the opinion of Roman historian Tacitus—who within a decade or so would himself command a legion—had a good chance of destroying the mutinous Batavians. "They might have been crushed," he would write.[99]

But then the vacillating Roman governor changed his mind yet again and sent Gallus another message, suggesting it might be better to let the Batavians be—but he did not give Gallus an order to either let the Batavians pass or stop them. As the mutinous cohorts approached Bonn, they sent delegates on ahead to urge Gallus to allow them to pass.

"We have no quarrel with the Romans, for whom we have so often fought," said the delegates. "We long for our native land and for rest. If no one opposes us, our march will be harmless. But if an armed force confronts us, we will make a way [through] with the sword."[100]

This incensed Gallus's subordinates, who demanded Gallus lead his men against the Batavians. With four of the 1st Germanica Legion's ten cohorts serving in Italy for Vitellius, Gallus had been left with three thousand legionaries plus several supporting cohorts of Belgae auxiliaries. So, the two forces were roughly equal, with the numbers slightly in Gallus's favor. At first, Gallus hesitated, but as his men reminded him that they outnumbered the mutineers, he gave in to them and a plan of attack was worked out. As the Batavians came marching down the road to the Bonn camp, Gallus's troops burst out of all four gates in a rush. They were accompanied and egged on by local farmers and hundreds of traders who lived outside the camp walls, all armed in a fashion, and bellowing for Batavian blood.

The Roman plan was to surround the Batavians. This they succeeded in doing, but the disciplined auxiliaries calmly formed a square,
with their ranks on all sides presenting walls of shields and darts ready
to be launched. The Belgae were the first to attack the square. They
were driven off with heavy casualties. Next, the 1st Germanica Legion
attacked, only to find itself being driven back as the square advanced
toward the Bonn camp like a slow-moving machine. Then, the legion
broke. Its men were driven back against the entrenchments outside the
walls of the camp, where many were slaughtered by the rampaging Batavians. Other members of the legion were crushed to death outside the
gates as thousands tried desperately to gain the protection of the camp.
To save the camp, their commanding general, Gallus, ordered the gates
closed.

The Batavians marched on, following the Rhine toward the sea.
Skirting around the large Roman base at Colonia Agrippinensis, today's Cologne, they linked up with Civilis outside Campus Vetera at
Xanten. Civilis was uncertain about what to do next, but for the moment he assembled his now sizeable army of 7,000 to 8,000 men and
led them in swearing allegiance to Vespasian. He also sent a message
to the legionaries behind the Old Camp walls, advising them to do the
same.

"We don't follow the advice of traitors or enemies," the legions replied, and, reaffirming their allegiance to Vitellius, they vowed to fight
Civilis to their last breath.[101]

This infuriated Civilis, who sent for the warriors that the
Bructeri and Tenteri tribes in Germany east of the Rhine had promised him, and within days thousands of Germans arrived, eager to
plunder Roman cities and camps. With these reinforcements, Civilis
launched an all-out assault against Campus Vetera, with each tribal
group operating as a separate unit. Crossing the outer ditches, the
rebels and their German allies went against the fortress's walls with
scaling ladders, but were driven off under a hail of catapult stones
fired from the walls.

The rebels, aided by Roman captives and deserters, even built a low siege tower on wheels. The tower's top was covered with rebel fighters. Others hid inside, ready to dig away at the camp wall once the mobile tower reached it. But once against the wall this machine was smashed to pieces by missiles from the legion catapults. Burning spears were also fired by the Roman artillery, with devastating effect on the attackers. Civilis called off the attack as his casualties mounted and, gauging that there were only a few days' supplies inside the camp, decided to starve the Roman troops into submission.

Once the elderly Governor Flaccus learned that Lupercus and his legions were trapped at Xanten, he decided to personally lead a force to his subordinate's aid. After sending letters throughout Gaul begging the support of Gallic tribes, Flaccus appointed the legate Dillius Vocula to lead a column down the Rhine. Probably aged in his forties, Vocula was commander of the new 18th Legion, with the five cohorts of the 22nd Primigenia Legion then also stationed at Mainz under a tribune or camp prefect also taking orders from him—the legate commanding the 22nd Primigenia had taken five cohorts of the legion to Italy earlier in the year as part of the army that installed Vitellius on the throne.

Vocula, a well-liked general, was instructed by Flaccus to lead his own six cohorts of the 18th Legion and other troops in his region along the western bank of the Rhine to relieve Lupercus, leaving the 4th Macedonica Legion and 22nd Primigenia Legion to garrison the Upper Rhine. As Vocula set off by land, Flaccus himself, suffering severely from gout, boarded a boat that would convey him down the river, landing him at each of his troops' overnight camps along the way. Vocula meanwhile sent orders to the 16th Gallica Legion, which was wintering outside Cologne, to link up with his force as he approached.

The column set off, followed by Flaccus on the river. At the first overnight halt, messengers arrived from the East and handed Governor Flaccus a letter from none other than Vespasian, in which the aspiring emperor sought Flaccus's support. To show his continued loyalty to Vitellius, Flaccus read this letter aloud to an assembly of his troops, then had Vespasian's messengers taken away in chains, to be delivered to Vitellius in Rome.

On arrival at Bonn, Flaccus's force linked up with Herrenius Gallus and his 1st Germanica Legion. The men of the 1st Germanica, who had been humiliated by the seven Batavian cohorts on their passage along the Rhine, blamed Flaccus for that humiliation, saying he should have done what he had originally said he would do, and come after the Batavians from the rear.

Flaccus realized that the men of the 1st had lost confidence in him. They were even accusing him of siding with Vespasian and deliberately allowing the Batavian cohorts to join Civilis. He wanted to tie up the Rhine legions in support of Vespasian, they said. Flaccus called another assembly. This time he read aloud the messages he'd sent to Gaul seeking help against Civilis. He also arrested the most vocal of the 1st Germanica legionaries who'd spoken against him.

The army marched on, and Flaccus sailed on, entering Cologne, where they were joined by large numbers of Gauls, untrained new recruits sent by the tribes in response to Flaccus's plea for Gallic militiamen. Continuing along the Rhine, the motley force reached Neuss, where it was joined by the five cohorts of the 16th Gallica Legion. At this point, Flaccus now had elements of three legions—the 1st Germanica, the 16th Gallica, and the 18th—plus several thousand auxiliaries and militiamen, in an army that numbered at least ten thousand troops.

The army marched along beside the Rhine for another day before Vocula chose a site for a marching camp on a rise at Gelduba, today's Krefeld, a little inland from a bend in the river. A dispirited Flaccus, no longer playing an active leadership role, remained in his tent after landing from the river. Vocula and Gallus, commander of the 1st Germanica, decided between them that the army would stay put at Krefeld to train the newly arrived raw Gallic recruits.

As part of this training, Vocula left Gallus in charge at Krefeld with half the army. He led the remainder, including the Gallic recruits, in raiding and pillaging nearby villages of the Gugerni, a German tribe from east of the Rhine whom the emperor Tiberius had settled on the western bank several generations back—and who were, in theory, Roman allies. This was supposed to give Vocula's troops a taste for German blood and plunder. But it led many of the rank and file, who supported Vitellius, to believe that Vocula and Gallus secretly supported Vespasian and his rebel friend Civilis and were deliberately wasting time to avoid hostilities with Civilis.

While Vocula was away raiding, his deputy Gallus, at Krefeld, was informed that a Roman cargo vessel carrying grain to the army had run aground on the Rhine's far bank. Northern Europe was in the grip of serious drought at the time, and it had reduced the level of the Rhine so much in this region that it was mostly mud, with the central channel so shallow that it was possible to wade across in neck-deep water.

When Gallus sent a small detachment of troops to secure the vessel, German tribesmen appeared on the opposite bank and attacked them. When Gallus sent a full cohort to support the first detachment, even more Germans emerged to enter the fight, pushing back the Romans and seizing the boat and its cargo.

The surviving legionaries returned to camp angry at being bested by the Germans, and blamed their general, Gallus. Accusing him of sending them into a trap, they dragged him from his tent, beat him, and extracted from him a so-called confession that he had been ordered by Governor Flaccus to betray his own men. Then they put him in chains. When Vocula returned to the Krefeld camp the next day with half the army, he had Gallus released, and arrested and summarily executed the legionaries who had led Gallus's beating.

While the force led by Flaccus, Vocula, and Gallus was making its way down the Rhine, German tribesmen had been rampaging along its southern bank from the "island," killing Roman allies. They particularly sought out Ubians, who were among Rome's oldest Germanic allies, at one village catching a cohort of Ubian auxiliaries off guard and massacring them. Civilis himself was building siege ramps toward the walls of Campus Vetera at Xanten, where Lupercus and his two legions were holed up. But the German tribes who joined him were impatient for glory and plunder, and when Civilis could no longer restrain them he let the Germans launch a night attack across the entrenchments while he stood back and watched.

The undisciplined tribesmen from east of the Rhine first piled up wooden logs around the Roman entrenchments, set fire to them, then feasted and got drunk before going against the camp walls. They were cut down in droves by the catapults, and if they reached the walls their scaling ladders were easily knocked down by the legionaries defending the camp. The fires lit by the Germans only illuminated them as targets for the Roman defenders, and finally Civilis realized the danger and had them extinguished.

At daylight, the Batavians joined the assault, bringing up a rickety double-storied siege tower. But the defenders battered it with long poles from the wall, and broke it in pieces. The legionaries even created a new kind of war machine, a grab dangling from a long pole. After seizing some attackers, the grab was elevated and its contents slung over the wall into the camp, where those unfortunate enough to be caught met the swords of waiting Romans. Defenders even sallied out to attack the enemy from the rear. The rebel attack faltered. Seeing the futility of such an undisciplined, uncoordinated assault, Civilis called it off, and again resorted to waiting and starving out the Romans.

While this was going on through the month of October, the Vespasianist army of Antonius Primus had reached Bedriacum, the site of emperor Otho's defeat and death that April. There, in a second battle on October 24, the troops of Vespasian crushed the army that Vitellius had sent from Rome to oppose them. They then went on to sack the city of Cremona. At Krefeld in the beginning of December, a prefect named Alpinius Montanus, who had commanded Gallic auxiliaries in the defeated army of Vitellius, arrived from Bedriacum. Montanus gave a firsthand account of the defeat of Vitellius's army, and brought a message from Antonius Primus for Governor Flaccus that called on Flaccus to swear his army for Vespasian.

This Flaccus did at an assembly of his army at Krefeld, as he read aloud copies of Primus's letters to Civilis in which the general called on the Batavian to rebel in Vespasian's name. But many of old Flaccus's rank-and-file legionaries only mouthed the oath of allegiance to Vespasian. Knowing that Vitellius was still in Rome with thousands of troops, they preferred to believe that their old commander in chief would still defeat Vespasian.

Montanus was sent downriver by Flaccus to pass on the news to Civilis, in hopes that the Batavian would terminate hostilities. When Montanus returned to Krefeld, he gave Roman commanders the impression that Civilis was indeed standing down—when, in fact, the opposite was true. While maintaining the siege at Campus Vetera with German fighters, Civilis sent his nephew Claudius Victor and a Batavian officer named Julius Maximus with his best troops, including his Batavian foot soldiers and cavalry, in hurriedly marching along the Rhine on Montanus's heels. Out of the blue, they launched a surprise attack on the sleepy Krefeld camp, where Flaccus had failed to put out pickets to warn of any rebel approach.

It was Vocula who took charge of the Krefeld defense, while old Flaccus cringed in his tent. The Roman general barely had time to assign his units their places in the battle lines that hastily formed outside the camp, as his legions took the center and auxiliaries the wings. The Roman cavalry charged, but, met by immovable lines of Batavian infantry and cavalry, they soon turned and rode back to their own lines in disorder, pursued by Batavian cavalry. On one Roman wing, Nervii auxiliaries, men from today's Belgium, suddenly broke and ran, allowing the Batavian infantry to charge into the flank of the legions, cutting them to pieces and driving them, step by step, back into their camp's outer ditch. There, hundreds of Roman legionaries surrendered and were hustled away by the Batavian cavalry.

Things were looking grim for the Romans until they had a piece of luck. A cohort of Spanish auxiliaries from the Vascones tribal area in northern Spain, men who'd been recruited only the previous year, arrived to join Governor Flaccus's army, with their route bringing them up behind the attacking Batavians. Word spread quickly through Batavian ranks that a Roman force was in their rear. Thinking that legions from Neuss or Mainz had arrived, the Batavians wavered and Vocula's legionaries found new courage.

The Romans succeeded in forcing the rebels back. With the bravest Batavians standing their ground and being cut down, Victor and Maximus were forced to order a retreat. The Romans had lost more men, both killed and captured, but they won the battle. Even so, Vocula chose not to immediately pursue the enemy and exploit his advantage.

When Victor and Maximus rejoined Civilis with their bloodied force and prisoners, Civilis paraded the captured Roman legionaries in view of Lupercus and his men of the 5th Alaudae and 15th Primigenia Legions, calling out to the Romans who lined the camp walls that he had won the battle at Krefeld. But a legionary among the prisoners yelled that this was a lie, that this battle had been a Roman victory. The man was immediately put to death, but not before Lupercus and his men knew the truth.

At Krefeld several days later, after licking his wounds and resupplying, Vocula led the relief army from the camp and down the road toward Lupercus's trapped force, leaving Governor Flaccus, who withdrew to Neuss. Once Vocula arrived outside Campus Vetera he wanted to delay to build a marching camp, but his legions demanded immediate action to free their comrades, and charged toward the rebels.

A hectic fight ensued, with Civilis leading the rebel counterattack on horseback. At one point, Civilis's horse was killed under him and the rebel leader was thrown to the ground. As word of this quickly spread, his men panicked, and the rebel army fled the field. Civilis managed to escape unharmed. But Campus Vetera had been relieved.

Instead of pursuing the fleeing, demoralized enemy, Vocula ordered his men to strengthen the camp's defenses and build new wooden guard towers, as if he expected the rebels would soon return. Then, after taking a thousand legionaries from Lupercus's force—one cohort from the 5th Alaudae and another from the 15th Primigenia—he added them to his army, taking away the 5th Alaudae's general Rufus to command them. He turned around and marched back the way he had come, leaving Lupercus and his depleted legions to hold Campus Vetera.

Seeing this, Civilis regrouped his forces. He surrounded Campus Vetera with part of his force, then pursued Vocula with the rest. Vocula returned to the Krefeld camp, then abandoned it and withdrew his army to Neuss, where old Governor Flaccus awaited. Civilis occupied the Krefeld post, as a Roman cavalry force sent by Vocula approached. It would have been at this point that the rebel who had earlier seized Centurion Aquilius's silver medal buried it at Krefeld. Civilis fought his way through the Roman cavalry, then withdrew to rejoin the Old Camp siege, leaving the Krefeld fort burning.

Meanwhile, at Neuss, Flaccus's legionaries learned that Vitellius had sent money from Rome to be distributed to his Rhine troops in order to retain their loyalty. They demanded the money from Flaccus. He distributed the cash, but he did so in the name of Vespasian. This incensed the rank and file, and a number of them dragged the old general from his tent at night and murdered him. They also went after Vocula, but the general succeeded in escaping the camp dressed as a slave, and hurried toward Mainz.

The Roman legions at Neuss were now in the control of their troops. But the men of two legions—the 1st Germanica and Vocula's own 18th—found their consciences and left Neuss, marching to join Vocula at Mainz. There, Vocula swore the men of these two units for Vespasian, with the resident 4th Macedonica Legion following suit.

As winter arrived, news reached the Rhine that Vitellius had been killed by his own troops at Rome in the last week of December, that Primus's army had fought its way into the city, defeating Vitellius's last loyal troops in bloody fighting, and the Senate had declared Vespasian emperor of Rome. At this point, had Civilis genuinely been a supporter of Vespasian he would have ceased hostilities, but he did no such thing.

Instead, pursuing his own agenda, he upped the ante by recruiting new allies to his cause.

By the start of AD 70, Julius Classicus, a Treveran from Trier and first among the Treveri for rank and wealth, was ready to join the rebel cause. Like Civilis, Classicus had commanded auxiliaries in the Roman army and served in Britain. Previously in command of the 6th Nerviorum Cohort, an infantry unit raised from the Nervii tribe in today's Belgium, Classicus now commanded Vocula's Treveran cavalry. To this point, he had faithfully followed Vocula's orders.

Classicus was to say, however, that his family had always been an enemy of Rome. He brought two more officers into his secret plot to join Civilis. One, Julius Tutor, was a fellow Treveran, while the other, Julius Sabinus, was a Gaul from the Lingone tribe, whose homeland was on the Seine River. Tutor and Sabinus met secretly at Cologne with leading members of their own tribes as well as Ubian and Tungrian Germans. All agreed with Classicus's view that, if they could eliminate the Roman generals who remained in command of the legions on the Rhine, their legionaries would become a leaderless rabble, and all of Gaul could be liberated by rebel forces. Sabinus the Lingone now deserted his unit and set off for his homeland, to lead his people in rising up to join Civilis. Classicus and Tutor remained with Vocula's army, biding their time.

In the new year, encouraged by word from Gallic chiefs that he had their support, Vocula again decided to rescue his comrades at Campus Vetera, and marched with his army from Cologne. As the Roman army neared Old Camp, Classicus and Tutor convinced Vocula to send them with their Treveran cavalry wing to scout the way ahead. But once they had separated from Vocula's force they set up their own camp a little way off. Shocked by this betrayal, Vocula retreated to Neuss with his legions. Classicus and Tutor followed with their cavalry and camped two miles from the Roman base. In the night, centurions and legionaries from Vocula's legions defected to the rebel cavalry camp, where Classicus offered them money to kill their general.

Ignoring advice from subordinates to flee, Vocula called a general assembly, and in a passionate speech, attempted to shore up the loyalty of his troops. Seeing his men unmoved, he returned to his pavilion and prepared to take his own life, before his freedmen and slaves talked him out of it. But this only delayed the inevitable. Later that night, deserters returned to the camp. A legionary from the 1st Germanica entered the general's tent and put him to the sword. Others seized Gallus, the 1st Germanica's commander, and Rufus, commander of the 5th Alaudae, putting them in chains.

At dawn, Classicus entered the camp, wearing the insignia of a Roman general, the scarlet cincticulus. With the legions assembled before him, he swore all the men to allegiance to the Empire of Gaul, an entity that at this point was no more than an aspiration. Classicus joined Civilis outside Old Camp with part of his force while Tutor took the larger part and entered Mainz.

The men of the legions stationed at Mainz arrested the tribunes in command of two of the units, while the camp prefect commanding a third contingent succeeded in escaping. Tutor entered the camp, put the two tribunes to death, then led the Roman troops in the camp and the townspeople in swearing loyalty to the Empire of Gaul. Tutor then moved on to Cologne. No Roman troops were based there, so taking the city and convincing the city senators of Cologne to switch their loyalty to the Empire of Gaul was not difficult. Once troops of the 1st Germanica Legion stationed at Bonn learned that Mainz and Cologne, the Roman administrative capitals of the provinces of Upper and Lower Germany, were in rebel hands, they voluntarily swore allegiance to the rebel cause, and awaited orders from Civilis. The Roman base at Vindonissa, modern Windisch in Switzerland, which had been the home base of the 21st Rapax Legion before it marched to Italy for Vitellius, was also taken over by rebel forces.

The only remaining loyal Roman army presence on the entire Rhine were the four thousand legionaries of the 5th Alaudae and 15th Primigenia under Lupercus at Campus Vetera. These men were on the verge of starvation and had resorted to eating grass, roots, and leather. Finally they agreed to go over to Civilis. Arresting Lupercus and his tribunes and senior centurions, these legionaries opened the camp gates to Civilis, and the legions begrudgingly swore allegiance to Civilis and his declared Empire of Gaul.

Lupercus and his officers were sent in chains by Civilis to Valeda, a German priestess who lived beside the Lippe River, but they never made it—rebels murdered the Roman officers en route. According to legend, Civilis trussed up other Roman centurions so his young son could use them for target practice with his child-size bow and arrow. Elements of seven legions—the 1st Germanica, 4th Macedonica, 5th Alaudae, 15th Primigenia, 16th Gallica, 18th and 22nd Primigenia— were now under rebel command, with the length of the Rhine from the North Sea to today's Switzerland in Civilis's hands, and all of Gaul open to him.

But almost as soon as Civilis was able to claim victory, the tide began to turn against him. In Gaul, Julius Sabinus had led the Lingones in an armed uprising, only for their Gallic neighbors the Sequani to remain loyal to Rome and go to war against them. The Sequani quickly defeated the Lingones, sending Sabinus into hiding. At the same time, Mucianus, the deputy of the new emperor Vespasian, arrived in Rome and took charge from Primus. As one of his first acts, Mucianus set in motion a campaign to retake the Rhine from Civilis, appointing two officers to lead it and dispatching orders to seven legions in Italy, Spain, and Britain to join it.

The overall commander of the operation was Annius Gallus, a former consul who had been one of Otho's generals in the short, unsuccessful war against Vitellius. Gallus had been incapacitated when his horse fell the previous April, however, so the lion's share of the work on the Rhine would fall to his deputy, the praetor Quintus Petilius Cerialis Caesius Rufus, a younger, fitter general. Cerialis was related to the emperor Vespasian by marriage, and had a lot to prove. During Boudicca's revolt in Britain, he had led two thousand men of the legion he commanded to annihilation in a rebel ambush. Then, just the previous December, Cerialis had led a cavalry force into an ambush outside the gates of Rome, as he attempted unsuccessfully to rescue Vespasian's brother Sabinus from the hands of Vitellius's troops. This time, he was determined not to fail.

While Gallus took his time marching for the Rhine, Cerialis hurried ahead with an advance force made up of the 21st Rapax Legion and an equivalent number of auxiliaries, plus the German troopers of the elite Singularian Horse, who had ridden for Otho against Vitellius. Until just weeks before, the 21st Rapax had been one of Vitellius's most loyal legions, but following the defeat at the Second Battle of Bedriacum its men had sworn for Vespasian. Ashamed of the submission to the rebels by their fellow legionaries on the Rhine, and keen to return to the Rhine and their de facto families there, the men of the 21st Rapax would prove fiercely loyal to Cerialis, this relative of their new emperor.

Leaders of the Gallic tribes were meeting at Durocortum, today's Reims in northern France, to decide their attitude toward Civilis's Empire of Gaul, when word arrived that a Roman force had crossed the Alps and was marching up through southern Gaul. Some leaders quaked at the news, but Civilis's representative at the meeting, the Treveran noble Tullius Valentinus, boasted that these fresh troops would simply be more fodder for rebel blades. When a vote was taken on whether all of Gaul would go to war with Rome, most of the tribes voted against, and Valentinus had to report to Civilis that they were on their own.

Meanwhile, the 1st Germanica and 16th Gallica Legions had been sent to Trier on the Moselle River by Civilis, along with the captive Roman generals Gallus and Rufus. Those generals were behind bars in Trier, but the legions were camped outside the city. With Valentinus away, the legions' men repented their oath to the Empire of Gaul and moved south, successfully reaching today's Metz, the capital of the Mediomatrici tribe, which had kept its loyalty to Rome. When Valentinus returned to Trier and found that the two legions had deserted the rebel cause, he flew into a rage and executed the generals Gallus and Rufus.

With unexpected speed Cerialis reached the Rhine with his ten-thousand-man Roman advance force. Splitting the force in two, he pushed down both sides of the Rhine at once, personally leading the 21st Rapax down one side while his deputy led the auxiliaries down the other. Among his auxiliary prefects, commanding the elite Singularian Horse cavalry wing, was none other than Civilis's nephew, Julius Briganticus, who hated his uncle. After liberating Windisch, the split force moved downriver toward Mainz. On the eastern bank of the Rhine, Cerialis's auxiliary infantry walked into an ambush set up by Julius Tutor, suffering heavy casualties.

But when word reached Tutor's men that the 21st Rapax Legion was approaching along the river's opposite bank, the legionaries in Tutor's force refused to fight fellow legionaries. Deserting Tutor, these legionaries marched for Mainz to place themselves back under Roman command. Tutor withdrew to Bingium, today's Bingen, where the Nahe River meets the Rhine, only to be surprised himself by Cerialis's deputy, who had regrouped his auxiliaries. Tutor's remaining troops were butchered, and Tutor fled down the Rhine to join Civilis.

At Mainz, Cerialis brought the returned legionaries into his force, then swung toward Trier. Some Treveran leaders, who until recently had been all for revolt, panicked and fled their city, but Valentinus levied every able-bodied Treveran into an army to repulse the Romans. Civilis and Classicus were marching to join him with their combined forces, sending messages to Valentinus not to engage in battle with Cerialis until they arrived. Outside Trier, Valentinus assembled his troops at a fortified hillside position beside the Moselle River that the Romans called Rigodulum.

As soon as the Roman commander Cerialis arrived at the Treveran position he launched an assault. Hoping to impress their general, the legionaries who had previously gone over to the rebels now showed outstanding bravery as they attacked uphill and overran the Treveri. Valentinus, trying to escape up the slope, ran into the waiting troopers of the Singularian Horse and was captured.

Trier threw open its gates to Cerialis, who entered and occupied it, forbidding his men to loot the city. He was asleep there early one morning a day or two later when he was abruptly awoken with the news that Civilis, Classicus, and Tutor had launched an attack on Trier and the legions encamped outside it. Once again Cerialis had allowed himself to be surprised by his enemy. Civilis had been opposed to this attack on the city, but Classicus and Tutor had talked him into it. By this stage he had dyed his hair red and was letting it grow long, as German warriors traditionally did when they went to war, and he led the assault on the city and the two legion camps outside it. Inside the city, the redheaded general Cerialis rose from his bed, grabbed his sword, and without even waiting for his attendants to strap on his armor, rushed out to lead the Roman counterattack.

Cerialis first drove off the rebels attacking the bridge that crossed the Moselle to Trier's main gate, then ran to the legion camps. He rallied the 1st Germanica and 16th Gallica Legions, which had only recently joined him from Metz, and which had been falling back, and then the 21st Rapax charged the rebels who were busy looting the camp. When the rebels were driven from the camp, Cerialis retained momentum by chasing them down the Moselle Valley.

At Cologne, where Civilis had left his wife, sister, and the daughter of Classicus, city leaders led a counter revolt, massacring a cohort of Germans stationed at the city by burning them alive in the barn where they slept. Then they arrested the rebel leaders' relatives and sent for Cerialis. After force-marching his army from Trier, the Roman general reached Cologne and made the women his prisoners. His army was soon bolstered by the arrival of the 14th Gemina Legion from Britain. Following the Battle of Bedriacum it had been sent back to its old station, Britain, only to be summoned back across the English Channel for this operation. On its march to Cologne, the 14th Gemina had accepted the surrender of Civilis's German allies the Nervii and Tungrii.

The revolt was not yet over, however. Civilis's original allies, the Canninefates, had sent warships against Rome's Britannic Fleet in the English Channel shortly after it delivered the 14th Gemina to Gaul, and sank half the Roman ships. The Nervii, to show their renewed loyalty to Rome, then sent a force of young men to punish the Canninefates, only for it to be swiftly wiped out.

Two more legions ordered by Mucianus to join Roman commander Cerialis arrived—one from Spain, the other from Italy. Now with a force of more than fifty thousand men, Cerialis advanced down the Rhine from Cologne. He found the legion base at Neuss burned out and abandoned. Continuing on, he came upon Campus Vetera. Civilis had broken an old Roman dyke to flood his path, and had formed up his army for battle. Civilis had decided to make a stand. He placed his Batavians on his right, with Gugerni on their outside. Ubians and Lingones filled his center. Beside the Rhine, the Bructeri and Tentheri Germans took the rebel army's left wing. Civilis addressed his men, declaring, "This day will either be the most glorious among the deeds of the past, or will be infamous in the eyes of posterity!"[102]

In the Battle of Old Camp that followed, as both sides were exchanging barrages of missiles, a Batavian deserter came to the Roman general Cerialis and promised to guide Roman cavalry via a dry route through the waterlogged ground, to enable an attack against the rebel right. Cerialis sent several hundred troopers with the man, whose information proved correct. This enabled the Roman cavalry to attack the Gugerni unexpectedly, from supposedly impassable ground. The charge broke the Gugerni, and the victory cry of the Roman cavalry was the cue for Cerialis to send his legions against the rebel center, which also broke. As heavy rain fell, Civilis and other rebel leaders escaped, fleeing all the way back to the Batavian "island."

Three more legions, along with the elderly operational commander Gallus, now arrived at Mainz from Rome. Retaining several legions, Gallus remained at Mainz, allowing Cerialis to continue the campaign. The operation would drag on for weeks, with riverside skirmishes as the rebels used hit-and-run tactics, even attacking Cerialis's own camp in a night raid, when the general was in bed with his German mistress. Among the Roman fatalities was Civilis's nephew Briganticus, commander of the Singularian Horse. Meanwhile, when one rebel raid backfired, Civilis, Classicus, and Tutor only escaped death by jumping into the Rhine. Swimming in the cold water, they were rescued by Germans in boats.

Cerialis sent messages offering a pardon to Civilis if he surrendered, and when Civilis heard that his own men were talking about handing him over and returning to Roman rule, he sent word to Cerialis that he wanted a parley, which Cerialis agreed to. The site for their meeting was a bridge that had been destroyed in the middle, on an unidentified river in today's Netherlands. Civilis stood at the Batavian end, Cerialis at the Gallic end, and the pair conversed by yelling across the gap.

As a result of this meeting, and the surrender terms offered and accepted, Civilis gave himself up to Cerialis. There the Roman record of him ends. Civilis is likely to have spent the rest of his life in house detention in an Italian city such as Ravenna, where Bato, the Dalmatian rebel, and Thusnelda, wife of the earlier German rebel Arminius, lived in comfortable exile.

Civilis's fellow rebel leaders did not fare as well. Of Classicus or Tutor we hear nothing, but the known fate of other rebels suggests both were executed. Valentinus the Treveran, we know, was captured, and executed on the orders of Vespasian's deputy Mucianus. Sabinus the Lingone was tracked down in hiding, and he and all his family were executed, with the Lingone leadership handing over seventy thousand armed rebels to the Roman military. Many of these Lingones would end up in new auxiliary units and posted to the far end of the Roman world.

The Batavi tribe again accepted Roman rule, with a new legion base built in their midst. The eight Batavian auxiliary cohorts that had rebelled were abolished and replaced with nine new Batavian cohorts filled with former rebels, which were immediately posted to Britain.

Batavian units were never again stationed on the Rhine, ensuring they would not become involved in the politics of their homeland.

Vespasian, the new emperor, punished the legions that had gone over to the rebels, despite the fact that they had returned their allegiance to Rome, been promised lenient treatment by Cerialis when they rejoined Roman ranks, and fought valiantly for Cerialis in the last weeks of the revolt. Vespasian was a hard-boiled soldier, and he had inherited the attitude of earlier emperors, who never pardoned a Roman legionary who voluntarily surrendered. These legions' fates were dictated by how prominent a role their legionaries had taken in the revolt. The 1st Germanica and 15th Primigenia Legions were abolished. The 4th Macedonica and 16th Gallica Legions were abolished and reconstituted as the 4th Flavia and 16th Flavia Legions. The 18th Legion was folded into the under-strength 7th Galbiana Legion in Spain, which became the 7th Gemina Legion. The Libyans of the four cohorts of the 18th in Egypt were apparently distributed around the legions in the East. The 5th Alaudae Legion, whose men were apparently considered not to have been ringleaders in the Rhine legion surrenders, remained in existence, but it was transferred well away from the Rhine to Moesia on the Danube.

As for Cerialis, the general who finally showed his mettle and put down the revolt, he was rewarded with a consulship and then dispatched by Vespasian to Britain in AD 71, to put down another rebellion, by Venutius the Briton.

Bust of the emperor Vespasian, who authorized the invasion of Commagene after Epiphanes covertly negotiated with Parthia. *Universal History Archive/ UIG/Bridgeman Images.*

XVII. EPIPHANES

THE PETULANT PRINCE. COMMAGENE, AD 72

The story of Epiphanes is the story of a rich, arrogant young prince who put his pride before his country, and as a result became a rebel against Rome and caused his father to lose his kingdom.

Located in the southeast of today's Turkey, Commagene had been a small but wealthy landlocked kingdom bordering Syria for hundreds of years by the time of the first-century Jewish Revolt in the Middle East. For much of this period Commagene had been an ally of Rome, acting as a buffer between Rome's eastern provinces and the powerful Parthian Empire. In AD 17, King Antiochus III, a cruel and unloved ruler of Commagene, died. His son and heir Antiochus IV was only a toddler, so, when Germanicus Caesar, then Roman commander in chief in the East, came through the region the following year, he placed Commagene under Roman control and installed one of his clients, Quintus Servaeus, as governor. At the same time, Germanicus sent little Antiochus and his sister Iotapa to Rome to be raised by his own mother, Antonia, the youngest daughter of Mark Antony.

In Rome, Antiochus and his sister lived at the Palatium and had as schoolmates and playmates a remarkable coterie of princes and princesses from around the Roman world, including Caligula, son of Germanicus, his sisters Agrippina and Drusilla, and Herod Agrippa, future king of Judea. Antiochus became thoroughly Romanized, taking the name Gaius Julius Antiochus. He also became a close friend of Caligula's. As soon as Caligula took the throne after the death of the emperor

Tiberius in AD 37 he installed Antiochus as king of Commagene, extending his realm to the Mediterranean. Caligula sent Antiochus and Iotapa home to Samosata, the capital of Commagene, cashed up with the equivalent of all the taxes Roma had levied on the country over the previous two decades. Antiochus was so grateful to Caligula that he renamed a city he rebuilt in west Commagene Germanicia Caesarea, after Caligula's now dead father Germanicus Caesar.

Just as Antiochus's father had married his own sister, a practice not uncommon in royal houses of the East, Antiochus married his sister Iotapa as soon as they returned home, and in AD 38 they had a son, Gaius Julius Archelaus Antiochus Epiphanes, followed by another son, Callinicus, and a daughter, another Iotapa. With Caligula becoming paranoid toward the end of his reign and mistrusting everyone near and far, he removed Antiochus from power. But, following Caligula's AD 41 assassination, Caligula's uncle Claudius was declared emperor by the Praetorian Guard, and Claudius restored Antiochus to his throne in Commagene.

Antiochus's eldest boy, Epiphanes, whose name meant "glorious," grew into an athletic, confident youth. When Epiphanes was just five years old he was betrothed in marriage to Drusilla, the daughter of King Agrippa of Judea, his father's boyhood friend. But once Epiphanes reached the marrying age of sixteen, he embarrassed his father by refusing to marry Drusilla, a famous beauty, because her father required him to adopt the Jewish faith. Instead, in AD 64, when Epiphanes was twenty-six, he married a distant relative, Claudia Capitolina of Alexandria.

Two years later, the First Jewish Revolt erupted in Judea and Galilee. Like other Roman client kings throughout the region, Antiochus IV sent a contingent of his own troops to join the Roman task force assembled to counter the revolt by the then Roman governor of Syria, Cestius Gallus. Gallus had sent to regional allies for 16,000 additional troops to join 14,000 legionaries and auxiliaries assigned to the task, and the allied troops were ordered to link up with Gallus at the Syrian port of Ptolemais.

King Herod Agrippa joined Governor Gallus bringing 3,000 of his own Jewish light infantry and 1,000 cavalry. King Sohaemus of the autonomous Syrian city-state of Emesa, which contained the mint that produced the pay of the Roman troops based in Syria and Judea, set off in the wake of the large Roman column as it marched to Ptolemais, bringing 1,500 of his personal cavalry and 2,500 foot archers. King Antiochus IV of Commagene, whose force would take the longest time to reach Ptolemais, sent 3,000 light infantry, 3,000 foot archers, and 2,000 cavalry who served under his scorpion standard.

In the past, during the early years of the reign of Nero, Antiochus had himself led his own military forces from Commagene in support of Roman operations. In AD 59 he had served under the tough Roman general Gnaeus Domitius Corbulo in Armenia, when Corbulo led several legions plus auxiliaries and allied troops against the forces of King Tiridates I of Armenia, brother of King Vologases of Parthia, ejecting Tiridates and setting a Roman puppet king on the Armenian throne. For supporting Corbulo, Nero added parts of Armenia to Antiochus's kingdom.

Perhaps limited by poor health, Antiochus did not personally participate in Corbulo's next campaign, in AD 62. Corbulo, who was governing Syria, was forced to intervene at the head of two legions after a Roman army led by the governor of Cappadocia, Lucius Caesennius Paetus, lost a battle against the Parthians, surrendered a Roman fortress, and retreated out of the country. Supported by troops from Commagene, Corbulo had driven out the Parthians and restored Roman control to Armenia.

It was possibly ill health that again prevented Antiochus from leading his forces when he sent the eight thousand troops to Gallus's army in opposing the Jewish rebels. We aren't told the name of the commander of the Commagene contingent, but it is likely that Antiochus's eldest son, the now twenty-eight-year-old Epiphanes, was champing at the bit to be involved and was bitterly disappointed when his father prevented him from taking part in the operation.

As it turned out, Epiphanes was fortunate not to be involved, for he avoided a military disaster. Gallus's task force of thirty thousand men reached Jerusalem, but after a brief siege the Roman commander withdrew his army and retreated all the way back to his palace in Antioch. En route, the Roman and allied forces serving under Gallus lost 5,630 men, killed at the hands of Jewish partisans, who harassed them almost all the way to the Mediterranean coast. Several senior officers, including the general commanding the 6th Ferrata Legion, were among the dead, and the sacred eagle standard of the 12th Fulminata Legion was captured by the partisans. More importantly, Jerusalem and much of Galilee and Judea were left in Jewish hands as Antiochus's surviving troops returned to Commagene for the winter. The Roman commander Gallus died at Antioch that December.

In early AD 67, Nero summoned his best general, Titus Vespasian, to a meeting at Corinth in Greece, and gave him the job of terminating the Jewish Revolt. The army that Vespasian assembled for the task at Ptolemais included four legions, numerous auxiliary units, and once again, units of light infantry, archers, and cavalry supplied by allied kingdoms of the region, including a Commagene contingent. This time, Antiochus put his son Epiphanes at the head of his troops.

By the time Nero committed suicide in June AD 68, Vespasian's army had clawed back much of Galilee and Judea, with just several rebel-occupied cities and fortresses, including Jerusalem, Masada, and Machaerus, yet to be dealt with. With Nero's death, Vespasian brought operations against Jewish rebels almost to a standstill over the next twelve months, as he awaited fresh orders from a succession of new emperors—Galba, Otho, and Vitellius. The following July, when the Roman legions stationed in Alexandria, Syria, and Judea proclaimed Vespasian their emperor, in opposition to Vitellius in Rome, several rulers of eastern allied states including Antiochus of Commagene also swore allegiance to Vespasian.

By the winter of AD 69–70, the Commagene contingent in Vespasian's army was back home. By that time, Vespasian had handed his twenty-nine-year-old son Titus the task of taking Jerusalem from the Jewish rebels, and by the end of AD 69 Titus had assembled a fresh army at Ptolemais for the task. Antiochus was slow to send troops to support Rome a third time. It wasn't until well into the spring campaign that Epiphanes turned up outside the walls of Jerusalem to join Titus, leading a new Commagene contingent made up entirely of thousands of Macedonian mercenaries—almost certainly men from Antiochus's personal bodyguard.

Titus had halted his siege of Jerusalem to give the encircled rebels and the million civilians trapped in the city the opportunity to surrender, but when his peace bid was rebuffed by the rebels he resolved to press on with the siege. He was personally going around the four massive Roman siege ramps that were slowly growing against the city's walls, urging the legionaries working on them to toil harder and faster, when Epiphanes arrived with his reinforcements.

Thirty-two-year-old Epiphanes considered himself a fine soldier, and he chided Titus, a younger man who wasn't even old enough for membership in the Roman Senate, for the tardiness of his troops so far. Titus smiled and said he would join with Epiphanes in any attack he cared to launch with his Macedonians. But Epiphanes ignored him and promptly led a surprise attack against the city wall with his mercenaries. While the prince of Commagene indeed proved a valiant fighter, his Macedonians made no progress against the wall and its defenders, and they retired with numerous casualties. Epiphanes's only wound was to his all-consuming pride. To make things worse, Titus never used the Commagene contingent for frontline assaults after that. They would have been assigned to rear echelon duties such as guarding prisoners.

On the conclusion of the siege of Jerusalem with the capture of the city in September AD 70, the majority of units that had served in the Roman army during the campaign were dispatched to their bases, in several cases at new locations. Only the 10th Fretensis Legion remained, tasked with physically destroying the city stone by stone. By this stage, a new Roman proconsul, Lucius Caesennius Paetus, had arrived in Antioch to take over the governorship of the province of Syria. This was the very same Paetus who'd performed so badly in Armenia years before, but he was a client of Vespasian, having married Vespasian's niece Sabina, the daughter of his recently killed brother Sabinus, and Vespasian always looked after his clients.

At this point Prince Epiphanes returned with his troops to Commagene an unhappy man, and he would quickly have moved to the footnotes of Roman history had it not been for what he did next. Apparently, he felt that Titus had humiliated him outside Jerusalem, and he would have almost certainly discovered that Paetus, the new Roman governor of Syria and the most powerful Roman administrator in the East, was antagonistic toward his father, Antiochus, so Epiphanes opened up a secret dialogue with the king of Parthia, Vologases I, about bringing Commagene into the Parthian orbit. It is unlikely that Epiphanes's father, Antiochus, knew anything about this. Expanding his anti-Rome activities, Epiphanes also covertly encouraged the nobles of Commagene to refrain from meeting their annual tax obligations to Rome.

Inevitably, in AD 71, word that envoys from King Antiochus's court were conducting secret discussions with the Parthian king reached the ears of Rome's governor Paetus in Syria. The fact that Antiochus was having trouble collecting the annual Roman taxes from his nobles would also have alarmed him. As a result, Paetus wrote increasingly frantic letters to Vespasian at Rome, seeking permission to lead an army into Commagene and annex it as a Roman province, ostensibly to forestall Parthian annexation and restore the kingdom's tax payments to Rome.

Initially, Vespasian did nothing about Paetus's letters. He liked King Antiochus, who had always been a faithful Roman ally, and he knew from past experience in Armenia that Paetus could be easily panicked. He also knew that Paetus was a greedy man, and Commagene was the richest kingdom among all Rome's eastern allies; in annexing Commagene, Paetus would create the opportunity to pocket large sums.

On the other hand, it had taken much blood and treasure in Armenia to keep Commagene from Vologases' grasp two decades earlier, and Vespasian didn't want another costly war with the Parthians to regain it yet again. Besides, Antiochus's capital, Samosata, sat on the upper reaches of the Euphrates River, controlling an important river crossing into the kingdom of Osrhoene, a longtime Parthian ally. In the end, Vespasian chose not to risk allowing Commagene to fall into Parthian hands, and in AD 72 he authorized Paetus to invade and annex Commagene.

Paetus seemed not to expect much resistance, for he led just a single legion, the 6th Ferrata, known as the Ironclad legion, across Syria's northern border into Commagene from the base at Cyrrhus. The legion would have been accompanied by its usual complement of supporting auxiliary light infantry and cavalry, so the force that Paetus took into Commagene would have numbered around ten thousand men. King Antiochus's army probably totaled around twenty thousand men, but, despite being outnumbered two to one, Paetus was relying on shock and surprise to bring him swift victory.

Sure enough, marching rapidly northeast, Paetus's force reached Commagene's capital of Samosata without meeting any resistance. Only there, beside the Euphrates, did Antiochus's army hastily line up for battle. As for Antiochus himself, he had fled upon learning of the Roman invasion. He headed west into the Commagenian part of Cilicia with his bodyguards, leaving Epiphanes and his younger brother Callinicus to deal with the Romans.

The two armies faced off in battle order for a full day, and there may have even been an exchange of missiles, but among Commagene's troops there was little desire to fight their powerful longtime Roman allies, and by nightfall they had laid down their arms. Epiphanes, his pregnant wife, Claudia, and his brother Callinicus escaped across the Euphrates into Osrhoene, taking with them a number of wealthy tax-avoiding Commagene nobles, "a large group of men liable to taxation," as a contemporary inscription described them. From there they would enter Parthia proper and seek asylum with King Vologases.[103]

Vespasian officially annexed Commagene, making it a new front-line Roman province, with the 6th Ferrata Legion becoming the province's permanent military garrison. Stationed in Samosata, the legion built itself a new base overlooking the Euphrates. But Vespasian was concerned about the future of Antiochus and his family. For one thing, he didn't want them in the East, where they might become the focal point for Commagenians bent on restoring their royalty. He wanted Antiochus and his sons close. But he also wanted to ensure they were well looked after.

Firstly, the emperor began negotiations via envoys with Antiochus in Cilicia. Antiochus agreed to relocate permanently to Rome, where he would live in a palace as a wealthy and honored member of Vespasian's court. Simultaneously, Vespasian sent a trusted centurion on a mission to the Parthian capital. The highly decorated Gaius Velius Rufus had been the chief centurion of the 12th Fulminata Legion during the siege of Jerusalem, where he had come to know Epiphanes. His job was to convince Epiphanes and his brother to accompany him to Rome—not in chains, but with their entourage and a Roman military escort. Once there, they would join their father in permanent but luxurious exile.

Parthia's King Vologases admired and respected Vespasian. Back in AD 69 he had even offered to loan Vespasian forty thousand archers to help him take the Roman throne from Vitellius, an offer Vespasian had politely declined. Vologases would have been glad to rid himself of the two troublesome princes from Commagene, and he put no obstacles in the way of them accepting Centurion Rufus's offer.

So it was that Epiphanes, his wife and his brother, and the nobles of Commagene who had accompanied them to Parthia traveled out of Parthia with Velius Rufus and a legionary escort. Everywhere in the Roman world they passed through en route to Rome, the members of the Commagenian party were treated as honored guests. Not long after they reached Rome in AD 72 and reunited with King Antiochus, Epiphanes's wife gave birth to their newest child.

King Antiochus died in Rome several years later, after which Epiphanes moved, with imperial approval, to Athens, Greece, with his family. He died there in AD 92 during the reign of Vespasian's second son, Domitian. Aged just fifty-four, he was wealthy but forgotten, and he never again troubled Roman historians by acting as a rebel against Rome.

Bust of the emperor Domitian, object of Saturninus's revolt. *Bridgeman Images.*

XVIII. SATURNINUS

REVOLTING AGAINST DOMITIAN.
THE RHINE, AD 89

By the winter of AD 88–89, Lucius Antonius Saturninus could stomach no more of his emperor Domitian, who had been on the throne for seven years. As a senator, Saturninus had been a faithful client of Domitian's father, the emperor Vespasian, who had rewarded him with appointments to gubernatorial posts in Macedonia and Judea. Once Domitian succeeded his brother Titus as emperor in AD 81, the young ruler soon elevated Saturninus to the consulship and by AD 87 had appointed him to the important job of governor of the province of Upper Germany, which entailed command of four resident legions. On the face of it, Saturninus had every reason to be grateful to Domitian. But the governor had come to dread every move the emperor made.

Domitian had an insatiable thirst for personal glory, and was jealous of all others who earned it. This desire for glory manifested itself in several ways. Firstly, he spent money as if there was an endless supply. For public popularity, he established several lavish new festivals and public games, and, being a lover of chariot racing as Caligula and Nero had been, he added two new teams, the Golds and the Purples, to the four existing racing corporations. He built a massive new palace for himself on the Palatine Hill, one that far eclipsed all the earlier imperial palaces and even included a chariot racing course. He not only restored Rome's Temple of Capitoline Jupiter after it had been destroyed by fire for the second time in AD 80, he built a second temple to Jupiter on Capitol Hill. He also built a new forum in Rome, and a stadium, a concert hall, as well as the Naumachia, an artificial lake for the staging of sea battles for public entertainment. On Rome's Quirinal Hill he erected a temple dedicated to his family, the Flavians, on the site of his childhood home and that of his late uncle Sabinus. All of these architectural works were inscribed with Domitian's name as their benefactor, and when he restored a building he would have the original builder's name erased so that only he received credit.

Domitian's need for military glory had first shown itself in AD 70, just weeks into his father's reign, when, as a nineteen-year-old, he insisted on taking a lead in the operation to put down the Civilis Revolt on the Rhine. To humor him, his father's astute deputy Mucianus had taken the youth as far as Gaul while the general Petilius Cerialis, who was related by marriage to Domitian and his family, led the advance force to the Rhine. Mucianus and Domitian were still in Italy, on the way to Gaul, when one of the captured rebel commanders, Valentinus, a native of Trier, was brought before them. Valentinus was allowed to speak his piece before Mucianus ordered his immediate execution, as Domitian watched. It was said that even Caligula averted his eyes when men were beheaded in front of him, but Domitian never as much as blinked.

Once Mucianus and Domitian reached Lugdunum, today's Lyon, the capital of the province of Gallia Lugdunensis, Domitian sent secret emissaries to Cerialis as he led the campaigning army against Civilis, asking whether, should Domitian arrive on the scene, Cerialis would hand over command to him. Cerialis replied in patronizing terms, neither saying yes or no, and would later excuse Domitian's grab for power as "an idle and childish ambition."[104]

By AD 83, after two years as emperor, Domitian was becoming jealous of his own victorious general, Gnaeus Julius Agricola, the current governor of Britain, who was pushing through northern Britain and into Caledonia in a successful but grinding campaign designed to bring Scotland into the empire. For the AD 83 campaigning season, the thirty-one-year-old Domitian transferred vexillations from all four of Agricola's legions from Britain to the Rhine, where he combined them with the legions stationed there. Having gone to Gaul on the pretense of conducting a census in the Gallic provinces, he went instead to the Rhine and personally led this massive army across the river in a surprise attack on the Chatti in today's Bavaria, an unsuspecting German tribe that had a peace treaty with Rome.

In this campaign, Domitian's troops drove tribes from their forests and farmlands and established a line of forts in German territory, even paying locals for their land. On returning to Rome to celebrate what he claimed was a great military victory, Domitian held what Tacitus would call a "sham Triumph," taking slaves from the slave market and dressing them as German warriors to masquerade as Chatti prisoners of war in a triumphal parade through the streets of Rome.[105]

The following year, Domitian's exploit was easily eclipsed when Agricola won a massive victory in a set battle against the Caledonians at Mons Graupius in Scotland. Domitian said and did all the right things, praising Agricola in the Senate and awarding him Triumphal Decorations, the near equivalent of a Triumph. But the jealous Domitian was furious, and the following year he recalled Agricola to Rome. Realizing that his life was on the line, Agricola went into quiet retirement, but when a mystery illness took his life at the age of only fifty-three, it was widely rumored that Domitian had poisoned him. Other former consuls would be executed by Domitian—seven in six years. Even his own cousin Domitius Celer, who had escaped the siege of the Capitol alongside Domitian in AD 69, would fall victim to Domitian's paranoia.

In AD 85, Decebalus, the newly crowned king of Dacia, a kingdom that included today's Romania north of the Danube, led his army in crossing the great river and invading Rome's Danubian province of Moesia. The Dacians savaged the 4th Macedonia Legion, killing its commander, before withdrawing back across the river with loot and prisoners galore. The following year, Domitian led a punitive expedition to the Danube. While Domitian sat idly in a Danubian city, he sent his Praetorian Prefect, Cornelius Fuscus, across the river to punish the Dacians. Fuscus walked into a trap and was killed, and a legion, almost certainly the 5th Alaudae, was wiped out by the Dacians. Roman survivors fled across the Danube to Moesia with tales of a large, curved Dacian sword that sliced through Roman helmets and heads, as if cutting butter.

Terrified by these disasters, Domitian scuttled back to Rome, and in AD 87 he made preparations for a fresh Roman incursion into Dacia to punish Decebalus. In the autumn of AD 88, while he remained at Rome, he sent another Roman army across the Danube. Led by Tettius Julianus, a former consul and onetime commander of the 7th Claudia Legion, this army succeeded in crossing the Danube and mountain passes undetected by the Dacians to emerge close to Decebalus's capital, Sarmizegetusa, today's Varhely. At Tapae, a fortress that guarded the southern approaches to Sarmizegetusa, Julianus routed a Dacian army led by Decebalus's deputy Vezinas. The Dacian general escaped by pretending to be dead, but his army was devastated. Julianus, instead of withdrawing to Roman territory for the winter, camped in Dacian territory in preparation for an attack on the Dacian capital in the spring.

Well before Julianus's victory, Saturninus, the governor of Upper Germany, had been exchanging secret correspondence from his gubernatorial palace at Mogantiacum, today's Mainz, on the Rhine, with fellow senators at Rome, canvassing the idea of removing Domitian from the throne by force. It is likely that Saturninus feared he would be next to earn an undeserved death sentence from his unstable emperor. That summer, encouraged by the responses he'd received from Rome, Saturninus set in motion a plan to lead his legions in revolt. Taking a page from Vitellius's AD 69 playbook, he set out to attract the support of the army as a whole and overthrow the sitting emperor.

Whether Saturninus saw himself as a future emperor, or, like Vindex twenty years before, planned to place another senator on the throne, is unclear. Certainly, behind closed doors at Rome, various potential candidates to replace Domitian were being discussed; the retired general Agricola predicted confidentially to his son-in-law, the historian Tacitus, that he believed the Spanish-born soldier and states-man Marcus Trajan would one day become emperor.[106]

Saturninus was confident that the two legions based with him at Mainz, the 14th Gemina (later the 14th Gemina Martia Victrix) and the 21st Rapax, would follow his lead. He wasn't so sure about the two remaining legions in his province, or the four legions farther down the Rhine in Lower Germany. So he decided to bring the German tribes immediately opposite Mainz into his plan. He would pay them to join his legions on the march on Rome. To raise the money to pay the Ger-mans, Saturninus emptied the banks of his own legionaries at Mainz, without their knowledge.

Those legionary savings, accumulated over twenty years of legion service and administered by each legion's eagle-bearer, the sergeant ma-jor of the unit, would have amounted to more than twenty million sesterces if each soldier had an average of just 2,000 sesterces in the bank—legionaries were paid 900 sesterces a year, and centurions up to 20,000 a year, and on top of that they made significantly more money from donatives from the emperor and the sale of booty from their cam-paigns. Once the German tribes received their money from the em-peror, they agreed to mass on the eastern bank of the Rhine during the coming winter, when the Rhine was frozen over, then cross the ice to join his army.

As far as the tribes were concerned, part of the attraction of Sat-urninus's plan would have been the guarantee that, once Domitian had been done away with, the next emperor would launch no surprise attacks across the Rhine on those tribes who helped put him on the throne. It was still a dangerous plan, letting loose thousands of German warriors in Roman territory, but Saturninus believed the tribal leaders when they promised to return home once Domitian was out of the way.

Unfortunately for Saturninus, his plan leaked out at the last mo-ment—including the date, in January AD 89—that the German tribes would cross the Rhine. Certainly, to have legions intact for his winter coup, Saturninus would have canceled the usual winter furloughs that would have allowed thousands of his troops to leave their camps from December and return in March for the spring marching season, and this could have raised suspicions and prompted investigation by officers loyal to Domitian.

Saturninus addressed his two legions at Mainz during the usual January 1 assembly when legionaries annually renewed their vow of allegiance to their emperor, and had them swear to follow him instead. As this was happening, an army of several legions was marching up the Rhine from Cologne in the province of Lower Germany to counter him. Meanwhile, in Dacia, Julianus had received urgent orders to abandon the Dacian campaign and return to Moesia to support efforts against Saturninus. Packing up his winter camp, he hurriedly withdrew, returning to the Danube and re-crossing it. It is also reported that Marcus Trajan, who was commanding the 7th Gemina Legion in Nearer Spain, had received orders to march to the Rhine to help counter the attempted coup, and he appears to have set off for Germany with his unit. Domitian himself set off from Rome to take command of the efforts to counter Saturninus, accompanied by a number of senators who strapped on swords to demonstrate their fidelity to their emperor, plus a large Praetorian Guard escort.

Cassius Dio, writing his *Roman History* two centuries later, would name the general leading the force from Lower Germany as Lucius Maximus. Dio seems to have confused Lucius Laberius Maximus, previously a Praetorian prefect under Domitian and a man who never rose above Equestrian status, with Maximus's son, Manius Laberius Maximus. This Laberius Maximus, a senator, appears to have only been of legion commander rank.

The force Maximus led from Lower Germany arrived at Mainz close to the day the German tribes had agreed to cross the river to link up with Saturninus. On the appointed day, the anti-coup legions lined up for battle outside Mainz, as Saturninus's two legions did the same, and on the far bank of the Rhine, thousands of fully armed German warriors arrived to keep their appointment with Saturninus.

But nature would play a cruel trick on the rebel governor. It was an unusually mild winter that year, so much so that, on this very day, the ice covering the Rhine at Mainz began to melt and crack. Germans would have attempted to cross, only to crash through cracking ice into the freezing water, with scenes of ungainly rescue by their comrades following. Neither the Germans nor Saturninus possessed boats, so the German crossing of the Rhine was canceled, and Domitian would later be able to claim that the gods were on his side.

Having witnessed this calamity from their side of the Rhine, and faced by their comrades in arms of the legions of the Lower Rhine, Saturninus's legions suddenly rediscovered their allegiance to Domitian. Saturninus and his senior officers were arrested by their own men and handed over to Laberius Maximus in chains.

On searching Saturninus's quarters, Maximus discovered chests full of incriminating letters from senior Romans who had encouraged Saturninus to revolt. Finding letters from men he knew well, some probably his own relatives, Maximus burnt the lot, protecting their authors from blackmail, and preventing Domitian from learning their identities and executing them. Dio was highly impressed by this act, which put Maximus's own life at risk. "I do not see how I could praise him enough," he would write later.[107]

Domitian was still in Italy en route to the Rhine when news of Saturninus's arrest and the termination of the revolt was received. An elderly and infirm senator in Domitian's party who had reluctantly joined his emperor's party now said to him, "You have conquered, emperor, as I always prayed. Allow me to retire, therefore to my country estate."[108]

Domitian was jubilant at the news from Mainz—and the old man was indeed allowed to retire. But Domitian still wanted blood. While he returned to Rome, he expected Laberius Maximus to determine the guilty and dole out swift punishment. Sure enough, Saturninus was executed at Mainz, as would have been the senators commanding Saturninus's two briefly rebellious legions. At least one of the military tribunes serving as second in command of these legions would have met a similar fate, but the other, Julius Calvaster, saved himself with a unique defense. Calvaster, a handsome young man in his twenties, answered the allegation that he had frequently met in private with Saturninus leading up to the rebellion by stating that he had been having an amorous homosexual affair with his governor, not planning treason.

The severed heads of Saturninus and his executed officers were sent to Rome, where, on Domitian's orders, they were displayed on pikes in the Forum for their families and all of Rome to see. And, although he did not possess the incriminating letters Laberius Maximus had destroyed, Domitian embarked on a purge of senators whom he suspected of supporting or encouraging Saturninus to revolt. "It would be impossible to say how many he killed," Dio writes, because Domitian destroyed all record of those he executed in the wake of Saturninus's revolt.[109]

Manius Laberius Maximus, the general who put down the revolt, was rewarded by Domitian with a *suffect*, or replacement, consulship between September and December of that year. And as a consequence of the Saturninus Revolt, Domitian ordered the 14th Gemina and 21st Rapax Legions separated, with the Rapax transferred at once to Pannonia. Domitian also ruled that a maximum of one thousand sesterces per man could thereafter be held in legion banks, and required that only a single legion could occupy any base. Where two legions were at the same winter base, one had to move elsewhere and build themselves a new home from scratch. To cement the loyalty of the army's rank and file behind him, Domitian raised the annual salary of legionaries from 900 to 1,200 sesterces, the legionaries' first pay rise in a century.

Even though Saturninus failed to eliminate Domitian, fear and resentment of the increasingly erratic emperor would grow throughout Rome over the next five years, as his spending, including the big annual increase in army pay, emptied the civil and military treasuries. This culminated in the September 18, AD 96, assassination of Domitian. The forty-four-year-old emperor was murdered in his palace bedroom by freedmen on his staff—men closest to him and most trusted by him. One of his assassins had gone to the length of sabotaging the sword that Domitian kept by his bed, so that when the emperor reached for it in the night, he found, on drawing the sword from its scabbard, no blade attached to the hilt. Domitian became one of eight first-century emperors to die via murder or suicide. Only four died of illness or old age.

His wife of twenty-six years, Domitia, had come to fear for her own life at Domitian's hands, and was complicit in the plot. And while Domitian's Praetorian prefects played no active role in the murder, many Roman historians believed they were aware of it and turned a blind eye, as did many senators. Certainly, there was a swift, smooth, and bloodless transition to Domitian's successor as emperor, the elderly, highly respected senator Nerva, suggesting that Domitian's demise was expected and planned for. The army, whose loyalty Domitian had bought, was far from happy, however, and on its demand the assassins were executed rather than thanked.

Sellah coins produced by Simon Bar-Kokhba during his Jewish Revolt. © *Zev Radovan/Bridgeman Images.*

XIX. SIMON BAR-KOKHBA

SECOND JEWISH REVOLT LEADER.
PALESTINE, AD 131-135

Following the First Jewish Revolt of AD 66–73, Jews were banned from the destroyed city of Jerusalem, but they flourished elsewhere in Judea and beyond, confident of their ultimate reoccupation of Jerusalem and reconstruction of their Temple. A twentieth-century Jewish historian writes, "Every Jew believed in his heart that the day of his return to Jerusalem was not far off."[110]

Jewish opposition to Roman rule had bubbled up between 115 and 117 in Cyrenaica, Egypt, Cyprus, and Mesopotamia, only to be quickly quelled by Roman force of arms. In the summer of 131, when the emperor Hadrian visited the former Jerusalem, which had been home to the 10th Fretensis Legion since the year 70, he ordered a new city built, Aelia Capitolina, with temples to Jupiter and Venus, and a marble pig over the main gate—an insult to the Jews.

This incensed the Jews, who turned to Shimon-bar-Koziba, literally "Simon son of a Liar," who claimed descent from King David. Akiva ben Yosel, the most influential rabbi of the day, renamed him Bar-Kokhba, or "Son of the Star," implying he was the still-awaited Jewish Messiah. With this endorsement, Simon Bar-Kokhba attracted a vast Jewish following, to which he gave secret instructions to prepare for war in the coming year. The Jews of Judea and Galilee supplied the Roman army with weapons as part of the annual "tribute" they paid Rome, and now they began making faulty weapons, which were returned to them with instructions to make good. In this way, the Jews openly made weapons for themselves.

The entire population of Judea and Galilee was watched over by two resident legions, which had grown lazy through inactivity. When revolt erupted in the spring of 132, the Romans were caught completely by surprise, with tens of thousands of Jews taking up arms. It appears the rebels overran the 10th Fretensis base at the former Jerusalem, causing heavy Roman casualties, and cut off the 6th Ferrata Legion at its base at Caparcotna, later Legio, in Galilee. Rebel bands then roamed the countryside, killing Roman traders on the roads, ambushing cohorts on the march, and ransacking supply columns. When Christians in the province refused to join the rebels, they were killed.

With inland Judea and Galilee mostly in rebel hands, the Roman procurator of Judea, Tineus Rufus, who was based on the coast at Caesarea with part of the 10th Fretensis, sent panicked messages begging for help from the emperor, who was by then in Greece. Disgusted by the poor performance of the procurator and his legions, Hadrian ordered the governor of Britain, Sextus Julius Severus, one of his best generals, to cross the Roman world to Judea and take charge, giving him broad powers.

It was the spring of 133 before Severus and a detachment of Roman auxiliary troops from Britain arrived in Caesarea, aboard warships of the Misene Fleet from Italy. Severus wasn't in a position to commence operations against the rebels until the summer. Shocked to find the 10th Fretensis Legion drastically reduced by losses in the early stages of the revolt, Severus took the almost unprecedented step of granting citizenship to hundreds of sailors and marines from the warships that had brought him East, transferring them to the depleted ranks of the 10th Fretensis.

Because so many experienced centurions had been lost, Severus even made the prefect of one of the auxiliary units he'd brought from Britain a first rank centurion of the 10th Fretensis, a demotion. From Arabia, Severus summoned the 3rd Cyrenaica Legion, and from Syria, the 3rd Gallica Legion. A vexillation of several cohorts of the 4th Scythica Legion also joined him from their base at Raphanaea in Syria.

By this stage, Bar-Kokhba, styling himself "President of Israel," had set up his headquarters with a Sanhedrin governing council at Bethar, an ancient twenty-five-acre hilltop fortress eight miles southwest of Jerusalem. Canyons ran around three sides of the hill, and the rebels dug a moat across the stony saddle on the fourth side and improved the fort's walls. From there, Bar-Kokhba forwarded orders to his regional administrators and distributed his own currency, which he'd begun minting in AD 132 with inscriptions such as "Year 1 of the Liberty of Israel."

The Roman general Severus, adding the newly arrived units to the battered resident legions, created numerous mobile strike forces, which he sent throughout the region that summer. These troops took as prisoners any Jewish men, women, and children they found, locked them up, and starved them to death. Jews were forced to flee to Bethar for Bar-Kokhba's protection, and soon there were at least 200,000—many more, according to some Jewish sources—at the overcrowded fortress, where there was standing room only. Severus now surrounded and besieged Bethar while mobile units sought out Jews hiding in remote places.

By the spring of 135, Severus's siege army had been reinforced by two legions transferred temporarily from Moesia, the 5th Macedonica and the 11th Claudia. Employing a tactic used at the siege of Masada sixty-two years earlier, Severus's troops labored in oppressive summer heat building an earth ramp across the moat in the saddle to Bethar. One day in late August or early September, the legions surged into the fortress, killing indiscriminately. Simon Bar-Kokhba was among the dead. According to Cassius Dio, 530,000 Jews were killed during the campaign and many others died from starvation or illness.[111]

As the Roman troops went home, Hadrian changed the name of the province to Syria Palaestina, and banned Jews from even laying eyes on their former city of Jerusalem.

Bust of the emperor Marcus Aurelius, object of the revolt of Avidius Cassius.
Bridgeman Images.

XX. AVIDIUS CASSIUS

ACCIDENTAL EMPEROR. SYRIA AND EGYPT, AD 175

Gaius Avidius Cassius was one of emperor Marcus Aurelius's most trusted and successful generals. Born at the onetime legion town of Cyrrhus in Syria, the son of a freedman, he rose to senatorial rank before being appointed governor of Syria. Nobly and bravely had Cassius served his emperor and friend, between AD 162 and 166 repelling a Parthian invasion of Syria that had seen the 22nd Deiotariana legion wiped out, then driving the Parthians from Armenia and marching into the heart of Parthia and destroying one of its capitals, Ctesiphon.

In AD 175, Cassius received a letter from the empress Faustina, with whom it was rumored he'd earlier had an affair, informing him that the emperor, then based at Carnuntum and fighting the Iazyges tribe from beyond the Danube, was gravely ill and about to die. Faustina felt Cassius would make a far better emperor than Marcus's odious thirteen-year-old son, Commodus—the young emperor depicted in the 2000 movie *Gladiator*—and urged Cassius to declare himself emperor the moment that Marcus died. Subsequently receiving word that Marcus had passed away, Cassius immediately declared himself emperor, and the legions based in Syria, Palestine, and Egypt all swore loyalty to him.

The only problem was, as Cassius soon learned, that Marcus was not dead; in fact, he had recovered. But Cassius had come too far to back down. His declaration stood, and Rome had two rival emperors. This forced Marcus to hastily seal a peace treaty with the Iazyges. He then set off overland for the East with the empress and an army to deal with the usurper.

When news that Marcus Aurelius was coming swept through the legions in the East, support for Cassius began to evaporate. Three months and six days after Cassius had declared himself emperor, a centurion named Antonius from Cassius's mounted bodyguard drew his sword and slashed Cassius across the neck, then galloped away. But Cassius wasn't dead. So, a decurion, a squadron commander from his bodyguard, finished him off. The head of the accidental emperor was chopped off and sent to Marcus. But the emperor refused to look at his former friend's severed head, ordering it buried at once.

Although the threat posed by Cassius had been removed, Marcus continued his march to Syria to cement the loyalty of the eastern legions behind him. In July, the legions in Syria swore an oath of allegiance to him. Late in the year, the emperor set off back to Rome. That winter of AD 175–176, at Halala in the Taurus Mountains of Cappadocia, the empress Faustina, Marcus's beloved wife of thirty years, who had married him at the age of fifteen and given him sixteen children, suddenly died. No evidence survives as to whether she died from illness or accident, or was put to death on Marcus's orders for stimulating Cassius's grab for power. Or perhaps it was suicide. Marcus mourned her deeply, having her remains interred in the Mausoleum of her great-uncle the emperor Hadrian at Rome, and declaring her a goddess.

Marcus finally died in March AD 180, smothered by his own physicians as a favor to nineteen-year-old Commodus, according to the historian Cassius Dio, whose father was alive at the time. The lazy, cruel Commodus did succeed his father, and indeed turned out to be one of Rome's worst emperors. According to Dio, Rome under Commodus went "from a kingdom of gold to one of iron and rust."[112]

Jasper ring bearing the image of Postumus, first emperor of the rebel Gallic Empire. © *Christies' Images/Bridgeman Images.*

XXI. POSTUMUS, LAELIANUS, MARIUS, VICTORINUS, AND TETRICUS

THE GALLIC EMPIRE. GAUL, SPAIN, BRITAIN, RAETIA, AND THE RHINE, AD 260–274

For fourteen years in the third century, much of the Roman Empire beyond the Alps was ruled by a series of rogue emperors, in defiance of the established emperor of Rome, running a poorly documented Gallic Empire.

It began in AD 260, when Marcus Cassianus Latinius Postumus, the handsome Batavian-born Roman governor of Lower Germany, took advantage of chaos in the empire following the Parthians' capture of the emperor Valerian, and declared himself emperor of Gaul. Soon, he extended his rule to the German provinces, then Raetia, Britain, and Spain. Running a well-ordered administration and preventing German insurgency across the Rhine, Postumus subsequently beat off two attempts by Valerian's son and successor Gallienus to overcome him, although Gallienus did succeed in retaking Raetia. Gallienus's successor, the soldier-emperor Claudius II Gothicus, then succeeded in wresting Spain and part of southern Gaul from Postumus's control.

In 269, Postumus had to storm the city of Mainz after his governor of Upper Germany, Laelianus, declared himself emperor following Postumus's losses to Claudius II. Laelianus was killed, but when Postumus refused to permit his victorious troops to loot Mainz, he was killed by his own men. The murder was led by a common soldier, Marcus

Marius, who declared himself emperor.

Marius was swiftly disposed of by the Gallic-born Victorinus, the commander of Postumus's Praetorian Guard, who declared himself Emperor of Gaul. Now, the city of Augustodunum, today's Autun in northern France, declared loyalty to Claudius II, so Victorinus lay siege to it and overran it, only to be overthrown by Tetricus, a fellow Gaul and former member of Postumus's administration. Tetricus ruled until 274, when Aurelian, who had been the emperor of Rome since 270, marched into Gaul. Aurelian, fresh from four years of campaigning, having defeated German invaders of Italy, restored Roman control in the East by overthrowing Queen Zenobia, and put down a series of riots and minor rebellions led by underlings ranging from soldiers to mint workers.

At today's Chalons in the Champagne region of northeastern France, Aurelian confronted Tetricus and his army. There, following secret negotiations, Tetricus defected to Aurelian in return for his life. Aurelian then attacked Tetricus's leaderless rebel army, easily defeating it. It seems that Domitianus, one of Tetricus's deputies in northern Gaul, briefly declared himself Tetricus's successor, but Aurelian swiftly put him to the sword. Aurelian would parade Tetricus and his son and designated successor, also named Tetricus, in a Triumph he later celebrated at Rome, before releasing both into retirement in Italy.

As his coins from AD 274 show, Aurelian declared himself "Restorer of the World," and for the first time in decades, the Roman Empire was whole again. For the moment.

Relief from Palmyra depicting Queen Zenobia and a lady-in-waiting. *Bridge-man Images.*

XXII. QUEEN ZENOBIA

SENATOR'S WIFE, CONQUEROR OF THE ROMAN EAST. SYRIA AND EGYPT, AD 267–272

With the Roman East in chaos in the 260s, King Odaenathus of the rich Silk Road city-state of Palmyra in Syria, a Roman client kingdom, had combined his own army of heavy cavalry and mounted archers with Roman infantry to defeat Persian forces and regain Roman assets in the East. This had earned him the gratitude of the Roman emperor Gallienus, who was fighting a tide of barbarian invasions across the Danube and contending with the so-called Empire of Gaul created by the rebel governor Postumus. Rome's Senate was so grateful to Odaenathus for his efforts on its behalf in the East that it awarded him the title of Reformer and Commander of the Entire East. It also granted him *imperium*, making him superior to the governors of Rome's eastern provinces.

In 267, the king and his adult son by his first marriage, Septimius Herodianus—his Palmyran name was Hairan—were assassinated in Bithynia while returning from a military campaign. Who was behind this assassination is unclear. The actual assassin was said to be Odaenathus's cousin Maeonius, who immediately declared himself king, only to be killed himself within twenty-four hours of his declaration.[113]

Some writers suspect the assassination was engineered by Odaenathus's young second wife, Queen Zenobia, to elevate her own son to the throne. The theory is that Zenobia put Maeonius up to it, only to have him immediately executed as a traitor. Certainly, the day following Odaenathus's death, his younger son and Hairan's half-brother, the eight-year-old Vaballathus, was declared king by the army. Zenobia, who had apparently, and unusually, accompanied her husband on campaign, was simultaneously handed the powers of regent, to rule in her son's name until he came of age.

The queen's full Roman name was Zenobia Septimia. In Palmyran, a dialect of Aramaic, she was Bat-Zabbai, or Daughter of Zabbai. Just twenty-seven years of age on becoming unofficial ruler of Palmyra, Zenobia was, according to the often unreliable *Historiae Augustae*, an incredible beauty, with swarthy skin, black eyes, and teeth as white as pearls. She was an outdoors girl who had enjoyed hunting as a child, and was given an excellent education once she married the much older Odaenathus at the age of fourteen, so that by the time power came into her hands she was fluent in Palmyran, Greek, Latin, and Egyptian.

Zenobia was also very smart, and with her young son's elevation to the throne and inheritance of his father's Roman titles and powers, she exercised those powers with care, in the name of both her son Vaballathus and Rome. Over the next three years, Zenobia strengthened Roman fortresses along the Euphrates River, the border between Syria and Persia, and kept the Persians at bay. But with chaos in the West, which included five Roman emperors in ten years, ongoing rebellion in Gaul, and constant barbarian threats, Zenobia began to think about taking the East for herself. She would later claim that Cassius Longinus, her Syrian-born tutor in Greek, who later became her chief adviser, encouraged her to create a Palmyran Empire.

When the Roman emperor Claudius II, or Claudius Gothicus, died from disease in January AD 270 at Sirmium, in the Balkans, and with his successor, Aurelian, hard-pressed fighting German invasions of Italy, Zenobia saw her chance. That spring, to test the waters, she sent an army south into the Roman province of Arabia Petraea, led by a general named Zabdas. When Zabdas's army was confronted outside the capital city of Bostra by the province's Roman governor Trassus and his resident legion, the 3rd Cyrenaica, Zabdas overran the Roman force, killed the governor, sacked and destroyed Bostra, and took control of the province in the name of Vaballathus.

In October, given confidence by this success, Zenobia sent an army of 70,000 to 80,000 men into Egypt under Zabdas. With the Roman governor of Egypt, the prefect Tenagino Probus, away fighting Scythian pirates, Zabdas took Alexandria. In November, Probus regrouped his forces and retook the city, only to be driven out by Zabdas. Probus retreated inland to the Babylon Fortress on the east bank of the Nile River in today's Cairo, so named because, like ancient Babylon, it was surrounded by a moat. The moat didn't save Probus, who, with aid of Egyptian sympathizers of Zenobia, was swiftly captured and executed.

Arabia and Egypt had been conquered, and Syria readily hailed Zenobia as their queen. No longer did Zenobia claim to be a loyal Roman subject. Since January, her son's coinage had shown Vaballathus on one side and Aurelian on the other. That November, the Roman mint at Antioch, the Syrian capital, began minting coins bearing the image of Vaballathus alone. The Palmyran Empire had been born.

At the beginning of spring the following year, a Palmyran army marched north into the mountains of Central Anatolia, commanded by a general named Septimius Zabbai, whose name indicates he may well have been Zenobia's father. He was soon joined by Zabdas leading another army, and together they conquered the Roman province of Galatia. This was the zenith of Zenobia's conquests, for her empire was about to be challenged.

By the spring of 272, the fifty-seven-year-old Roman emperor Aurelian, a masterful strategist severe in appearance and attitude, was marching for the East with a vast army bolstered by new units such as the 1st Illyricorum Legion, recruited in the Balkans over the winter. At the same time, he dispatched a fleet across the Mediterranean to deal with Zenobia's six-thousand-man garrison in Egypt.

That summer, having marched from the Danube to the Bosporus and then through today's Turkey, Aurelian entered Syria without encountering opposition and advanced on Antioch, where Zenobia was based. On flat ground outside Antioch, at Immae, Zenobia's general Zabdas waited with the confident Palmyran army. The cavalries of both sides charged. When Aurelian's lighter cavalry turned and fled, the heavily armored Palmyran cataphracts pursued under the hot summer sun, only to be lured into a trap Aurelian had devised. After a long chase, the Roman cavalry turned as one and charged the wearied Palmyran horses. Caught by surprise, many Palmyran cavalrymen were butchered.

Deprived of his cavalry, Zabdas withdrew his unsettled infantry to Antioch, and in the night Zenobia and her troops abandoned the city, in good order retreating south along the Orontes River to the Syrian city of Emesa, or Homs, as we know it today. Come daylight, Antioch opened its gates to Aurelian, who spared the city and its leaders, sending a signal to all Zenobia's subjects. After overcoming the Palmyran garrison of nearby Daphne, Aurelian remained at Antioch gathering reinforcements locally, including Roman troops who had served under Zenobia, and a levy of Palestinians equipped with clubs.

Within weeks, the Roman army marched south to Emesa, where Zenobia had also garnered reinforcements. Zabdas again formed up his army on flat ground, ideal cavalry terrain. Once again the cavalries of both sides charged, and the Romans turned and supposedly fled, luring much of the Palmyran cavalry away. The remaining Palmyran riders, once dispersed, became fodder for the Roman infantry that swarmed around them at close quarters. Even the Palestinian club-men proved formidable cavalry slayers. As the Palmyran army was overrun, Zabdas escaped the carnage. With Zenobia and her family, he fled inland, due east to Palmyra itself, leaving in such a hurry and traveling so light that Zenobia had to leave behind her national treasure.

Aurelian took Emesa's surrender, then followed Zenobia east. For several weeks, Zenobia withstood a Roman siege of Palmyra. More than once the Romans breached the city walls, only to be repulsed by desperate defenders. But Zenobia, seeing inevitable defeat, slipped from the city one night with her children and fled east to the Euphrates, planning to seek refuge with the Persians. While looking for a river crossing, she was discovered by Roman border guards, and was returned in chains to Aurelian outside Palmyra. Once Palmyra's defenders learned their queen had been captured, they surrendered, with Aurelian sparing the city and its inhabitants. All of Syria now threw its loyalty behind Aurelian, while, in Egypt, Aurelian's troops took control. The war was over, and the rebel Palmyran Empire was at an end.

At Emesa, Aurelian conducted trials of Zenobia and all her rebel leadership. Zenobia's defense was that she had been led into rebellion by Cassius Longinus and other advisers. All defendants were found guilty, and it's believed that Cassius Longinus, Zabdas, Septimius Zabbai, and all other senior advisers to Zenobia were executed on Aurelian's orders. If Aurelian recognized their Roman citizenship they would have been decapitated, but, as they'd rebelled against Rome, it is possible Aurelian crucified them. Zenobia and her children were spared, to accompany Aurelian to Rome and be paraded as trophies in his planned Triumph.

In 274, with Zenobia imprisoned at Rome, the Palmyrans again revolted, declaring five-year-old Septimius Antiochus, a possible relative of Zenobia, their new king. Aurelian's legions reacted swiftly, overrunning Palmyra, massacring the population, and looting and destroying the city.

According to the *Historiae Augustae*, Zenobia's young son, the Palmyran king Vaballathus, died on the journey to Rome. Whether as a result of illness or suicide, or whether Zenobia killed her son to prevent his humiliation in Aurelian's Triumph and subsequent traditional execution by garroting, we don't know. We do know that Zenobia herself was led through the crowd-lined streets of Rome in a double Triumph for Aurelian's victories over Zenobia and the Empire of Gaul. This was in the spring of AD 275, before Aurelian resumed campaigning in the East. Wearing golden chains, Zenobia was accompanied by her two youngest sons by Odaenathus, Hairan II and Timoleus.

Also led in chains in this Triumph were Tetricus, last emperor of Gaul, and his son of the same name. Showing uncharacteristic magnanimity, Aurelian allowed Tetricus and his son to live in secluded retirement in Italy, and permitted Zenobia and her sons to live as well.

Zenobia took up residence with her boys at or near the palatial Hadrian's Villa at Tibur, today's Tivoli, outside Rome.

According to tradition, Zenobia married a Roman senator and lived a long and settled life. During the 364–375 reign of the emperor Valens, her descendants were recorded among the Roman aristocracy. Zonaras reported that she also had daughters, one of whom married Aurelian, but this was demonstrably untrue; Aurelian's only wife, Ulpia Severina, who married him before 270, outlived him, and for a time she ruled in her own right following Aurelian's death.[114]

Aurelian celebrated Zenobia's defeat by declaring himself "Restorer of the East" on his coinage. Yet just months after celebrating his Triumph at Rome, Aurelian, Zenobia's nemesis and one of the Roman Empire's last unifying emperors, was killed by his own officers in Thrace in September 275.

Palmyra would be substantially rebuilt and repopulated during the later reign of the emperor Diocletian, and significant ruins remained until they were heavily damaged by Islamic State terrorists in 2015.

BRITISH COIN OF CARAUSIUS.

From an unique Gold Coin in the British Museum.

Coin produced by the rebel Carausius at his London mint, bearing his image.
Granger/Bridgeman Images.

XXIII. CARAUSIUS AND ALLECTUS

REBEL ROMAN EMPERORS OF BRITANNIA.
BRITAIN, AD 286–293

B etween the years 284 and 286, while Diocletian was sole emperor of the Roman Empire, Frankish and Saxon pirates from Germany roved the English Channel and North Sea in hundreds of ships, ravaging Roman shipping. On land, massive marauding bands of Gallic bandits, collectively called the Bacaudae, made travel, trade, and tax collection impossible. While some of these Bacaudae were runaway slaves, many were Roman citizens, Gallic farmers who took up arms under the Gallic leaders Amandus and Aelianus, initially around Lugdunum, today's Lyon in north-central France.

Diocletian sent his deputy Maximian to deal with the Bacaudae. By 286, Maximian, who had risen from farmer to general through military skill and determination, had eliminated the rebels. This success sponsored his promotion to co-emperor with Diocletian, with Maximian in charge of the Roman West while Diocletian ruled the East. As Maximian headed back to his capital, Milan, after dealing with the Bacaudae, he left a deputy to deal with the remaining problem, the sea pirates. This deputy was Marcus Aurelius Mausaeus Valerius Carausius, admiral of the *Classis Britannicus*, Rome's Britannic Fleet.

Carausius was a native of the Menapi tribe, whose territory roughly encompassed today's Belgian coast as far as the Rhine. His family had apparently gained Roman citizenship during the reign of Marcus Aurelius. Carausius was a seaman who had served as a maritime pilot prior to joining the emperor's service, and he knew the Belgian coast like the back of his hand. To deal with the pirates, Carausius came up with a novel strategy. Instead of putting hundreds of warships to sea to try to anticipate where the pirate fleets might next strike, and intercept them, Carausius identified ports being used by the pirates. Using commando-style raids, he would land legionaries to await the return from raids of pirate ships. When the ships arrived, Carausius's troops would strike.

Carausius, a massive, bearded, bull-necked man, made careful preparations at the headquarters of the Britannic Fleet, Bononia, today's Boulogne-sur-Mer on the French coast. Maximian had left him 10,000 to 15,000 troops from the army used to eliminate the Bacaudae, including four cohorts of the Praetorian Guard from Rome.

To carry his troops, Carausius employed his Britannic Fleet, built more warships, and commandeered Gallic cargo vessels. Within a matter of months, he was ready to wage war on the pirates. Carausius achieved his first successes very quickly, capturing pirate ships complete with booty from their latest raids. But when word reached Maximian in Milan that Carausius was devastating the pirate fleets, he was also told that Carausius was keeping all the booty and sharing it with his troops. Admiral Carausius had proven as bad as the pirates. Furious, Maximian decreed the arrest of Carausius, and marched for Gaul to seize him.

When warning of the arrest order reached Carausius, he simply embarked his troops and sailed for Britain. Over the winter of AD 286–287, Maximian arrived at Boulogne with an army, only to find that Carausius had escaped. Storms that lashed the Gallic coast then derailed Maximian's plans to cross the English Channel to tackle Carausius. One account claimed the storms actually destroyed Maximian's fleet, but as Carausius controlled Roman shipping on the Channel, Maximian is unlikely to have had many ships at his disposal.

With raiding Alemanni Germans now flooding across the Rhine into Roman territory, the western emperor withdrew to deal with this latest threat, leaving Carausius for another day. The following spring, Maximian and Diocletian jointly invaded Germany. With Maximian crossing the Rhine from the legion base at Mogantiacum, today's city of Mainz at the junction of the Rhine and Main Rivers, Diocletian marched into Germany from the East via the province of Raetia, which covered much of today's Switzerland, Bavaria, and the Tyrol. For a time, the emperors' joint scorched-earth campaign cleared Rome's Rhine frontier of the Alemanni Germans. But Roman consolidation was not possible because Diocletian was soon forced to return to the East to combat other threats, leaving Maximian to withdraw to Milan.

Carausius, meanwhile, bluffing his troops into believing he'd been appointed deputy emperor in charge of Britain by Maximian, sailed his fleet around northern Britain and landed on the west coast of England, northwest of Eboracum, today's York. The capital of the province of Britannia Secunda, one of the four provinces into which Britain had been divided by Diocletian, York had been built as a riverside legionary fort by campaigning Roman general Cerialis in AD 71 as he went after the Brigantic Revolt leader, Venutius.

Not only did Carausius's landing take Roman authorities in Britain by surprise, but he slipped in between the legions then based in Britain—to the north, the 2nd Augusta Legion and 20th Valeria Victrix Legion; to the south, the 6th Victrix Legion at York. Archaeological evidence points to British towns in the region being burned at this time as Carausius advanced southeast on York, with Carausius no doubt telling his men they were putting down an insurrection against Rome's authority as he allowed them to loot and burn.

Outside York, Carausius was met by a force apparently based around the five thousand men of the 6th Victrix Legion. There is no report of a battle ensuing, and it's likely the silver-tongued Carausius talked the outnumbered 6th Victrix troops into coming over to him without a fight. Before long, the 2nd Augusta and 20th Valeria Victrix were also bowing to Carausius's authority, and all of Britannia was his.

Carausius subsequently used the title *imperator*, literally meaning "commander," normally given to Roman generals by acclamation of their troops after a great victory. This suggests Carausius had wide popular support from the military in Britain. That year of 287, when Carausius minted the pay of the troops now under his command, he styled himself Augustus of Britain and put his image on the coins.

Hunkering down for a long stay, Carausius built forts at potential landing sites along the south coast of England to counter amphibious landings by Maximian's troops. One such fort was at Clausentum, today's Bitterne Manor in suburban Southampton. Carausius continued to pay his Roman troops for another six years. Throughout this time, Britain was no longer part of the Roman Empire; it stopped contributing taxes and military recruits to Rome, and it took no orders from the emperor Maximian.

Emboldened by his success, "Emperor" Carausius crossed the Channel and reoccupied Boulogne. Then, to jointly control and exploit northern Gaul, he allied with the Franks, a confederation of aggressive German tribes originating between the Rhine and Weser Rivers, and brought Frankish mercenaries into his army. Frankish warriors, identifiable by their short hair, mustaches, and tunics of broad horizontal stripes, fought without helmets or armor and used battle-axes to fearsome effect. As the Franks increasingly settled in Gaul they would give their name to today's nation of France—named for *Francia*, Latin for "land of the Franks."

On March 1, 293, however, an appointment in Milan sealed Carausius's fate. That day, the western emperor Maximian appointed a Caesar, or deputy emperor, of the West, to serve under him and counter the likes of Carausius. At the same time, at Nicomedia, the eastern emperor Diocletian similarly appointed a Caesar for the East. The understanding was that, after Diocletian and Maximian had served twenty years as co-emperors, they would go into retirement and their Caesars would replace them on the eastern and western thrones. This four-part leadership team became known as the Tetrarchy.

The man appointed Caesar, or deputy emperor, of the western empire was forty-three-year-old Flavius Valerius Constantius, known as Constantius Chlorus, or Constantius the Pale, apparently due to his pallid complexion. Constantius's eldest son was Constantine, the future Constantine the Great. In 293, Constantine's father headed for war against the rebel Carausius—at the very same time that eighteen-year-old Constantine was heading for Egypt to commence his military service as a junior tribune in the army of Galerius, Caesar of the East.

Constantius marched into Gaul with a Roman army made up of troops from legions based on the Rhine. Arriving outside Boulogne, he lay siege to the port, as Carausius's forces made a stand there. Setting his legionaries to work, Constantius built two earth dikes out into the English Channel. When linked, the dikes cut off the port from the sea, preventing the rebels from escaping by water and blocking any resupply or reinforcement from Britain. Surrounded, the rebels surrendered Boulogne.

After Constantius captured Boulogne, he ordered a number of legion cohorts that had served under Carausius to march across the empire to Egypt to join the Caesar of the East, Galerius, on a campaign there. As for the four thousand men of the four Praetorian Guard cohorts that had gone over to Carausius back in 286, who were among the surrendered troops at Boulogne, they were discharged on the spot by Constantius. Stripped of their arms and equipment, these elite Italian troops were left to their own devices to return home to their families in Italy.

Meanwhile, when news of the loss of Boulogne reached troops serving under Carausius in Britain, they revolted, and assassinated him. But instead of returning their allegiance to Rome, they made Carausius's deputy Allectus their new leader and new emperor of Britain. Allectus had held the post of Carausius's treasurer, but according to legend he had been a smith prior to his army service and had personally made the sword he wore. Now, the blacksmith with pecuniary skills ruled Britain. But Carausius's British empire had been primarily funded by plunder from Gaul, and with access to Gaul now cut off by Constantius, the only way that Allectus could pay for the continued loyalty of his troops was by plundering the Britons, which he proceeded to do.

Across the Channel, with Boulogne in his hands, Constantius ignored Britain for the moment. Instead, he secured his rear. Throughout 294–296 he systematically retook northern Gaul from the Franks and defeated Alemanni German forces at the mouth of the Rhine, restoring Gaul to Roman control. Through this period, Constantius had added to the ships he'd captured at Boulogne to create two invasion fleets, one based at Boulogne, the other near the mouth of the Seine River in Normandy.

Spring was the customary time for launching Roman military campaigns, and the western emperor Maximian marched from Italy in the first half of 296 with an army whose role would be to cover the Rhine while Constantius did the heavy lifting in Britain. This freed up Constantius to launch an amphibious operation against Allectus in Britain. Constantius's deputy for this operation was Maximian's new Praetorian prefect Julius Asclepiodotus, who was of Greek heritage and had been a consul of Rome four years prior. He had also previously served as Praetorian prefect to three emperors: Aurelian, Probus, and Diocletian. Constantius gave Asclepiodotus command of the southern invasion force at the Seine, with orders to land in the vicinity of today's Southampton, close to Allectus's fleet, which was stationed at the Isle of Wight. At Boulogne, Constantius himself took charge of the northern landing force, with the Thames River and Allectus's capital, Londinium, today's London, as his objective.

As both fleets set sail with the tide, the English Channel was flat and calm, but filled with thick fog that severely reduced visibility. We don't know what month this was, but the presence of fog doesn't necessarily narrow it down—fog at Southampton is common in winter but can also manifest in August, in midsummer. This fog proved a barrier to Constantius's ships, which lost contact with each other and became separated. To Asclepiodotus, however, it proved a boon, enabling him to slip by the enemy fleet and land his troops near Southampton, probably at Calshot Beach.

Dividing his force into two divisions, giving the second division the task of cutting off the enemy's retreat, the prefect set out to find his foe. Allectus was in the vicinity, and learning of the landing, he led his troops to counter the invasion. Running into one of Asclepiodotus's divisions in the fog, the rebel troops put up a brief fight before turning and running. Allectus fled along with his men. As he ran, he threw away his *cincticulus*, his insignia of rank, a knotted golden waistband that identified commanding generals. Near the town of Callevra Atrebatum, today's Silchester, Allectus and his men ran into Asclepiodotus's second division, and the second self-declared emperor of Britain died in a slaughter of his men.

Meanwhile, several ships from Constantius's fleet located the Thames in the fog, made their way upriver, and landed troops at London. There, leaderless Frankish mercenaries garrisoning the city surrendered. Once the fog cleared, Constantius's flagship pulled up beside the London wharf. The story goes that he was greeted by a crowd of Londoners, who, relieved to be rid of the depredations of the rebels, welcomed the deputy emperor with joy. According to one legend, the locals even took pieces of the sail and mast of the warship that had brought Constantius, as souvenirs. A medallion subsequently minted by Constantius to celebrate the event shows him victoriously riding a horse into London after landing.

As for the Frankish prisoners taken in London, they were massacred. According to Geoffrey of Monmouth's *History of the Kings of Britain*, they were decapitated beside the Walbrook, the stream that ran through Roman London from north to south between Cornhill and Ludgate Hill, with their heads tossed into the river. Hundreds of skulls were indeed found in the bed of the Walbrook in 1838, but these were subsequently dated to the second century—although no recorded second-century event at London explains why they ended up in the stream.

Constantius remained in Britain for several months after defeating Allectus. There he "restored what had been lost to those who had been despoiled" by Carausius and Allectus, and reorganized and put his stamp on the administration across Britannia as he installed new governors answerable to him.[115]

It is also possible that Constantius left the Praetorian Prefect Asclepiodotus to govern a British province, or even put him in overall charge in Britain; we don't hear of him again. In Geoffrey of Monmouth's later mangled account, Asclepiodotus was a British-born king who ruled the island for ten years. Perhaps the truth of the matter was that Prefect Asclepiodotus indeed ruled in Britannia for a decade, as a Roman governor.

As Constantius departed London he left behind a number of auxiliary units that he'd brought to Britain, as a mobile reserve in support of units on Hadrian's Wall. Constantius returned most of the remaining troops who had followed Carausius and Allectus to their original bases. The three legions resident in Britain prior to the rebellion remained in Britain, although the indications are that at least the 2nd Augusta was punished for its role, perhaps for too enthusiastically embracing the oppression of the Britons. It was reduced in status, substantially reduced in size, and posted to coastal defense duties at Richborough in Kent.

Memories of Carausius and Allectus, the rebel Roman emperors of Britain, would morph into stories passed down through generations of Britons and told in the Middle Ages about mythical native kings of Britain who had defied foreign occupiers.

Statue of the emperor Maxentius, object of the African revolt of Domitius Alexander. *Bridgeman Images*.

XXIV. DOMITIUS ALEXANDER

REBEL ROMAN EMPEROR OF AFRICA.
NORTH AFRICA, AD 308–310

In the late summer of AD 310, a Roman fleet approached the North African city of Carthage in the night, carrying five thousand crack troops including men of the Praetorian Guard. This was an amphibious landing force, sent from Italy to invade the provinces of North Africa and deal with Lucius Domitius Alexander, an elderly Roman administrator who had declared himself emperor of Africa.

To understand Alexander's bold move, it's necessary to go back to October 28, AD 306. On that day, an almost bloodless military coup was staged in Rome. The Praetorian Guard, led by two of its tribunes and a tribune of Rome's City Guard, installed thirty-year-old Maxentius, son of recently retired emperor Maximian, as emperor of the West, with Maxentius's appointment endorsed by the Roman Senate. For centuries past, the Praetorian Guard had served as the Rome-based imperial bodyguard, accompanying the emperor everywhere. But Diocletian, the now retired emperor of the Roman East, who'd been born and raised in today's Croatia in the Balkans, hadn't trusted the haughty Italians of the Praetorian Guard. Downgrading them to field troops during his reign, he had authorized the disbandment of four Guard cohorts that had served under Carausius, the rebel governor of Britain, and his successor, Galerius, had recently ordered the abolition of the entire Guard.

This military coup—installing Maxentius on the throne in Rome—was an act of Praetorian self-preservation. In binding themselves to Maxentius, the Guards secured their continued existence. And Maxentius rewarded the Praetorians, not only with privileges but by increasing the unit's size to twelve thousand men.

Maxentius's crowning was popular in Rome, with the Senate and public broadly behind the young man, who had been born in Rome and was one of their own. Just a single senator protested, and he lost his head to a Praetorian centurion's sword. Rome hadn't been the empire's capital for decades, but with Praetorian Guard and Senate support, Maxentius promised to make Rome great again. It was a promise he quickly set about keeping, launching major building projects, to the delight of the Roman populace.

Maxentius's elevation to the throne was in defiance of the existing complicated imperial power-sharing arrangement. Reigning as emperor of the Eastern Empire from Nicomedia since May 305 was Galerius, former Caesar, or deputy, of now retired emperor Diocletian. Galerius's Caesar was Maximinus Daia, his nephew and adopted son, who was based in Antioch in Syria. Since the recent death of Constantius, emperor of the West, Flavius Valerius Severus, one of Galerius's generals, had become emperor of the West, with Constantius's son Constantine as his deputy. And these existing emperors were determined to dethrone Maxentius.

At the urging of Galerius, Severus, the official emperor of the West, marched on Rome from Milan, with his army, to deal with young Maxentius. But Maxentius was joined at Rome by his retired father Maximian. Severus's troops had previously served Maximian, and once they arrived outside Rome most of these troops defected to Maxentius and his father. Severus, forced to flee to Ravenna on the northeast coast of Italy, surrendered to Maximian, who, within months, had him executed. Maximian then attempted to wrest power from his son, only for the Praetorian Guard to stand with Maxentius, forcing Maximian to flee to Trier. There, he was granted asylum by his son-in-law Constantine.

Galerius had then led an army from the East to deal with Maxentius, but a little way north of Rome his troops had become mutinous, so

Galerius had withdrawn, returning to the East. To replace the murdered Severus as official emperor of the West, Galerius appointed another of his generals, Licinius, to the post, but based him in the Balkans, with Constantine at Trier as his Caesar. Galerius had then turned his attention elsewhere, ignoring Maxentius. This left Maxentius in control of Italy, Sicily, Sardinia, and North Africa.

Since Maxentius's governor, based in the provincial capital of Carthage, had returned to Rome in 308, the acting governor of the Roman provinces of Africa was the elderly Lucius Domitius Alexander, a *vicarius*, or vicar—the term literally means "substitute"—an official who usually only ran one of the twelve departments within a province. Alexander, enjoying his newfound power, let the troops in the African provinces do as they wished.

As was the custom, once Maxentius had taken the throne in Rome he had sent portraits of himself to Africa to head processions at the opening of games at the circus and amphitheater throughout the year. But with the departure of Maxentius's loyal governor, troops of Africa's resident legions had ceased to carry the portrait of Maxentius at the head of ludi parades. At one time there had been a single legion, the 3rd Augusta, in the African province, but Diocletian had stationed seven across North Africa, from Egypt to Mauretania. Knowing that Galerius, the emperor of the East, did not recognize Maxentius as the Augustus, or emperor, of the West, legionaries in Africa had started carrying the bust of Galerius in games parades, as a protest against the western "usurper."

As Alexander's troops became increasingly restive, Maxentius sent demands to Carthage for Alexander to send his son to Rome as a hostage to ensure his good behavior. When Alexander refused to do this, Maxentius withdrew the official imperial mint from Carthage and transferred its artisans to Italy, eliminating Alexander's ability to pay his troublesome soldiery. Alexander set up his own rudimentary mint, and the troops under Alexander were so incensed by Maxentius's actions that they rebelled and declared Alexander emperor of Africa, swearing their allegiance to him.

To counter Alexander, Maxentius planned to personally lead an army to Africa in 307 to put down the revolt, until the augurs told him the omens were inauspicious. Instead, Alexander cut off the export of grain to Rome, forcing Maxentius to institute food rationing in Italy. Alexander also ceased to send Rome the taxes annually gathered in his provinces, adding the money to his own little empire's treasury.

Finally, in 310, the omens were declared right for dealing with the rebel emperor, and Maxentius dispatched his Praetorian prefect, Gaius Volusianus, with an army made up of his most loyal troops, with orders to return Africa to his control. Those troops would have included cohorts of the Praetorian Guard, the 2nd Parthica Legion and the Herculean Legion. They boarded warships of an Italian battle fleet controlled by Maxentius, and sailed for Carthage.

A coin issued by Alexander at Carthage that spring depicted three military standards on its reverse—the eagle of a legion, the standard of a legionary cohort, and the standard of an auxiliary unit, suggesting that this was the extent of the military force that had enthroned him and was loyal to him. If that were the case, Alexander still fielded more men than Volusianus, but the Maxentians were much more experienced and highly disciplined.

Alexander and his troops were taken completely by surprise. In the face of Prefect Volusianus's fixed ranks, the locally based troops melted away. With his men deserting him, old Alexander was forced to hurriedly retreat west to the inland city of Cirta, in today's Algeria. Volusianus followed, surrounded Cirta and stormed it. "Emperor" Alexander was taken prisoner, and garroted on Volusianus's command, suffering the Republican Roman punishment for leaders who rebelled against Rome. In every city and town through the province, military and civil leaders who had supported the rebellion were also executed, with their property seized and added to the assets that supported Maxentius's imperial treasury at Rome.

Leaving new officers in command of the province's military and a prefect named Zenas at Carthage to govern in Maxentius's name, Volusianus was able to return to Rome with his army. He brought with him large shipments of grain for the people of Italy, which ended grain rationing, and military reinforcements for Maxentius, among them units of nimble Numidian cavalrymen and Berber *Mauri feroces*, or ferocious Moors, light cavalry from Mauretania.

Volusianus arrived back in Rome in time for the October 28 celebration of the anniversary of Maxentius's accession to the throne. As a reward for a job well done in Africa, Volusianus was appointed Rome's city prefect by Maxentius, effective for twelve months until the following October 28.

The victory of Maxentius, a son of Rome, over Alexander was celebrated joyously by the populace at games on his October 28 anniversary, as the self-proclaimed Invincible Prince took their plaudits at the Circus Maximus. Some historians even suggest that, to celebrate his victory, Maxentius ordered the construction of a triumphal arch beside the Colosseum and was planning to conduct a Triumphal procession through the city on its completion. If this was the case, that arch would still be incomplete two years later when Constantine, Maxentius's brother-in-law, marched with an army from Trier to Rome. On October 28, 312, aided by the treachery of several of Maxentius's chief advisers—including Volusianus, the man who had retaken Africa for him—Maxentius was defeated, dying during the Battle of the Milvian Bridge just to the north of Rome.

Constantine had Maxentius's head severed and paraded through Rome on the end of a spear. He then sent it to Africa, where it was shown to the troops loyal to Maxentius stationed there, to prove that the Invincible Prince was dead. Constantine then mounted the throne, becoming emperor of the West. But after a stay of just several weeks, he departed Rome. Taking away the city's power thereafter, he would only visit Rome twice more during his lifetime, establishing his capital at Byzantium and renaming it Constantinople. The triumphal arch beside the Colosseum was completed within several years and became the Arch of Constantine, celebrating Constantine's defeat of Maxentius on Rome's doorstep.

Whether the arch was initiated by Maxentius to celebrate his victory over Alexander, or was, as some historians believe, created from scratch by the Senate for Constantine, it broke all the rules that applied to Roman Triumphs and their associated triumphal arches. Triumphs and arches had traditionally been awarded by the Senate for victories by a Roman general over foreign enemies, not over fellow Roman citizens. In the first century BC, Julius Caesar had set a dubious precedent by celebrating Triumphs for victories over Senatorial armies in Africa and Spain in which foreign allies and auxiliaries had participated. The later Triumphs of the emperors had tended to abide by the old rules, but now, in these dying days of the Roman Empire in the West, traditions were being thrown to the wind.

Soon, foreign invaders would bring about the breakup of the Roman West, and the pan-continental Roman Empire that had existed since the late first century BC would be no more.

NOTES

I. SERTORIUS

1–4. Plutarch, *Sertorius*, *Lives of the Noble Grecians and Romans*.

5–7. Velleius Paterculus, *Compendium of Roman History*.

8. Frontinus, *Stratagems*.

9. Velleius.

10–11. Plutarch.

12. Velleius.

II. SPARTACUS

13. Seneca, *Dialogues and Letters*.

14. Appian, in *Roman History*, says just seventy-four men carried out this surprise attack, not 300. He may have confused this number with the seventy-two gladiators who escaped from Capua.

15. I have adopted Barry Strauss's suggestion in *The Spartacus War* that Lentulus's battle as described by Sallust in his *Histories* was likely to have been this one in Picenum. But the interpretation of Sallust's meaning about the camp, with men emerging with officer's cloaks from kitbags, and the "selected cohorts," is mine.

16. Plutarch, *Crassus*, *Lives*.

III. VERCINGETORIX

17. Caesar, *Civil War*.

IV. LABIENUS

18. Cassius Dio, *Roman History*.

V. SEXTUS POMPEY

19. Sallust, *Histories*.

20.   Plutarch, *Antony, Lives*.

21.   Tacitus, *Annals*.

22–26.   Appian.

27.   Velleius.

28–29.   Appian.

30.   Dio.

31.   Velleius.

VI. THE TWO BATOS

32.   Dio.

33.   Velleius.

34.   Dio; Velleius.

35–36.   Velleius.

37.   Suetonius, *Twelve Caesars*.

38–41.   Velleius.

42.   Suetonius.

43.   Velleius.

VII. ARMINIUS

44.   Tacitus, *Annals*, for Segestes's full speech and Varus's response.

45.   These details are on the memorial erected to Caelius by his brother and found at Xanten in modern times.

46–47.   Velleius.

48.   Suetonius.

49.   Seneca.

50–54.   Tacitus, *Annals*.

VIII. TACFARINAS

55–57.   Tacitus, *Annals*.

IX.   PISO

58.   Josephus, *New Complete Works of Josephus*, 'Jewish Antiquities'; Suetonius; Dio; Tacitus, *Annals*.

59–68.   Tacitus, *Annals.*

X. SACROVIR

69.   Holder, *The Roman Army in Britain.*

70.   Tacitus, *Annals.*

71.   Tacitus, *Histories.*

XI. SCIBONIANUS

72.   Josephus, 'Jewish Antiquities.'

73.   Dio.

74.   Suetonius.

XII. VENUTIUS

75.   Tacitus, *Annals.*

76.   Tacitus, *Histories.*

77.   Tacitus, *Annals.*

78.   Tacitus, *Histories.*

79–81.   Tacitus, *Annals.*

82–83.   Tacitus, *Histories.*

84.   Holder.

85.   Tacitus, *Agricola.*

XIII. BOUDICCA

86.   Dio.

87.   Tacitus, *Agricola.*

88–89.   Dio.

XIV. MENAHEM, ELEAZAR, JOSEPHUS, JOHN, AND SIMON

90.   Josephus, *New Complete Works*, 'Life of Josephus.'

XV. VINDEX

91–93.   Dio.

94.   Tacitus, *Histories*.

95.   Pliny, *Letters of the Younger Pliny*.

XVI. CIVILIS

96–102. Tacitus, *Histories*.

XVII. EPIPHANES

103.   The Velius Rufus inscription AE 1903.368 speaks of this "large group of men liable to taxation," which Centurion Rufus conducted from Parthia to Rome with Epiphanes and his brother.

XVIII. SATURNINUS

104.   Dio.

105.   Tacitus, *Histories*.

106.   Tacitus, *Agricola*.

107–109. Dio.

XIX. SIMON BAR-KOKHBA

110.   Yadin, *Bar-Kokhba*.

111.   Dio.

XX. AVIDIUS CASSIUS

112.   Dio.

XXII. QUEEN ZENOBIA

113.   *Historiae Augustae*.

114.   Zonaras, *Epitome Historiarum*.

XXIII. CARAUSIUS AND ALECTUS

115.   Rogers and Nixon, *In Praise of Later Roman Emperors*, Pan VI.

BIBLIOGRAPHY

Anonymous, *Historiae Augustae*, trans. D. Maggie (Cambridge, MA, Loeb Classical Library, 1932).

Appian, *Roman History*, trans. H. White (Cambridge, MA, Loeb Classical Library: Harvard University Press, 2000).

Caesar Augustus, *Res Gestae Divi Augusti*, trans. F. W. Shipley (Cambridge, MA, Loeb Classical Library: Harvard University Press, 2002).

Caesar, G. J., *The Civil War: Together with the Alexandrian War, the African War, and the Spanish War by Other Hands*, trans. J. A. Gardner(London: Penguin, 1967).

—, *The Conquest of Gaul*, trans. S. A. Handford (London: Penguin, 1982).

Carcopino, J., *Daily Life in Ancient Rome* (London: Pelican, 1956).

Cassius Dio, *Roman History*, trans. E. Cary (Cambridge, MA, Loeb Classical Library: Harvard University Press, 2004).

Cicero, *The Letters to His Friends*, trans. W. Glynn Williams (Cambridge, MA: Harvard University Press, 1965).

Dando-Collins, S., *Blood of the Caesars: How the Murder of Germanicus Led to the Fall of Rome* (Hoboken: John Wiley & Sons, 2008).

—, *Caligula: The Mad Emperor of Rome* (Nashville: Turner, 2019).

—, *Cleopatra's Kidnappers: How Caesar's Sixth Legion Gave Egypt to Rome and Rome to Caesar* (Hoboken: John Wiley & Sons, 2007).

—, *Conquering Jerusalem: The AD 66–73 Roman Campaign to Crush the Jewish Revolt* (Nashville: Turner, 2021).

—, *Constantine at the Bridge: How the Battle of the Milvian Bridge Created Christian Rome* (Nashville: Turner, 2021).

—, *Legions of Rome: The Definitive History of Every Imperial Roman Legion* (London: Quercus, 2010).

—, *Mark Antony's Heroes: How the Third Gallica Legion Saved an Apostle and Created an Emperor* (Hoboken: John Wiley & Sons, 2007).

—, *Nero's Killing Machine: The True Story of Rome's Remarkable Fourteenth Legion* (Hoboken: John Wiley & Sons, 2005).

—, *The Great Fire of Rome: The Fall of the Emperor Nero and His City* (Cambridge, MA.: De Capo Press, 2010).

—, *The Ides: Caesar's Murder and the War for Rome* (Hoboken: John Wiley & Sons, 2010).

Frontinus, *The Stratagems*, trans. C. E. Bennett (Cambridge, MA, Loeb Classical Library: Harvard University Press, 2003).

Geoffrey of Monmouth, *The History of the Kings of Britain* (London: Penguin, 1977).

Gibbon, E., *The Decline and Fall of the Roman Empire* (Chicago: Encyclopaedia Britannica, 1989).

Grant, M., *Gladiators* (Harmondsworth: Penguin, 1967).

—, *Roman History from Coins* (New York: Barnes & Noble, 1995).

Gregory of Tours, *History of the Franks* (London: Penguin, 1974).

Henry of Huntingdon, *The History of the English* (London: Longman, 1879).

Hill, G. F., *Historical Roman Coins: From the Earliest Times to the Reign of Augustus* (London: Constable, 1909).

Holder, P. A., *The Roman Army in Britain* (New York: Palgrave Macmillan, 1982).

Josephus, *The New Complete Works of Josephus*, trans. W. Whiston (Grand Rapids, MI: Kregel, 1999).

Keppie, L., *The Making of the Roman Army: From Republic to Empire* (Totowa, NJ.: Barnes & Noble, 1994).

Matyszak, P., *Sertorius and the Struggle for Spain* (Barnsley: Pen & Sword, 2013).

Philo Judaeus, *The Works of Philo*, trans. C. D. Yonge (Peabody, MA.: Hendrickson, 1994).

Pliny, *The Letters of the Younger Pliny*, trans. B. Radice (London: Penguin, 1969).

Plutarch, *The Lives of the Noble Grecians and Romans* (the Dryden translation) (Chicago: Encyclopaedia Britannica, 1952).

Rogers, B. S., and C. E. V. Nixon, *In Praise of Later Roman Emperors: The Panegyric Latini* (Berkeley: University of California Press, 1995).

Sallust, *The Histories*, trans. H. Maffett (Farmington Hills, MI: Gale Ecco, 2010).

Seneca, *Dialogues and Letters*, trans. C. D. N. Costa (London: Penguin, 2005).

Sher, F. C., *The Revolt of Avidius Cassius* (Madison: University of Wisconsin-Madison, 1992).

Speidel, M. P., *Ancient German Warriors: Warrior Styles from Trajan's Column to Icelandic Sagas* (London: Routledge, 2004).

—, *Riding for Caesar: The Roman Emperors' Horse Guards* (Cambridge, MA: Harvard University Press, 1994).

Star, C. G., *The Roman Imperial Navy, 31 BC–AD 324* (Cambridge, Heffer & Sons, 1960).

Strauss, B., *The Spartacus War* (New York: Simon & Schuster, 2009).

Suetonius, *The Twelve Caesars* (London: Penguin, 1989).

Tacitus, P. C., *The Annals* and *The Histories*, trans. A. J. Church (Chicago: Encyclopaedia Britannica, 1952).

—, *The Agricola* and *The Germania*, trans. H. Mattingly and S. A. Handford (London: Penguin, 1970).

Vegetius, *The Military Institutions of the Romans*, trans. J. Clark (Harrisburg, PA: Military Service Publishing, 1944).

Velleius Paterculus, *Compendium of Roman History*, trans. F. W. Shipley (Cambridge, MA, Loeb Classical Library: Harvard University Press, 2002).

Watts de Peyster, J., *The History of Carausius* (Whitefish, MT: Kessinger, 2009).

Webster, G., and D. R. Dudley, *The Rebellion of Boudicca* (New York: Barnes & Noble, 1962).

Wells, P. W., *The Battle That Stopped Rome: Emperor Augustus, Arminius, and the Slaughter of the Legions in the Teutoburg Forest* (New York: W. W. Norton & Co., 2003).

Wightman, E. M., *Roman Trier and the Treveri* (New York: Praeger, 1970).

Wilkes, J. J. (ed.), *Documenting the Roman Army in Britain; Essays in Honor of Margaret Roxan* (London: Institute of Classical Studies, 2003).

Wiseman, E. J., *Roman Spain* (New York: Bell, 1956).

Yadin, Y., *Bar-Kokhba: The Rediscovery of the Legendary Hero of the Last Jewish Revolt Against Imperial Rome* (London: Weidenfeld & Nicolson, 1971).

Zonaras, J., *Epitome Historiarum* (Delhi: Pranava, 2020).

Zosimus, *New History*, trans. R. T. Ridley (Sydney: Australian Association of Byzantine Studies, 1982).

INDEX

ABOUT THE AUTHOR

STEPHEN DANDO-COLLINS is the multi-award-winning author of forty-six books, including biographies and nonfiction works on ancient Rome, Greece, and Persia, as well as American, British, French, and Australian history including World War I and World War II. These works focus on military history, with Stephen considered an authority on the legions of imperial Rome. He has also written several successful novels and children's novels. His books are widely published in the US, UK, Canada, Australia, and New Zealand, and they appear in translation in Spain, Italy, Poland, the Netherlands, Albania, Russia, Korea, and Latin America.